Recent Economic Thought Series

Warren J. Samuels, Editor
Michigan State University
East Lansing, Michigan, U.S.A.

Other titles in the series:
Feiwel, G.R., *Samuelson and Neoclassical Economics*
Wade, L.L., *Political Economy: Modern Views*
Zimbalist, A., *Comparative Economic Systems: Recent Views*

This series is devoted to works that present divergent views on the development, prospects, and tensions within some important research areas of international economic thought. Among the fields covered are macromonetary policy, public finance, labor and political economy. The emphasis of the series is on providing a critical, constructive view of each of these fields, as well as a forum through which leading scholars of international reputation may voice their perspectives on important related issues. Each volume in the series will be self-contained; together these volumes will provide dramatic evidence of the variety of economic thought within the scholarly community.

Labor Economics

Labor Economics: Modern Views

edited by
William Darity, Jr.
University of North Carolina, Chapel Hill

Kluwer-Nijhoff Publishing
A member of the Kluwer Academic Publishers Group
Boston The Hague Dordrecht Lancaster

Distributors for North America:
Kluwer-Nijhoff Publishing
Kluwer Academic Publishers
190 Old Derby Street
Hingham, Massachusetts 02043, U.S.A.

Distributors outside North America:
Kluwer Academic Publishers Group
Distribution Centre
P.O. Box 322
3300AH Dordrecht, The Netherlands

Library of Congress Cataloging in Publication Data
Main entry under title:

Labor economics.

(Recent economic thought)
Bibliography: p.
Includes index.
1. Labor economics — Addresses, essays, lectures.
I. Darity, William A., Jr. 1953-
II. Series.
HD4901.L13 1984 331 83-13541
ISBN-13:978-94-010-8985-2 e-ISBN-13:978-94-009-5636-0
DOI: 10.1007/978-94-009-5636-0

I INTRODUCTION

REFLECTIONS ON THE STATE OF THE ART IN LABOR ECONOMICS

William Darity, Jr.

Preliminary Remarks

As Rhonda Williams observes in the lead chapter in this volume, modern labor economics has become, for the most part, an extensive branch of applied microeconomics. Williams' observation has been echoed by Paul McNulty (pp. 260–1) who, in an interesting recent study of the history of labor economics, made the following comment

> Perhaps the most fundamental point to be made about the current state of labor economics is that at no other time in the history of the field has it been more closely aligned with its parent discipline. The study of labor by economists is generally characterized by the same analytical approach that their colleagues are bringing to bear upon problems in other subdivisions of the field: the formulation of hypotheses based generally on observations consistent with economic theory and empirically tested with econometric techniques applied to such data as are available.

Obviously, this tendency is not unique to labor economics as a particular subdivision of the "dismal science." Virtually all other subfields increasingly have been absorbed by the style and fashion of the empirical neoclassical economics. The macroeconomists continuously seek to convince themselves of the legitimacy of their enterprise by demonstrating that aggregate behavioral relationships in their standard models have appropriate "microfoundations." Even development economics, perhaps the most eclectic (and perhaps, as a consequence, the most often denigrated as fuzzy and nonrigorous) of the subfields, has undergone a recent invasion led, ironically, by labor economists who aim to transform it into a thoroughly conventional arm of the larger discipline.[1]

Labor economics was not always this way. In fact, at the outset, labor economics, arguably, was not economics at all. In the United States, the earliest substantial investigations of the conditions of work and working people stretched far beyond the limits of economics — at least the limits set by the classical schoolmaster J.S. Mill in the preface to his *Principles.* Labor studies in the late 19th century were spearheaded by such broad-ranging social researchers as Richard Ely and John R. Commons, who instinctively thrust beyond any disciplinary lines. Their electicism could be nurtured in the academic-intellectual environment of the latter years of the 1800s because of the general looseness in disciplinary barriers. Their careers were not nurtured, however; they stood too close to the unions' side of the labor struggles. McNulty (p. 133) has highlighted, in this context, the remarkable flexibility of the boundaries of the social sciences at that time — a flexibility epitomized by the seminar series at Johns Hopkins where Ely was a central figure. What he neglects to highlight was the political climate that enveloped the development of labor studies.

Moreover, the early students of labor on the American academic scene conceived of themselves as standing in opposition to classical economics and its ideological hand maiden *laissez-faire.* Those scholars who had been trained as economists, but who had deep reservations about the standard economics, found a refuge within labor studies. It was an outpost where they could conduct research outside of the terms of the orthodoxy. The late 19th century researchers in labor economics laid the foundation for the institutionalist movement (as well as a power base for Commons at Wisconsin), a movement that consciously viewed itself as hostile toward conventional economics. McNulty (p. 163) has put it bluntly, if somewhat trenchantly: ". . . the earliest labor economists were generally unequivocal in their rejection of economic theory [due in part to] the individualist bias in the classical model as well as the neoclassical theory of marginal utility." For the early labor economists, group activity rather than a reduction to the individual lay at the base of their analyses.

This subfield with its subject matter so close to the heart of the social struggles that dominated the turn of the century thus became the domain of the nonconformist economists. As disciplinary boundaries tightened, their efforts remained hardest to classify. Their frequent inclination to sympathize with the union movement further distinguished and isolated them from the mainstream. While economic theory proper preached of the dangers of unionism in obstructing the normal adjustment capability of the market, the early labor economists supported unionization to bring fairness to the bargaining process for wages and to bring improved conditions to the workplace.

Accompanying this sympathetic stance toward unionism was a growing concentration of labor courses on the topic of organized labor (McNulty, p. 142). Paradoxically, this highly eclectic subfield had made its subject matter more and more narrow. In its eclecticism, it also had become more divorced from mainstream economics.

One senses that its practitioners began to grow more and more nervous that they might not, in fact, comprehend that which they rejected so adamantly. There was a tendency among other economists to stigmatize the labor economists as economists whose grasp of theory was weak. McNulty (p. 173) says, in fact, that this was often true — although there were exceptions like Veblen's brilliant student, Robert Hoxie.

By the close of the 1930s, labor economics appeared to be a dying field. It was devoid of the best theorists; some of the most hostile individuals from within the mainstream would have claimed it had none at all. The institutionalist movement was not on the verge of supplanting neoclassicism. Labor courses were devoted almost exclusively to the study of the history and problems of organized labor.

One could argue in hindsight that the subfield was either doomed to extinction or ripe for revolution. It, in fact, received the latter — but not a reenervating insurgency that produced a new economics. Rather, the labor economics revolution of the 1940s and 1950s — led by the Chicago School — pulled labor economics fully within the fold of the mainstream. Labor economics became applied or empirical microeconomics. The sweep of its scope now is panoramic. Trade unionism became a mere side-dish in the face of such entrées as racial and sexual discrimination, the distribution of income, occupational attainment, the relationship between unemployment and inflation, differences in unemployment rates across various demographic groups (e.g., teens versus the elderly), the structure of families, marriage and divorce, the relationship between growth and equity, and so on.

The reversal in approach and emphasis in labor economics is so marked that by the end of the 1970s a textbook could appear that is thoroughly and unapologetically neoclassical from start to finish. The authors (Bellante and Jackson, p. 305) only make a single reference to the remnants of dissent from the mainstream in one paragraph on the next-to-the-last page of their book by encouraging their readers to examine the work of dual labor market theorists and radicals on the labor market. Then they immediately instruct students to examine critiques of those approaches as well. Of course, in a text pregnantly subtitled "Choice in Labor Markets," they did not find it worthwhile to discuss those approaches in any part of their book.

Ingrid Rima's text, which is far more open to alternatives to neoclassical labor economics, devotes several chapters to themes more familiar to the proponents of the older brand of labor economics — wage contours, segmented labor markets, and the like. But she still feels compelled to worry about the connection between these phenomena and microeconomic theory.

Rima's concern for microfoundations reveals a deeper problem that besets the latter-day institutionalists in their attempts to strike out on a separate path from the neoclassicals. Their discoveries about various institutional features of the labor market that seem, at first glance, to undercut the relevance of the neoclassical approach tend to be only a temporary puzzle. With sufficient ingenuity and time, the neoclassicists always can find a means of reconciling empirical phenomena with utility maximization. A case in point is Walter Oi's famous neoclassical explanation for the existence of labor market segmentation via his treatment of labor as a "quasi-fixed factor." Since the institutionalists, for a variety of reasons, refuse to cross the boundaries of orthodox social science altogether into Marxism, they always will be confronted with this vulnerability (see, e.g., Saul Hoffman's comment below on chapters by Blau and Datcher). All of their contributions can be reworked in a completely neoclassical vein. Marxism has been subjected to the same sort of reworking, but the transformation is never as smooth. To the extent that institutionalists construct models by relaxing assumptions of the neoclassical model of perfect competition, the neoclassical model of perfect competition constitutes their standard reference point. In chapter 6 of this volume, Sam Friedman discusses this problem in great detail in an essay that evaluates the status of the current dissent in labor economics.

The key point is, today, institutionalists and Marxists constitute a tiny minority of practitioners of labor economics. Once, in the United States, the institutionalists were a majority in the subfield of labor economics. For idealists, this reversal came about because the superior research approach ultimately prevailed. For materialists, there were concrete developments in the class composition of American society involving professionalization, technocraticization, and the ideological function of economists that turned the subfield upside down. McNulty wrestles noncommittally with a sociological analysis of the change in orientation in labor economics. The objective of this book is to gather in one place a set of seven chapters and four comments that provide the beginnings of a fruitful assessment of the consequences of the intellectually conservative revolution of the 1940s and 1950s for labor economics. It was conservative in a conceptual and imaginative sense; it was radical in its demands for rigor. To conduct the assessment the contents of this book combine papers from those who are active practitioners of labor economics as well as those who are economists working in other subfields. It is a diverse potpourri that should prove stimulating to the reader.

Survey of the Book's Contents

While embracing the approach of applied microeconomics, labor economists have explicitly and, more often, implicitly accepted the associated methodological position of "Positive Economics." Economists are not known for belaboring the finer points of the philosophy of science. On the rare occasions when the matter of methodological approach is raised, economists will refer the inquirer to Milton Friedman's famous essay "The Methodology of Positive Economics" and consider the subject closed. This is unfortunate; Friedman's essay constitutes extremely weak methodological underpinnings. Two economists with a serious knowledge of methodological issues but with vastly different ideological perspectives have both concluded that there are glaring theoretical shortcomings in Friedman's development of "Positive Economics." They also agree that neither Friedman nor his disciples actually follow his methodological prescriptions (Blaug, pp. 103–20; Katouzian, pp. 45–84). Moreover, less idiosyncratic and more general positivist positions than Friedman's are far from unassailable as well (Blaug; Katouzian).[2]

Rhonda Williams in chapter 1 examines whether labor economists follow the premises of positivism as described by Karl Popper. She concentrates on the empirical research involving human capital theory. In concluding that there is a marked gap between actual practice and the professed or ostensible methodological position of the labor economists, Williams leaves the door open for the possibility that there is a, as of yet unarticulated, coherent methodological position that is consistent with actual practice in labor economics. But, as she demonstrates convincingly, actual practice is clearly inconsistent with Popperian falsificationism. Thus labor economics fails to meet its own norms for maintaining scientific status.

Williams suggests that Popper's criteria for scientific inquiry, if followed, can produce a common ground for competition between the neoclassical, institutionalist, and Marxist paradigms. This is an interesting suggestion. However, Marxism frequently is premised on an entirely different conception of science from the ultraempiricist orientation of both the neoclassical and institutionalist approaches. It may be inappropriate to draw all three traditions into the same race.

The second chapter in the book is an impressive survey of a burgeoning region of labor economics — the literature on sex discrimination in the labor market. It is impressive both in its comprehensiveness and its dispassionate assessment of a host of frequently incompatible studies. The author, Francine Blau, has written what may remain for a while the definitive survey article on this topic.

To summarize, Blau's conclusions can be reduced somewhat inelegantly to four major points: (1) human capital theory suggests that wage and occupational differences are attributable to productivity differences between the sexes; (2) this explanation does not account fully for the empirically significant incidence of wage and occupational differences between men and women with equivalent productivity-linked characteristics; (3) therefore sex discrimination must operate in the labor market; but (4) there is an absence of a satisfactory theory of the *persistence* of sex discrimination in competitive labor markets.

The persistence of labor market discrimination under competition is *the* conundrum for neoclassicals. One escape route has been a tendency among those thoroughly committed to the human capital project to minimize the existence and/or importance of such phenomena; Thomas Sowell's perspective is representative of this tendency. Alternatively, those labor economists who acknowledge that discrimination matters have tended to invoke market imperfections as the source of persistence. This means, in turn, that they obligate themselves to explain the persistence of the imperfections in the face of ongoing or potential competitive pressures (e.g., the "contestable markets" literature in the subfield of industrial organization) — or they must dismiss the existence of competition in the marketplace. Few have considered the possibility that the difficulty might lie with the contemporary neoclassicals' market structure concept of competition in the first place.[3] Problems such as the nature of competition that could subvert the coherency of the entire discipline's normal practices rarely will surface in subfields distant from the immediate arena of dispute. Only in the earlier history of labor economics when contention with the marginalists was a going enterprise did such problems occupy a great deal of the time and energy of labor economists. Today the subversive aspects of worries over the limitations of the market structure notion of competition are far less pronounced. When it is discovered that persistent labor market discrimination and labor market competition are irreconcilables, the inclination is to question the former rather than the latter.

Blau's work also suggests, at least, two further issues associated with trends in the development of labor economics. First, her chapter makes it plain that labor economists attack average differences in economic performances between the sexes, the races, or various ethnic groups in exactly the same way. Research on sex discrimination and race discrimination in the subfield of labor economics looks indistinguishable if one substitutes black and white for male and female. The difficulty here is the fact that sex and race are not conceptual equivalents, a difficulty masked by the current ideological use of the all-encompassing term "minorities." Reinforcing the peculiarity is the argument frequently made about male employees' "taste for discrimination" toward women. Yet, men generally live with women, marry women, sleep with women, and rear children with women — while ostensibly preferring homosocial workplace groupings. Obviously, no such paradox is as blatant in the case of white workers having a "taste for discrimination" toward blacks. Compounding the confusion in the use of identical research tactics for sex and race discrimination is the additional obvious fact that members of both sexes come in all races, and members of all races come in both sexes.

Second, the issue of economic inequality between ascriptively different groups has become a major research topic in labor economics. This has occurred to such an extent that now labor economists seem to be the only researchers in economics exploring this topic. Why sexual, racial, or ethnic economic differences have become the purview of labor economists alone is a curious event that demands exploration. It is a serious shortcoming of McNulty's book that he makes no mention of how or why these themes were allocated to the labor economists after World War II.

Somewhat obliquely, Blau's chapter indicates that, in their research on sexual differences in labor market experiences, economists have displayed only a tangential (at best, statistical) interest in the nature of parenthood (fatherhood versus motherhood), the historically changing role and structure of family life, and the role of the legal-judicial system in affecting family life. If anything, the analysis of the family also has been assimilated into the domain of applied empirical microeconomics (e.g., Becker). As the approach of the subfield has grown more narrowly economistic — while its research topics have broadened dramatically — labor economists typically have lost a serious interest in and knowledge about the research of scholars in social anthropology, sociology, legal studies, and psychology. But that body of research seems eminently relevant to the study of sexual differences in labor markets.

Julianne Malveaux's chapter on the continued observation of a marked racial discrepancy in unemployment rates points toward many of the same themes and puzzles that emerge in Blau's contribution. Coupled with Blau's work, it provides the reader with a thorough view of how labor economists handle sex and race gaps. As suggested above, labor economists tend to handle both in the same way.

It is notable that Malveaux's discussion of the self-investment variant of the human capital argument opens the door wide for the entry of the rational expectations hypothesis (REH) throughout all of labor economics. It need not remain confined to the Phillips curve controversy, but it can easily spread across all efforts to model participants in the market for labor as rational optimizers. Blau's discussion of Kenneth Arrow's "perceptual equilibrium" as a self-fulfilling prophecy carries the same message. The use of the REH in labor economics is likely to become more pronounced since "rationality" and "rational expectations" are natural allies.

The assumption of "rationality" is the subject of Samuel Myers, Jr.'s challenging comment on the Blau, Dickens, and Malveaux contributions to this book. Myers wonders why all three proceed to accept, without reservation, the conventional view of individual decision-making characteristic of neoclassical microeconomics. Drawing on the work of organization theorists and researchers concerned with decision making in environments with nonquantifiable uncertainty, Myers suggests that the authors should have considered seriously models where individuals "satisfice" or display "bounded rationality."

There is, in addition, a subtle contrast between the Blau and Malveaux chapters in their respective attitudes toward the marginal productivity doctrine. Although Blau is not convinced that differences in productivity between the sexes fully explain differences in earnings, she generally seems willing to accept the validity of viewing productivity as a characteristic possessed by individuals. Malveaux is more uneasy; her chapter is suggestive of deeper problems with the conceptualization of productivity as an attribute of individuals, independent of their work context and the machinery they use in their workplace.[4] Malveaux's work hints that disputes that arose in the area of capital theory over the nature of productivity and over the legitimacy of marginal productivity as an explanation of the functional and/or size distribution of income are slowly seeping back into more critically minded discussions in labor economics.

In contrast, in the fourth chapter, Linda Datcher unabashedly accepts the marginal productivity doctrine. She implicitly adopts the view that increased educational attainment raises individual marginal products which, in turn, raises individual market earnings. With this assumption in mind, she examines the literature on the connection between an individual's social background and educational attainments. She then assesses what labor economists have said about the sources of racial differences in educational attainment in the broader context of the debates over the conditions required to achieve "equality of opportunity" in the United States.

Social background for Datcher is a mixture of the endowments bestowed upon an individual by his or her family and by their immediate community.

Datcher is concerned with the contribution relatives and neighborhoods make toward human capital formation. Her project is premised on a prior commitment to human capital/marginal productivity theory.

As a consequence, her discussion bears an intimate relationship to a recently burgeoning literature that attributes individual and group differences in economic achievement to cultural inheritance. Representative of this literature is Thomas Sowell's book *Ethnic America* and the conjectures about intergenerational transmission of economic status of Datcher's colleague, Glenn Loury. Loury refers to a racial or ethnic group's "social capital" which it bestows on succeeding generations. Depending upon the quantity and quality of the group's "social capital," its offspring will have varying degrees of success in the labor market.

Datcher treats the "social capital" approach as distinct from human capital theory. This is conceivable only if one treats human capital theory as meaning solely a pure self-investment model. The "social capital" approach, by placing the emphasis on parental and neighborhood investments in children, could be contrasted with a pure self-investment model.[5] However, if patterns of self-investment are conditioned by parental and community influences, the approaches tend to overlap. Furthermore, there are few labor economists who would equate human capital theory with a pure self-investment model. At least as early as the late Victorian era, economists sought to connect the advantages or disadvantages children received from their parents with the children's subsequent economic achievements. For example, all the essentials of the "social capital" approach appeared in chapter 4 of Book VI of Marshall's *Principles.* What really was at stake was the degree of upward mobility in a class-based society, but economists from Marshall to the present generally have shied away from an authentic analysis of class, race, and labor.[6]

Datcher's tacit acceptance of a strong positive connection between schooling and earnings lays the basis for further potential controversy over her chapter. Sources of skepticism are, at least, a couple of books from the early 1970s by Ivar Berg and Christopher Jencks. In fact, Jencks (p. 265) concluded his book by challenging the capacity of the school system to function as a vehicle for promoting economic equality at all

> As long as egalitarians assume that public policy cannot contribute to economic equality directly but must proceed by ingenious manipulations of marginal institutions like the schools, progress will be glacial.

Jencks (p. 265) then argued that equality — racial or general — will require a form of socialism, or, in his words, "political control over the economic institutions that shape our society." Disturbingly, this leaves open the question of whom should exercise such control. But Jencks' contention does stand in marked contrast with Datcher's optimistic conclusions about the schools as instruments of economic equality. Datcher suggests that the schools can prevent new generations from remaining locked into their parents' or their community's economic status. In addition, Datcher acknowledges at the start of her chapter that education's equalizing role can be diminished "when differences in social origin result in large differences in the quality or quanitity of educational attainment." Yet none of the empirical studies she surveys make any reference to the quality of schooling. The outcomes they explore are based strictly on years of schooling without regard for content, difficulty, or level of mastery by the student. This omission is especially glaring in the Bowles-Gintis study discussed in her contribution.

A related problem is the subtle distinction between schooling and education. Education relevant to increasing an individual's earnings must include on-the-job training, which also is not captured by the dependent variable in these studies. Thus Datcher's chapter really examines, somewhat narrowly, what labor economists have had to say about the effects of social background on attained years of formal schooling.

The fifth chapter in the volume is a survey by William Dickens of a somewhat more specialized area of labor economics — the literature on occupational safety and health regulation. It represents a region of the subfield that overlaps significantly with the subfield of industrial organization. Not only does Dickens do a yeoman's job of covering the existing literature, but he also endeavors to offer further original contributions to the literature.

Throughout his writing, Dickens adopts an idealist view of progress in economic science — as if the discipline moves forward in terms of its analytical method and its capacity to know. This divorces the analysis of the development of economic thought from any important connection with the social context within which it evolves. In Dickens's chapter the research of labor economists on occupational safety and health is not placed in an historical or ideological milieu but is evaluated instead via a cataloguing of what has been achieved and what remains to be done. What makes his paper compelling is the detail he marshalls to demonstrate that a great deal remains to be done. Nevertheless, this method of evaluation is based on the idealist view of the history of thought.[7]

While sharing Dickens's idealist view of the history of thought, Stephen Woodbury, in his extended comment, expresses reservations about Dickens's methodological position. While both of them share the view that predictive power is the test of a sound theory, Dickens opts for giving the lead to testing assumptions rather than hypotheses generated by untestable assumptions. Woodbury, on the other hand, assigns responsibility entirely to hypothesis-testing. Their disagreement echoes back to the confused state of methodological ideals and actual research practice in labor economics raised by Williams in the lead chapter. Where exactly does a priorism end and empirical testing begin for those committed to positivism in some sense?

Strictly speaking, Dickens does not propose a critique of labor economics en masse in his review essay. His critique applies to what he views as the false application of the perfect competition model to the occupational health and safety literature. He advocates fuller development of models of imperfect competition as the route toward superior insight. Thus, Dickens' complaint is not with economic theory per se, but with the excessive application of the perfect competition model where, in his view, it does not belong.

Dickens does not address why so many economists working in this area stick with the perfect competition model instead of pushing on with development of imperfect competition models. Perhaps the answer is purely ideological. A large number of economists in Washington, D.C., in the age of Reaganomics, are quite willing to argue, unlike Dickens, that the perfect competition model should serve as the fulcrum for the design of occupational safety and health policy. Ironically, such a position renders empirical work largely unnecessary. Any departures from perfect competition could be attributed to state intervention in the marketplace, which ought to be lifted, leaving only optimal competitive market outcomes.

The connection between inquiry and policy in this area is as direct as any in labor economics. This is, in Dickens' view, the way it ought to be, since he takes the position that policy implications should guide scientific inquiry. Thorstein Veblen would have argued that policy-motivated research, however, produces "pragmatic knowledge." "Scientific knowledge" requires a sufficient degree of detachment on the part of the researcher — inclusive of a detachment from the policy arena. Veblen's interesting line of demarcation raises the deeper question, because of the wide variety of ways in which the topics pursued by labor economists are perceived as policy-relevant, of whether labor economics is a subfield solely engaged in the pursuit of "pragmatic" rather than "scientific" knowledge.

It also is worth noting that Dickens reveals a region of labor economics where the use of the rational expectations hypothesis has become quite prevalent. Dickens himself has taken the somewhat unusual step of examining the relationship of the hypothesis to psychologists' findings about individual decision making. He is one of the few labor economists who has seen fit to reach beyond economic theory to develop his models. This has led him toward a provocative treatment of the phenomenon of cognitive dissonance in a collaborative paper with George Akerlof.

But the central issue in the chapter by Dickens is one mentioned above in the context of Blau's work on sex discrimination: Is the best path away from the perfect competition model the development of an endless array of imperfect competition models that relax the assumptions of the perfect competition model or dispensing with the neoclassical market structure concept of competition altogether in favor of an alternative conception that is not beset with the same problems?

The sixth chapter by Samuel Friedman is probably the most detailed evaluation available on the theoretical and empirical content of dual and segmented labor markets. The extent and complexity of the work on dual and segmented labor markets that Friedman uncovers belies Rima's (p. 235) claim in her textbook that "little has thus far been accomplished in the realm of empirical testing . . ." Friedman also provides a valuable clarification about the distinction between dual (industries) and segmentalist (jobs) approaches.

Friedman views both strands as attempts by economists with a lingering attachment to the institutional movement to construct a non-Marxist alternative to neoclassical economics. Contributions to this literature, such as Michael Piore's, descend in near linear fashion from the research of John R. Commons and John T. Dunlop. The work of David Gordon, Richard Edwards, and Michael Reich on segmented workplaces offers a radical vision of the market for labor closer to Marxism, but still is permeated by the concepts and raison d'etre of conventional economics. Friedman argues further that these developments among the dissenting fringe of labor economists constitute a pragmatic attempt to construct a labor economics compatible with their New Left democratic socialist politics.

Somewhat surprisingly, Friedman accepts the empiricist bias of the radical-institutionalist literature, despite posing an external critique of the perspective. Friedman's critique is external in the sense that he evaluates the dualist and segmentalist work on the basis of criteria separate from the premises of applied microeconomics. Friedman raises the fundamental issue of why labor economists conceive of, and focus their attention on, labor markets. A similar issue is raised in a direct but more compressed fashion by Paul Zarembka in his comment on four of the chapters in this book. Friedman, while critical of the radical-institutionalist literature, seeks to extract those insights which are fruitful for a richer understanding of labor-power and the labor-process. Friedman's study reestablishes the fundamental significance of Marx's concept of the reserve army of the unemployed. A satisfactory theory of unemployment and the analysis of the sexual, racial, and ethnic composition of the labor force ought to find its starting point with the concept of the reserve of labor. Successful research attempts in this direction have been undertaken by sociologists — in the 1940s by Oliver Cox and more recently by Edna Bonacich (pp. 17–64) in her development of the "split" labor market hypothesis. Rhonda Williams discusses this approach toward the close of her chapter in this book.

Samuel Friedman's paper also evokes another fascinating theoretical conclusion, although he does not state it himself. Radicals tend to dismiss human capital theory altogether as an ideologically motivated move on the part of bourgeois economists to transform laborers into capitalists. This tendency is blatant in the following passage written by Nobel Laureate and scion of the human capital approach, Theodore Schultze (1978, p. 381, emphasis added)

> . . . neither classical economic theory nor the economic theory of socialism explains the development that accounts for the extraordinary rise in the value of human time; in the United States, for example, real hourly wages increased more than fivefold from 1900 to 1972. It is obvious that the observed high price of the services of labor cannot be explained by a theory of subsistence wages or by a theory of labor exploitation. Although a very large share of national income accrues to labor (in the United States about 80 percent), Marx's labor theory of value is of no avail. Laborers have become *capitalists* as a consequence of the value of their human capital . . .

Seventeen years earlier, Schultze (1961, p. 3, emphasis added) made a similar observation

> *Laborers have become capitalists* not from a diffusion of the ownership of corporation stocks, as folklore would have it, but from the diffusion of knowledge and skill that have economic value.

The usual radical repudiation of comments along these lines from mainstream labor economists is that they overlook the fact that labor-power must be sold to employers regardless of differences in quality. Marx (p. 1040, emphasis in original) plainly recognized the heterogeneity of the commodity, labor-power

> . . . *labour-power socially combined* and the various competing labour-powers which together form the entire production machine participate in very different ways in the immediate process of making commodities, or, more accurately in this context, creating the product. Some work better with their hands, others with their heads, one as a manager, engineer, technologist, etc., the other as overseer, the third as manual labourer or even drudge. An ever increasing number of types of labour are included in the immediate concept of *productive labour,* and those who perform it are classed as *productive workers,* workers directly exploited by capital and subordinated to the process of production and expansion.

The crucial distinction for Marx was not between high and low quality labor-power but between productive and unproductive labor. The latter distinction did not depend upon whether or not a laborer receives wages; Marx (p. 1041) wrote "Every productive worker is a wage-labourer, but not every wage-labourer is a productive worker." Unproductive labor functionally was labor that did not contribute directly to the creation of profit.

Aspirations for upward mobility increasingly became oriented toward movement from productive to unproductive positions (Marx, p. 1041). Professional services increasingly became concentrated in the tier of unproductive occupations (Marx, pp. 1041–2). Thus the usual radical repudiation of Schultze's remarks misses the inner meaning of the postwar resurgence in human capital theory. Whereas human capital theory in its variants that stress educational attainment explain little about the allocation of workers across productive occupations, it may well provide a strong description of the allocation of workers across unproductive occupations. Schultze's assignment of great importance to human capital is a direct consequence of the visible rise of unproductive labor in the mid-twentieth century (see Zarembka, pp. 19–22). Hence the paradox: Human capital theory as a theory of schooling, individual productivity, and labor market achievement has little relevance for the experience of productive laborers but a great deal of relevance for unproductive laborers.

It is the unique position of a segment of unproductive laborers — professional intellectuals and intelligentsia — that provides the transition into the final chapter of this book. Kathryn Allen investigates the area of labor economics that represents the direct region of overlap between applied microeconomics and macroeconomics — the controversy over the Phillips curve. Allen compares the Keynesian, monetarist, and new classical schools' positions on the short- and long-run relationships between inflation and unemployment. Both the monetarists (á la Milton Friedman) and the new classical school presuppose that if economic agents know the true path of prices, they will negotiate money wage rates that will clear the labor market. The monetarists assume the adjustment to market-clearing will be slow due to adaptive expectations; the new classical school assumes the adjustment will be rapid because expectations of future prices are formed rationally. The orthodox Keynesians now argue that even with perfect foresight both employers and employees have sound (rational) reasons for setting wage contracts that do not clear the labor market (e.g., Begg, pp. 134–70).

Allen's major point is that the debate is taking place among members of the same class — a class comprised of intellectuals or the intelligentsia. Their debate and the attention devoted to it signals their ascension to power above both capital and labor. Therefore, Allen is arguing that the significance of the Phillips curve controversy is not primarily over the fine points of the debate but the message it delivers about a change in power relations in U.S. society. Zarembka expresses brief skepticism about this position in his comment, while applauding Allen's efforts to go far outside of the terms of discussion pursued by Blau, Datcher, and Dickens. But Allen has identified what may be the central issue for Marxists today: Is it sufficient to conceive of class struggle as being limited to capital and labor, or should Marxists acknowledge the existence of a separate and significant class — a managerial class — that is a serious contestant for power and proceed with their analyses on that basis?[8] At stake, in the latter instance, is the generation and perpetuation of social hierarchy.

Conclusions

The seven chapters and four comments in this book either directly or indirectly identify all the major issues in labor economics. These ideas have implications for the entire discipline. Several issues are summarized in the following twelve questions:

1. Is there a systematic and coherent methodology that actually is practiced by labor economists?
   a. If so, how does that methodology compare with extant conflicting views of the nature of science (e.g., should a scientist predict or explain)?
   b. If not, does this undermine the validity of all the research undertaken by labor economists?
2. How should the irreconcilability of labor market discrimination and competition be resolved?
   a. Does the failure lie with the concept of labor market discrimination?
   b. Or, does the failure lie with the neoclassical concept of competition?
   c. Does "split" labor market theory constitute a successful alternative?
3. Should the same approach to discrimination be applied to sexual, racial, and ethnic differences in the labor market?
4. What are the implications — conceptual and ideological — of the focus on the market for labor by labor economists?
5. How should uncertainty about the future and expectations be handled in models of individual choice?
6. To what extent should individual choice form the basis for the analysis of behavior in the labor market?
7. Do dual and segmented market approaches constitute a distinct alternative to neoclassical labor economics?

8. What is the role of culture and parental assets in influencing an individual's labor market performance; moreover, what exactly is culture?
9. What is the valid scope of the human capital/marginal productivity theory?
10. What are the analytical consequences of adoption of Marx's concepts of the reserve of labor and productive versus unproductive labor?
11. Is an idealist or materialist theory of the history of ideas superior in the analysis of the development of labor economics as a subfield of economics?
12. Are labor economists themselves members of a distinct social class whose activities promote their own class interests?

The chapters and comments in this volume do not provide definitive answers. But they are evocative and provocative, raising the issues that merit serious consideration for those concerned about the ongoing development of labor economics. These are the modern issues in modern labor economics. It is not really surprising that due to the conservative nature of the revolution of the 1940s and 1950s that the subfield finds itself circling back to the same issues that were present at its inception.

Notes

1. Epitomizing the emergence of an empirical neoclassical development economics is the work of Gary Fields at Cornell University's School of Labor and Industrial Relations group.

2. Blaug does commit himself, although far from blindly, to Popperian falsificationism. Katouzian, while sympathetic, expresses still more reservations. The nagging issue is what are the criteria for deeming a hypothesis false.

3. The inadequacy of the neoclassical market structure concept of competition was raised more than fifty years ago by Piero Sraffa when he observed that neoclassical competition could not accommodate successfully economies of scale. He was, and still is, correct.

4. Lester Thurow tried to force the issue with the marvelous set of puzzles he posed for proponents of marginal productivity theory in a clever appendix to his book *Generating Inequality.* But no defenders of marginal productivity theory have taken up the cudgel to reply to Thurow.

5. To the extent that parents are characterized as choosing the community in which they live, the "social capital" approach really boils down to a parental-cum-cultural determinants version of human capital theory.

6. Sociologists, in contrast, have been inclined to grapple enthusiastically with the race and class matrix — although in more of a Weberian than a Marxist vein. For a work of recent vintage, see William Wilson's *Declining Significance of Race.*

7. For a demonstration of the antithetical materialist analysis of the history of thought, see Krishna Bharadwaj's fine set of lectures on the transition from classical political economy to marginalist/neoclassical economics.

8. My own research has led me to take Allen's position seriously and to explore the implications of the rise to dominance of the managerial class (see Darity).

References

Akerlof, George, and Dickens, William T. "The Economic Consequences of Cognitive Dissonance." *American Economic Review* (June 1982), 302–19.

Becker, Gary. *A Treatise on the Family*. Cambridge: Harvard University Press, 1981.

Begg, David K.H. *The Rational Expectations Revolution in Macroeconomics: Theories and Evidence*. Baltimore: Johns Hopkins University Press, 1982.

Bellante, Don, and Jackson, Mark. *Labor Economics: Choice in Labor Markets*. New York: McGraw-Hill Book Co., 1979.

Berg, Ivar. *Education and Jobs: The Great Training Robbery*. Boston: Beacon Press, 1972.

Bharadwaj, Krishna. *Classical Political Economy and the Rise to Dominance of the Supply and Demand Theories*. Calcutta: Orient Longman, 1978.

Blaug, Mark. *The Methodology of Economics, or How Economists Explain*. Cambridge: Cambridge University Press, 1980.

Bonacich, Edna. "The Past, Present and Future of Split Labor Market Theory." In Cora Bagley Marrett, and Cheryl Leggon (eds.) *Race and Ethnic Relations Vol. 1*. Greenwich: JAI Press, 1979, 17–64.

Cox, Oliver. *Caste, Class, and Race*. New York: Modern Reader, 1970.

Darity, William, Jr. "The Managerial Class and Surplus Population" *Society* (November-December 1983), 54–62.

Fields, Gary. "Industrialization and Employment in Hong Kong, Korea, Singapore, and Taiwan." In Walter Galenson (ed.) *Foreign Trade and Investment: The Newly-Industrializing Asian Countries*. (forthcoming 1983).

Friedman, Milton. "The Methodology of Positive Economics." In *Essays in Positive Economics*. Chicago: University of Chicago Press, 1953.

Gordon, David, Edwards, Richard, and Reich, Michael. *Segmented Work, Divided Workers: The Historical Transformation of Labor in the United States*. Cambridge: Cambridge University Press, 1982.

Jencks, Christopher et al. *Inequality: A Reassessment of the Effect of Family and Schooling in American*. New York: Harper Colophon Books, 1972.

Katouzian, Homa. *Ideology and Method in Economics*. New York and London: New York University Press, 1980.

Loury, Glenn. "A Dynamic Theory of Racial Income Differences." In Phyllis Wallace, and Annette M. La Mond (eds.) *Women, Minorities and Employment Discrimination*. Lexington, Mass.: Lexington Books, D.C. Heath, 1977.

Marshall, Alfred. *Principles of Economics*. 8th edition. London: Macmillan Press, 1920.

Marx, Karl. "Appendix; Results of the Immediate Process of Production." *Capital. Vol. 1*. New York: Vintage Books, 1977.

McNulty, Paul J *The Origins and Development of Labor Economics: A Chapter in the History of Social Thought*. Cambridge: M.I.T. Press, 1980.

Mill, J.S. *Principles of Political Economy with Some of Their Applications to Social Philosophy*. London: Longmans, Green, Reeder, and Dyer, 1869.

Oi, Walter. "Labor as a Quasi-Fixed Factor." *Journal of Political Economy.* (December 1962), 538–55.

Piore, Michael J. "Notes for a Theory of Labor Market Stratification." In Richard C. Edwards, Michael Reich, and David M. Gordon (eds.) *Labor Market Segmentation.* Lexington: Lexington Books, 1975.

Rima, Ingrid. *Labor Markets, Wages, and Employment: An Introduction to Labor Economics.* New York: W.W. Norton, 1981.

Schultze, Theodore W. "Investment in Human Capital." *American Economic Review* (March 1961), 1–15.

______. "Migration: An Economist's View." In William H. McNeill, and Ruth S. Adams (eds.) *Human Migration: Patterns and Policies.* Bloomington: Indiana University Press, 1978.

Sowell, Thomas. *Ethnic America: A History.* New York: Basic Books, 1981.

______. *Markets and Minorities.* New York: Basic Books, 1981.

Sraffa, Piero. "The Laws of Returns Under Competitive Conditions." *The Economic Journal.* (December 1926).

Thurow, Lester. *Generating Inequality.* New York: Basic Books, 1975.

Veblen, Thorstein. "The Place of Science in Modern Civilisation." In *The Place of Science in Modern Civilisation and Other Essays.* New York: Russell and Russell, 1961.

Zarembka, Paul. "The Capitalist Mode of Production: Economic Structure." *Research in Political Economy.* Vol. 1. Greenwich: JAI Press, 1977, 3–28.

II ESSAYS

1 THE METHODOLOGY AND PRACTICE OF MODERN LABOR ECONOMICS: A CRITIQUE

Rhonda M. Williams

Today's student of labor economics quickly learns that the dominant approach to his or her field of inquiry has come to share much with the methods employed by all neoclassical practitioners of applied microeconomics. Like most developments in the history of social science, the current synthesis of labor economics and mainstream economic theory developed gradually and amidst considerable controversy.[1] Nonetheless, under the influence of Chicago's H. Gregg Lewis and his protégés, the post-World War II years have witnessed the meteoric rise of a "modern labor economics" whose theoretical foundations and empirical techniques are at one with the corpus of orthodox economic theory.

Insofar as the establishment of an independent journal signifies the ascendance of a particular field of endeavor, the 1983 publication of the *Journal of Labor Economics* by the University of Chicago Press is evidence of the profession's recognition of the significance of labor economics as an independent field of study. In recognition of the importance of the post-war synthesis, this chapter's critical appraisal of both the methodology and practices of modern labor economics and their most outspoken critics will confine itself to labor economics in its aforementioned form.

Our discussion emphasizes what the author perceives to be a potentially disturbing gap between the espoused methodological principles of neoclassical economists and the actual methods used by those who conduct and evaluate research in labor economics. Accordingly, the first section constitutes (1) a brief primer on the key methodological issues which have shaped modern economists' understanding of the procedures appropriate to their inquiries in "positive" economics (we suggest that the great debate about the rule of assumptions in theory lead to the reaffirmation of economists' commitment to falsificationism and, to varying degrees, instrumentalism) and (2) a summary of Imre Lakatos' criteria for the evaluation of scientific research programs and their applicability to the evaluation of labor economists' theories. The second section critically assesses the extent to which practitioners of labor economics adhere to their own standards; in particular, we focus on both state-of-the-art human capital research and applications of the human capital model to the analysis of racial income inequality. By limiting our discussion to human capital theory, we necessarily present only a partial treatment of the neoclassical labor economists' research agenda. Nonetheless, the growth of human capital research in the past two decades suggests that a reasonable assessment of its strengths and weaknesses will provide a good first approximation to the state of the art. The next section addresses the methodological implications of current challenges to the orthodox treatment of labor economics — i.e., dual labor market and Marxist theories. Finally, we conclude with a brief summary of our appraisal of modern labor economics and suggest future directions which may enhance labor economists' efforts to steer clear of methodological muddles.

Methodology and Modern Economics

Unlike their nineteenth century counterparts, who were predominantly verificationists,[2] the majority of contemporary mainstream economists are self-proclaimed falsificationists. Their methodological mission, as practitioners of economic science, is the generation of theories and hypotheses whose predictions can, at least in principle, be falsified empirically. Having accepted that their business as social scientists is the development of testable theories, most economists also share the conclusion that economic theories should stand or fall on their predictive power. The profession also appears united in its rejection of "naive falsificationism," the doctrine which holds that a theory can be refuted by a single test, and in the affirmation of a more sophisticated version of falsification which demands several tests before discarding a theory. In their popular introductory textbook, Richard G. Lipsey and Peter O. Steiner (1981, p. 27) describe the evolution of science as follows:

> When theories fail to predict better than available alternatives, theories tend to be rejected. The progress of any science lies in finding better explanations of events than are now available. Thus, in any developing science, one must expect to discard present theories and replace them with demonstrably superior alternatives.

Lipsey and Steiner assert that the progress of economic science must be gauged in terms of its ability to generate better explanations of economic phenomena; however, not all supposedly theoretical explanations lend themselves to the making of predictions (e.g., Darwin's theory of evolution or Freudian theories of psychology), and prediction requires correlation but not identification of a causal mechanism. This distinction between explanation and prediction becomes methodologically significant when we are confronted with predictively powerful economic theories whose behavioral explanations ascribe motives to economic agents that bear no resemblance to categories which we, as homo sapiens, use to describe and understand our behavior. Although the previously cited passage is a somewhat ambiguous guide to the evaluation of such theories, Lipsey and Steiner's other comments strongly suggest that prediction is the desideratum of theorizing — "A successful theory enables us to predict the consequences of various occurrences" (p. 22).

Not surprisingly, Lipsey and Steiner's position corresponds to the dominant viewpoint held by the majority of those in the economics profession. At the risk of exaggeration, we suggest that the modern (post-1950) resolution of the criteria crisis (i.e., by what criteria should economists judge their work?) was provided by Milton Friedman in his now classic essay "The Methodology of Positive Economics" (1956), written during an era when there was much in-house debate about the realism of the behavioral assumption of profit-maximization, which constitutes the core of neoclassical theory of the firm. Because Friedman's essay fails to distinguish among the various types of assumptions which economists use — motivational and behavioral assumptions, assumptions which invoke convenient fictions, definitional assumptions, assumptions which define the realm of a theory's applicability, etc. — much confusion emerged in subsequent discussions of this thesis.[3] Nonetheless, Friedman struck the decisive blow on behalf of falsificationism when he convinced the majority of his colleagues that a scientific theory should be judged not on the basis of the relevance or realism of its assumptions, but rather by its "predictive power for the class of phenomena which it is intended to explain" (p. 27). Moreover, Friedman goes on to assert that truly important hypotheses must be descriptively false in their assumptions, since they are but abstractions of the crucial elements of the phenomena to be explained. Finally, Friedman claims that it is indeed valid to use assumptions to specify the circumstances under which a theory holds, but not to determine the circumstances for which it holds, since a well-constructed theory details, inter alia, its realm of applicability (pp. 30–33).

We are therefore justified in assuming that individuals and firms are, respectively, utility and profit maximizers, not because we believe that they actually undertake the solution of constrained optimization problems, but because they behave as if they were optimizing agents. The strength of Friedman's conviction is made all the more clear in his discussion of the cigarette industry, where he argues that the nature of the problem at hand (rather than the attributes of the cigarette industry) determine whether or not the industry should be treated theoretically as if it were perfectly competitive (pp. 43–44). As Blaug observes, it is at this juncture that Friedman reveals his truly instrumentalist orientation — i.e., scientific theories in general, and economic theories in particular, are no more than instruments for generating hypotheses and predictions. Hence, we need not be disturbed by economists who, in one instance, assume competitive behavior in the cigarette industry and in the next, assume noncompetitive behavior, since these assumptions are but convenient tools for the generation of predictions.

Much more could, and probably will, be said about Friedman's famous essay on the irrelevance of assumptions. For our purposes, two additional comments are warranted. First, Friedman does acknowledge (in a footnote!) that independent studies of actual behavior, designed to ascertain the extent to which assumptions actually correspond to agents' self-understanding, may be extremely valuable in suggesting leads to follow in accounting for divergences between predicted and observed results; that is, in constructing new hypotheses or revising old ones" (p. 40, footnote 23). Assumptions are thus not completely irrelevant to the assessment of theories, only largely irrelevant. Second, Friedman's tenacious advocacy of instrumentalism leaves unanswered questions for those inclined to apply his methodological prescriptions: Should we rest easy on the laurels of predictive power, or should we ask more of economic theory than predictive accuracy? Insofar as one takes seriously the position espoused by Harre and other critics of Friedman, he would insist that a truly scientific explanation must posit an intervening causal mechanism which makes necessary the relationships between observed phenomena.[4]

Because even those predictions derived from the most rigorously axiomatized theory need not provide explanations, we are left in a bit of a quandary. We should note that the prevailing view within the profession embraces the instrumentalist methodology, despite its potential failings.[5] Our critique in the second section will therefore proceed from the assumption that neoclassical labor economists are practicing falsificationists generally unconcerned about the relevance of their assumptions.

Before turning our attention to the methodological and empirical status of modern labor economics, we will pursue a line of inquiry related to the larger implications of falsificationism. In principle, there must exist circumstances under which the true falsificationist would abandon his theory. However, as Thomas Kuhn so aptly observed, few scientists will completely discard a body of theory (for example, neoclassical theories of labor market behavior derived from the assumption of utility-maximizing individuals) simply because some empirical evidence exists counter to that theory (Kuhn, 1970). Only when an alternative theoretical construction exists, and only after long periods of debate, will one disciplinary matrix replace another. These issues obviously become important in our forthcoming consideration of the challenges to orthodox labor theory posed by dual labor market theorists and Marxists, and are elaborated in the concluding portion of this section.

Our appraisal of the methodological practices of labor economists will also be greatly aided by reference to the insights of Imre Lakatos (1978), who proposed an approach to falsificationism which recognizes the intransigence of existing theoretical frameworks. Lakatos proposed the "Methodology of Scientific Research Programs" (MSRP) as a means of scientific appraisal. Lakatos argued that individual theories (e.g., human capital theory or economic theories of discrimination) are inappropriate units of analysis; when evaluating the stature of a given body of scientific thought, the focus should be on clusters of interrelated theories or "scientific research programs" (SRP). For example, neoclassical economic theory constitutes an SRP. When confronted with a series of falsified hypotheses, an SRP's practitioners begin to augment its assumptions. These auxiliary assumptions can either enhance or detract from the substantive content of the theory. An SRP is said to be "theoretically progressive" if its successive reformulations lead to an accumulation of empirical content (i.e., new hypotheses and predictions) and "empirically progressive" if the new hypotheses survive empirical testing. "Degenerative" SRPs are typically characterized by endless ad hoc adjustments that render the theories consistent with new facts and "immunize" the existing corpus from further onslaughts (Blaug, 1980, p. 36).

Equipped with these methodological tools, we now can turn our attention to the specifics and applications of the human capital research program, which, as we shall suggest, constitutes a subprogram of the more broadly defined neoclassical SRP.

Human Capital Theory: Progress or Degeneration?

Again employing the terminology suggested by Lakatos, we justify our treatment of human capital theory as a research program by distinguishing its "hard core" from its "protective belt." The "hard core" of a research program constitutes the set of beliefs deemed irrefutable by the methodological decisions of its practitioners; the "protective belt" is the flexible portion of an SRP in which the hard core and auxiliary assumptions are combined to formulate testable hypotheses (Lakatos, pp. 49–52). Blaug has summarized the core of the human capital research program as "the idea that people spend on themselves in diverse ways, not for the sake of present enjoyments, but for the sake of future pecuniary and nonpecuniary returns" (Blaug, 1976, pp. 822–855). Individuals are therefore choosing health care, deciding to migrate, or choosing formal education and on-the-job training as if they were maximizing a lifetime stream of future benefits. As mentioned previously, our evaluation of the human capital research program will proceed according to the falsificationist and instrumentalist standard espoused by the majority of the profession. However, for those inclined to evaluate scientific theories in terms of their explanatory power, Darity's criticism of the behavioral implications of the many human capital theories which populate the "protective belt" is worthy of note:

> If the world is one of subjective uncertainty in the Keynes-Shackle sense of people not knowing the probability distributions for the rates of return associated with various actions they can take today, then the self-investment model makes little sense as a guide to human behavior. In a world of subjective uncertainty, attempts to estimate earnings equations that rely on adaptive or rational expectations are clearly misspecifications of the actual processes at play. (Darity, 1982a, p. 84)

In what remains of this section, we consider the empirical evidence amassed on behalf of several theories in the protective belt of the human capital research program. As we consider theories of the demand for schooling, on-the-job training, earnings functions, and racial income inequality, it should be recalled that our primary concern is (1) the extent to which these theories lend themselves to falsification; (2) both the severity of, and results from, the tests compiled to date; and (3) the extent to which human capital theories predict actions not predicted by rival theories (independent corroboration).

Turning first to formal education, the principle prediction of human capital theory is that the demand for noncompulsory (upper secondary and postsecondary) education is a function of both the private costs (direct and indirect) of schooling and variations in the earnings differentials associated with additional schooling. Thus, Becker notes that human capital theory would have ex ante predicted the increase in American college attendance during the post-World War II years on the basis of a consistently high rate of return to educational self-investment (Becker, 1975, pp. 169–73). However, as Blaug has observed, human capital theorists are not unique in their ability to predict these enrollment changes; during the late 1960s and early 1970s, several researchers estimated demand functions for higher education in theoretical models which treat education as a pure consumption good.[6] These predictively accurate models suggest that Becker's initial predictions have not been independently corroborated.

Richard Freeman's 1971 study of scientists' career choices extended the human capital protective belt to include specialization decisions (Freeman, 1971). Although Freeman's analysis incorporated the lag effect of today's earnings on the supply of scientists four years hence and proxies for the nonpecuniary aspects of jobs which influence occupational choice, as well as controlled for labor demand in the market for college-trained scientists, his use of starting salaries as a proxy for lifetime earnings prohibits the testing of the crucial hypothesis of interest — i.e., that human capital investment is undertaken with an eye to life-cycle benefits. We must therefore conclude, as did Blaug, that this hardly constitutes a strong test of the pecuniary implications of human capital theory. And, as in the aforementioned general analysis of trends in college enrollment, researchers applying orthodox consumer theory have been able to predict successfully, for at least one college, changes in student subject choices;[7] again, the protective belt is not independently corroborated.

As a final reflection on the demand for schooling, we must ask to what extent human capital theory is useful to the analyst interested in those countries where the supply of higher education slots is determined by government policy. Unless we model the decision-making process of educational policy-makers, human capital tests of demand functions must ultimately be construed as simultaneous tests of supply functions. In those European countries where access to higher education is rationed, tests of the hypothesis that subject choice is sensitive to relative earnings must be conducted in a theoretical framework which first specifies the process whereby a young person gains access to higher education.

Formal classroom education is but one outlet for productive self-investment. Virtually every contemporary labor economics textbook also treats at great length the nature of on-the-job training. Becker's model of general versus specific training laudably predicts that employees must pay for general training, whether it be of the sort presumably provided in the classroom or on-the-job general training. Workers are viewed as engaging in postschool human capital investment by choosing occupations that pay workers less than their marginal products. The choice of such a job enables the worker to enhance future earnings by foregoing current earnings while pursuing training. This model predicts that age-earnings profiles will be concave, and this prediction thus far has been confirmed for the United States and for a wide variety of nations throughout the world.

There are, however, at least three problems which advocates of training models must confront. First, as Blaug notes

> . . . any psychological theory of "learning curves," in which appreciation over time is partly but only partly offset by depreciation and obsolescence, will likewise account for concave age earnings profiles. (1976, p. 831)

Second, in neither practice nor in principle is it easy to separate costly off-the-job, in-plant training (whether it be general or specific) from either costless on-the-job-learning-by-doing or on-the-job-doing-under-supervision. Since learning by doing is unavoidable, it is questionable whether it is legitimate to treat it as an endogenous variable subject to individual choice. Full treatment of the training problem would require the construction of a structural model which (1) completely specified the determinants of occupational choice (nonpecuniary and pecuniary occupational attributes, uncertainty, capital market constraints which effectively constitute barriers to occupational entry, etc.), including the training opportunities offered by different firms and occupations, and (2) a firm-specific production function which incorporated firm's joint production of goods (or services) and training opportunities.[8] Such a theory would obviously require an extensive treatment of internal labor markets.

A third problem confronting the developers of labor training models (Mincer, 1974) is their need to assume that human capital markets attain an equilibrium in which private rates of return to successive years of schooling are equalized at the margin. However, as Psacharopoulos and Hinchliffe (1973) have shown, the overwhelming available international evidence (including the United States) indicates that private rates of return decline with successive years of schooling. A true believer in the irrelevance of assumptions would not, of course, find such counterevidence disturbing; we simply suggest, as might Friedman, that future formulations of labor training models might benefit from consideration of the apparent disequilibrium tendencies in human capital markets.

Finally, we should comment on Yoram Ben-Porath's efforts (1967, 1970) to model the aforementioned process of sequential individual decisions according to the tenets of optimal control theory. The optimal control approach to human capital acquisition assumes that individuals possess an initial given human capital stock which can generate a lifetime of earnings subject to an exogenously determined rate of depreciation. Individuals can use their stock to earn or learn, but not both. Ben-Porath's model leads to two, by now unstartling, predictions: age-earnings profiles are concave and investment in training occurs early in the life cycle. His later efforts to test the model with data were unsuccessful, largely due to his discovery that it is impossible to allow for both earning and learning on the job. Suffice it to say that human capital theories of postschooling labor training have yet to experience rigorous testing.

This is not, however, the case for the hypothesis that years of schooling and earnings are positively correlated. Age-earnings profiles indisputably reflect the positive relationship between numbers of years of schooling and income. Literally thousands of human capital earnings functions have been estimated for samples from a wide variety of populations. The results overwhelmingly demonstrate a positive rate of return from schooling. On the basis of these results, many human capital theorists infer that schooling is indeed the link between productivity and earnings. It is at this point that the consensus deteriorates and the schooling/earnings function controversy begins.

Our objective at this juncture is not the presentation of an in-depth survey of the vast accumulation of earnings function results.[9] Rather, our concern is illumination of the methodological issues which have shaped the environment within which this research has been, and continues to be, conducted. We suggest that these concerns fall into two basic groups: (1) the role of schooling and (2) the general appropriateness of the specification used in the estimation of earnings functions.

Human capital earnings functions generally assume the following form

$$\ln Y = \alpha_0 + \alpha_1 S + \alpha_2 EXP + \alpha_3 EXP + BZ + E \qquad (1.1)$$

where:
- Y = earnings
- EXP = experience (years in a specific job or in the labor force)
- S = years of schooling
- Z = a vector of ascriptive traits (age, race, sex, family background) hypothesized to be determinants of income
- α_i, B = parameters to be estimated
- E = random variable

The role of schooling controversy centers around the interpretation of α_1, the supposed rate of return to schooling. At least three alternative explanations of schooling's correlation with earning have been offered. Whereas human capital theorists argue that education is productivity-enhancing (due to its develoment of cognitive skills), advocates of the screening or credentials thesis suggest that in the presence of insufficient information about prospective employees, firms use education credentials as a screening device to distinguish new workers in terms of ability, affective traits, and trainability. Radical theorists view education as a concomitant force in the reproduction of inequality which socializes young people for their roles in a class-based society.

Although we do not intend to resolve this debate here, we should note that the controversy was considerably heightened by the results from both the Coleman report (1966) and Christopher Jencks' study (1972) of inequality. Whereas the Coleman report results indicated that both schooling and the amorphously defined family background (a composite of family income, parental occupations and educational levels, number of siblings, etc.) contribute to learning and therefore earnings, Jencks concluded from his study that earnings are determined primarily by luck. Jencks et al. found that neither parental education, student test scores, nor schooling expenditures exhibit a statistically significant relationship to earnings. Mosteller and Moynihan (1972) further fanned the fires of controversy when they found no significant link between educational expenditures and achievement, holding years of schooling constant. Given the absence of evidence which demonstrates the interdependence between resource expenditure and either earnings or educational achievement, the claim that education and marketable productivity are related rests on rather tenuous empirical grounds: only on the extensive margin are earnings and schooling related. Indeed, most practitioners who estimate earnings functions admit that using years of schooling as a proxy for productivity constitutes measurement error, since what is actually desired is a measure of "productive knowledge."

A second area of major concern might be best described as specification and measurement problems. It is widely recognized that because schooling itself is a choice variable in the human capital model (an individual invests in schooling as long as the present value of benefits exceeds that of costs, assuming that his internal rate of time preference exceeds alternative rates of return), years of schooling must be treated as an endogenous variable in a more fully specified structural model.[10] In such a model, time preference would also warrant treatment as an endogenous variable, since it is arguably determined by initial income endowments as well as tastes.

Another thorny problem which continues to plague estimators of human capital earnings functions is the appropriate treatment and measurement of ability. Because human capital theory generally assumes more able individuals undertake more self-investment, ability's absence from the earnings specification biases estimates of α_1 (i.e., estimates of schooling's impact on earnings are contaminated by the unobserved impact of ability on earnings). Earnings function estimators generally have dealt with this problem in one of two ways — either estimate the equations without ability and evaluate the results in light of the potential biases (Datcher, 1982, p. 34) or include some test-score measure of ability. I.Q. test scores and other aptitude test scores are used frequently. The latter approach is, of course, not an entirely satisfactory solution, given that we have no way of directly measuring intelligence. Similar measurement problems arise in the quantification of family background in the modelling of family background's direct and indirect (via the demand for schooling) impact on earnings and in the use of experience as a proxy for investments in on-the-job training.

After many years of estimating earnings functions, few would disagree that the task proved to be more complicated than was imagined initially. Recognition of the aforementioned complexities has led to the development of improved specifications, as have, for example, efforts to address sample selection problems. Nonetheless, the human capital research program is still in the early phases of specifying and testing a fully specified structural model (complete with both the demand and supply equations which generate the reduced form earnings function and equations which specify the endogenous determination of time preference and years of schooling) consistent with the theoretical implications of the human capital model. Once again, the tests to date are not altogether convincing, given the gap between theory and econometric specification.

We are not, of course, the first to note some of the more troubling inconsistencies in human capital theory. Although he did not specifically address the aforementioned problems which confront the estimator of earnings functions, Lester Thurow's 1975 analysis of earnings distribution in the United States revealed many empirical realities which contradict the predictions of human capital theory. Thurow noted that the shape of the distribution of earnings in the mid-1960s was not consistent with "the distribution of augmentable human capital, or at least that part of it reflecting education" (Thurow, 1975, p. 59). More simply stated, there were (and continue to be) more low-income individuals than would be predicted from the number of persons with low levels of education.

Economists' efforts to resolve this paradox reveal their tendencies to invoke what Karl Popper (1972, p. 61) has described as auxiliary "immunizing stratagems" to shield the protective belt of human capital theory from serious refutation. As Thurow aptly observed, the standard strategy used to explain the divergence between the distribution of earnings and education is to "postulate the existence of some unobservable, non-normally distributed ability" (*op. cit.*, p. 61) such as motivation or the willingness to accept risk. These explanations can be further complicated by postulating that the interaction of innate abilities and acquired human capital leads to a final distribution of earnings which varies greatly from that generated by the sum of the two characteristic distributions. If we assume (1) the more innately gifted acquire more human capital and/or (2) the variance in the returns to human capital are larger than the returns to innate ability/effort, almost all distributions of earnings become instantly explicable in terms of the distributions of, and returns to, these innate attributes.

Arguments of this form share the common attribute of irrefutability. Since we cannot yet satisfactorily measure innate ability, the invocation of assumptions about either its distribution or nonlinear interaction with acquired human capital is destined to yield hypotheses which cannot be falsified; theories based on assumptions of this form can be formulated so as to be consistent with almost any empirical finding. What, then, has happened to our methodological norm of falsificationism? It has been replaced by the easier doctrine of verificationism, which, as its nineteenth century practitioners showed, leads to endless justifications for ignoring apparent refutations of an economic prediction, but produces no criteria by which we might reject a particular theoretical construction.[11]

Human capital analyses of black-white wage differentials also have fallen prey occasionally to this perplexing tendency to generate unfalsifiable propositions. It is, however, to their credit that human capital theorists have been quite explicit about explanations of racial wage differential: blacks tend to accumulate less human capital, and the market, in its impersonal fashion, simply rewards blacks according to the lower value of their marginal products. Discrimination therefore disappears from the labor market and recedes into the background market of human capital acquisition or development.

An in-depth review of the empirical studies on black-white wage differentials would obviously take us well beyond the scope and intentions of this chapter, and the author elsewhere has addressed at great length the theoretical and empirical dilemmas which plague this literature and preclude the placing of much confidence in its results (Williams, 1983). Our methodological discussion of the human capital research program can, however, beneficially draw on insights developed in earlier analyses.

First, among those economists who do not view the convergence of the black-white earnings differential in the 1960s and 1970s as the by-product of voluntary black withdrawal from the labor force (e.g., Richard Freeman, James Smith, and Finis Welch), explanations of the convergence assume one of two forms — a decline in white "tastes for discrimination" (Freeman, 1973, 1978) or qualitative improvements in the stock of black human capital (Smith and Welch, 1977). Because Freeman's test of the hypothesis that "tastes for discrimination" have declined seems more like a disturbing confusion of theory and fact rather than a powerful statistical test, we direct our methodological comments to his and Smith and Welch's shared emphasis on changes in racial differences in human capital.

Freeman argues that the remaining observed black-white wage gap is the product of continuing racial gaps in the quality of home-produced human capital. Or, put differently, black families are still less effective in their efforts to socialize their children than white families. Smith and Welch adopt a slightly different view and contend that observed improvements in the relative economic position of blacks already reflect an upgrading in the quality of black human capital. Although they disagree about the timing, both Freeman and Smith and Welch nonetheless support the human capital view of racial income inequality, which predicts that a decline in racial differences in human capital will lead to the demise in the black-white wage differential.

The straightforward nature of this prediction facilitates its testing (albeit imperfectly) with conventional techniques. The available evidence strongly indicates that convergence in human capital characteristics has not led to the demise of the racial wage gap. We suggest that the evidence produced below casts considerable doubt on the current validity of the Freeman/Smith-Welch hypothesis.

One of the more obvious implications of the human capital explanation is that blacks and whites with similar characteristics should experience similar successes in the labor market. Neither the evidence on earnings nor unemployment support this hypothesis. For evidence on earnings, we look to Linda Datcher's (1982) study of the impact of family backgrounds and neighborhood characteristics on socioeconomic achievement. Although Datcher's recursive model of educational attainment and earnings is not without its own econometric problems,[12] her analysis of the impact of family background on education and earnings is a revealing test of human capital theory. Datcher's simulations do indeed suggest that neighborhood characteristics (as a source of externalities) are an important component of family background's impact on education and earnings. However, of even greater importance is her finding that, as of 1978, whites continued to experience greater benefits (i.e., more years of schooling and higher earnings) from a given augmentation of human capital than did blacks. In other words, convergence in human capital characteristics may be necessary, but certainly is not sufficient, to guarantee the closing of the black-white earnings gap.

A second and equally damaging body of evidence which strongly challenges the human capital explanation of racial income inequality is found in unemployment studies and statistics. Smith and Welch argue that human capital upgrading is particularly important in explaining the economic gains of younger black cohorts; decreasing wage inequality between blacks and whites is primarily the result of the decline in racially based human capital differences. However, as Robert Hill's (1978) collection of unemployment data reveals, black and white youth with comparable educational achievements experience dramatically different levels of unemployment (table 1–1). Hill's data shows that blacks who have attended college have higher unemployment rates than white high school dropouts. It is difficult to explain these racial unemployment gaps simply in terms of racial differences in educational attainment.

The most frequently pursued resolution of this paradox has been provided by job-search theory, which views unemployment as a voluntary, productive activity because the unemployed have, on the basis of their preferences and the availability of social insurance programs, decided to search for a job and can do so better when out of work. Social insurance programs (AFDC, unemployment compensation, food stamps, public housing) reduce the burden of joblessness and are particularly attractive to low-wage earners (for whom the opportunity cost of not working is low), and thereby prolong unemployment. However, quit-search activity has been shown to be empirically the least important source of unemployment,[13] and Clark and Summers' important study revealed that (1) relatively few of the unemployed use job-search techniques that conflict with the demands of holding a job and (2) neither job search nor temporary layoffs explain a large part of measured unemployment (Clark and Summers, 1979). Given that the greatest share of the unemployed are job losers and the smallest share are job leavers, job-search theory empirically continues to constitute a dead end for the human capital theorist in search of alternative explanations of the racial unemployment gap.

This somewhat less than comprehensive survey of the state of neoclassical labor economics indicates that its cornerstone, the human capital research program, may be in somewhat of a methodological crisis. We have seen that its explanations of the private demand for education have been corroborated only in their weaker forms, and that empirical models derived from traditional consumer theory have been equally as successful in predicting changes in private demand for formal education.

Human capital theory's treatment of post-school labor training continues to pay insufficient attention to its various forms (some more costly than others) of on-the-job-training, and rate of return calculations continue to produce unexplained differences in the payoff to different forms of human capital investment, although the labor training and schooling models presume equilibrium in human capital markets. Our discussion of earnings functions revealed that schooling and earnings are clearly related

Table 1-1. 1976 Unemployment Rates, by Race and Education (youths, age 16-24)

	Blacks	*Whites*
High school dropouts	37.1	22.3
High school graduates	23.6	10.8
College (1-3 yrs)	27.2	8.2

on the extensive margin but that the relationship between educational resources and productivity is weak, at best. More seriously, tests of human capital theory based on earnings functions are weakened by a host of specification problems which complicate the task of interpreting results. We also observed that human capital models (unless shrouded by immunizing stratagems regarding distributions of unobservable innate abilities) generate predictions about the state of racial parity in labor markets which the existing empirical evidence simply does not support.

The aforementioned dilemmas constitute prima facie evidence that the human capital research program currently exhibits some degenerative tendencies. We cannot, however, judge a research program in isolation — it must be evaluated in relation to the explanations of rival theories intended to explain similar phenomena. Dual labor market theory and Marxian economics currently constitute the major alternative approaches to orthodox labor economics. Methodological analyses of these alternative paradigms will be constrained by the degree to which they purport to explain the same phenomena as neoclassical theorists. The third section is restricted, therefore, to (1) a juxtaposition of dualist and neoclassical theories of labor training and internal labor markets, and (2) consideration of both dualist and Marxist theories of racial income inequality. Again, we focus on these particular issues because they provide a logical point of comparison for the three competing views of the labor market.

Dualist and Marxist Theories of Labor Market Structure: An Abbreviated Overview

The modern development of the institutional alternative to neoclassical visions of the labor market owes much to the research of Peter Doeringer and Michael Piore (1971), who view contemporary labor market structure as historically conditioned by the progress of specialization in capitalist economies characterized by cyclical fluctuations. Because capitalists control production, subgroups of the work force are required to bear the costs of "flux and uncertainty" inherent in the process of capital accumulation (Piore, 1979a, 1979b). Piore argues that the basic duality between capital and labor leads to divisions among workers as well — i.e., capitalists will give different treatment to those workers employed in capital-intensive methods of production. More specifically, in order to have a trained work force in the presence of skill specificity, on-the-job training, and workplace customs, an employer will invest in certain segments of his work force just as he invests in physical capital. Production processes which necessitate the creation of a stable work force lead to the evolution of "primary jobs," which are well-paying, secure, and offer opportunities for career mobility. "Secondary jobs," in contrast, are created largely in marginal firms whose production processes do not require the development and retention of a stable work force and are characterized by their low pay, absence of fringe benefits, and lack of opportunities for intrafirm upward mobility.

Dualists thus explain the rise of internal labor markets in terms of capital's response to economic flux and uncertainty in competitive markets characterized by enterprise-specific skills, on-the-job training, and workplace customs. Their theory predicts that employers will invest in workforce training and, having done so, attempt to stabilize the employment relationship. However, as Doeringer and Piore noted in their early work, "an understanding of the origins of internal labor markets can be approached through study of the canons of conventional theory" (*op. cit.*, p. 28). Neoclassical theory easily accounts for the existence of internal labor markets by assuming that there are nonwage, training, and hiring costs associated with hiring workers. Once these costs have been incurred, employers view their work force as a "quasi-fixed" factor of production.

At least since the publication of Walter Oi's 1962 paper on labor as a quasi-fixed factor of production, neoclassical theorists have been comfortable with the existence of both internal and external labor markets and explain the former's emergence as the result of efficiency considerations. Dual labor market theorists are thus unable to argue convincingly that their analysis of internal labor markets constitutes a qualitatively significant breakthrough in the history of economic thought. Dualists have, however, offered an explanation of the persistence of racial income inequality which is, at least on the surface, distinguishable from neoclassical theory. But, as the subsequent discussion reveals, these distinguishing characteristics fade upon closer examination.

As was previously noted, dual labor market theorists characterize the labor market as a two-tiered caste system of occupations (subsequent analyses recognized three distinct tiers). Next, it is argued that racial income inequality primarily is the result of the disproportionately large number of blacks employed in low-paying, dead-end jobs characteristic of marginal, technologically primitive firms, and that this employment pattern continues irrespective of black labor's accumulation of human capital. Unlike their white counterparts, blacks initially employed in the secondary sector are likely to remain there, regardless of the quantity of their acquired or innate human capital. Early theorists also hypothesized that human capital is not a determinant of earnings in the secondary sector.

Turning first to the earnings equations, the dual labor market theorists hypothesize that primary sector jobs offer significantly higher rewards to given levels of human capital than do others (the secondary market) and that the primary market also offers greater incremental rewards for increases in labor quality than does the secondary market. Both Paul Osterman (1975) and Russell Rumberger and Martin Carnoy (1980) apply the same method for testing the incremental form of the segmentation thesis, which amounts to estimating separate human capital earnings functions for each occupational segment. Using different data sets (Osterman uses the 1967 Survey of Economic Opportunity, Rumberger and Carnoy use a 1/1000 sample from the 1970 Census), they arrive at the same conclusion — the economic returns to additional years of schooling are higher in the primary than in the secondary sector.

However, this finding is neither sufficient to establish the existence of labor market segmentation defined as the existence of a differential in the level of job rewards for comparable workers on a lifetime basis, including opportunities for growth of skills and pay, (Ryan, 1980) nor inconsistent with neoclassical theory. Figures 1-1 and 1-2 clarify the first assertion:

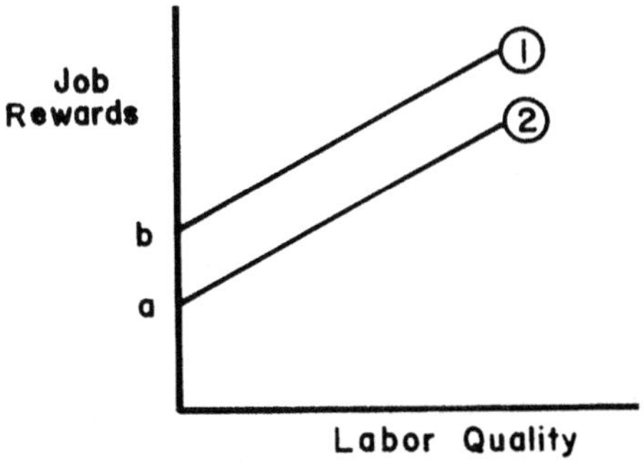

Figure 1-1. Total Rewards Derived from Employment under Segmentation: The Noncompetitive Case

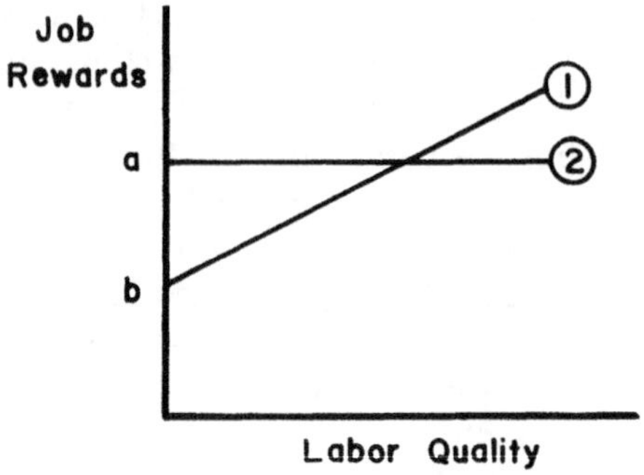

Figure 1-2. Total Rewards Derived from Employment under Segmentation: The Competitive Case

In figure 1–1, the total reward derived from employment in segment 1 for labor of a given quality exceeds that of segment 2, even though the incremental rewards to labor quality are identical in each job. On the other hand, figure 1–2's reward functions are not inconsistent with competitive theory. Even if individuals spent their entire working lives employed in only one segment, the starting level (b) of job rewards in segment 1 would be bid down or up by an excess supply of, or demand for, applicants until the present values of the two reward streams were equalized. More generally speaking:

> if (1) increased levels of schooling and experience allow individuals to move between segments and (2) wage flexibility prevails, the existence of differential effects *within* segments carries no necessary implications of intersegment differences in average levels of job reward for comparable workers. Individuals will be expected to sort themselves by segment so that persons with low levels of schooling and experience will be found in segments which offer low incremental rewards — and high with high. (Ryan, 1980, p. 10)

To the extent that incrementalist arguments have been made in defense of dual labor market theory, its proponents provided neoclassical theorists with ample reason to view segmentation as, at best, a descriptive language for the consequences of technological developments (e.g., firm specific skills) and institutional manifestations of these developments (i.e., internal labor markets). Critics also have challenged the aforementioned econometric technique of estimating separate earnings functions for each segment. Glen Cain (1975, 1976) noted that any sample truncation on the values of the endogenous variable (such as wages or annual income) will negatively bias the schooling and experience parameters; that some segments offer higher lifetime rewards for a given labor quality than do others is dismissed less easily, since it implies that those who gain access to, say, internal labor markets attain significantly higher lifetime rewards than do comparable outsiders.

As was noted above, segmentation theory explains racial income inequality in terms of labor immobility — i.e., there exists a boundary between secondary and primary labor markets not crossed by blacks, regardless of their stock of human capital. We now briefly review two principle studies of intersegment mobility.

Paul Andrisani (1973) analyzed the occupational mobility of a noninstitutional sample of young men, aged 14–24, from the National Longitudinal Survey of Young Men. All of the sample members had completed twelve or fewer years of school, were not enrolled in school between 1966 and 1968, and were classified occupationally on the basis of their first job after leaving school. Because young men seem to select their first jobs in an unsystematic fashion and are therefore highly mobile, Andrisani viewed his sample as a potentially severe test of segmentation theory. His model assumes the probability that a young man finds his first job in the primary sector as a function of the young man's socioeconomic status, years of schooling, mental ability, and the level of aggregate demand at the time of entry. Andrisani's results can be summarized as follows:

(1) The process whereby young men first enter primary or secondary labor jobs was considerably random. However, in a tight labor market, blacks were significantly more likely than whites to begin their careers in secondary jobs.
(2) The probability of movement from the secondary to the primary sector exceeded that of confinement to the secondary sector. Confinement to secondary employment did not seem to be the result of a lack of education.
(3) Higher levels of educational attainment increase the probability that white youths start their careers in the primary sector.
(4) White young men were more than two and one-half times as likely than blacks to start out in primary jobs, and almost twice as likely to move from the secondary to the primary segment.

Andrisani's results, therefore, dispute the existence of an impenetrable boundary between segments for white youths but not for blacks. Black high school graduates were no more likely to begin their working lives in the primary sector than their less well-educated peers, and experienced no mobility advantage. Once again, black and white labor of comparable quality experienced qualitatively different levels of job rewards.

Russell Rumberger and Martin Carnoy (1980) also used their 1/1000 sample of the U.S. Census to investigate labor market mobility between 1965 and 1970. Because they had information on only two years, their data reflects only net mobility; the high rate of economic expansion between

1965 and 1970 may have rendered their results somewhat atypical. They model the probability of intersegment mobility as a function of educational attainment, marital status, age, industrial sector, vocational training, and having a Spanish surname.

Rumberger and Carnoy's analysis revealed that, on average, both blacks and whites were more likely to leave secondary employment than remain. However, whites were more likely to make the transition than blacks (note the similarity with Andreasani's results). Among men age 20–24, blacks were twice as likely to stay in secondary jobs than whites, which suggests that while secondary employment is a way station for most whites, it is a permanent situation for most young black men.

Rumberger and Carnoy's mobility probability model produced the following results:

(1) For both races, having less than a high school education reduced the probability of movement from the secondary to the primary; however, for whites but not blacks, having at least a few years (1–3) of college increased upward mobility between sectors and within the primary sector.
(2) Conversely, having a college education significantly reduced downward mobility for whites but again, not for blacks. Vocational training increased the probability of upward mobility for both races.
(3) Being married increased the likelihood of upward mobility (*ceteris paribus*) for whites, but not for blacks.

Like Andrisani, Rumberger and Carnoy's results suggest that intersegment mobility is not uncommon for the majority of the population, but for the black minority, upward mobility is less common and less likely to be affected by human capital and "stability indicators," such as marriage. These studies are, therefore, additional prima facie evidence that human capital acquisition would be insufficient to improve the earning opportunities of black men.

Andrisani and Rumberger and Carnoy's results thus severely challenge human capital conceptions of the labor market's tendency to reward comparable workers equally. Neoclassical explanations of this apparent anomaly require either the assumption of market imperfections (imperfect information about black workers keeps them locked into bad jobs) or, that due to human capital decisions made in the past and under different circumstances, skilled blacks may find themselves stuck in secondary jobs. In a dynamic economy, some cohorts may not have time to correct initial choices (Wachter, 1974). Besides having all the attributes of the aforementioned immunizing strategems, this neoclassical response fails to explain why information about black workers is so much "noisier" than information about observationally equivalent whites or why the market treats skilled blacks differently than skilled whites.

So far, we have not mentioned the dualist explanation of how blacks initially become crowded in secondary jobs. As a final note on the dualist approach, we observe that its explanation of racial crowding is remarkably similar to previously mentioned human capital explanations of racial income inequality. Piore (1975) argues that blacks have been inadequately socialized and lack the culturally created values necessary for success in primary jobs. Piore's theory of labor supply draws a connection between subcultures and occupations. Whereas most white youth make the transition to stable adult life necessary for access to primary work, black youth fail to make this transition. The instability of black life — both at home and within the larger community — predisposes young blacks to secondary jobs. Although his understanding of the labor market differs from that of mainstream labor economists, Piore ultimately explains the persistence of racial income inequality in similar terms — i.e., its continuation is the result of home- and community-generated differences in the development of market-valued attributes.

Piore's hypothesis is severely challenged by all the aforementioned studies and data which indicate that ascriptively similar blacks and whites are rewarded unequally in the labor market. In hopes of stimulating continued research on racial income inequality, we close this section with an alternative Marxist theory of discrimination and suggest that it may offer a theoretically progressive approach to the study of black-white earnings differentials.

The Marxist analytic tradition is arguably more amenable to the persistence of discrimination because it begins with the recognition that the capitalist mode of production generates a labor surplus (unemployment). Because Marxist theory presumes the existence of a reserve army of labor created by the process of capital accumulation, it becomes possible and reasonable (given the underlying conflict between capital and labor) for groups of workers who have managed to secure positions in the active portion of the work force to engage in actions to exclude other workers from their hard-fought economic gains. Capital introduces new workers (activated from the reserve army) because they can be paid less for the same quantity of labor time.

This framework obviously redirects our emphasis in the analysis of racial earnings differentials. First, it seeks to explain earnings inequalities among ascriptively different groups on the basis of who gains entrance to which jobs and in what order, rather than in terms of invariable productivity characteristics. Second, it seeks to ground our understanding of labor market discrimination in an analysis of white labor's perspective and action in the context of its conflict with capital. Thirdly, although groups of ascriptively different workers may enter the active work force with essentially the same capacity to perform the required tasks, an equitable distribution of individuals across occupations is not expected, because those workers who first entered the labor force operate at an advantage in relation to the latecomers. Finally, this analysis differs substantively from that developed by radical economist Michael Reich (Reich, 1981) who argues that though capitalists need not be the actual agents of discrimination, there exist conditions under which its reproduction is conducive to the maximization of profits. White capitalists, therefore, foster racism and institute black-white wage differentials in order to divide and weaken the working class.

We present an alternative Marxist framework which assumes the existence of both a job hierarchy and a reserve of surplus labor. The latter serves as (1) a source of labor during periods of expanded capital accumulation and (2) constrains the demands of those workers already employed in preferred jobs of the hierarchy. Established workers are assumed to engage in behavior which protects their occupational turf and, therefore, their income. Because they are actors in a mode of production defined by the commoditization of labor power and the necessity of a surplus pool of labor, workers' struggles against one another are shaped by their efforts to avoid becoming part of the reserve army.

Oliver Cromwell Cox laid the foundations for this analysis in his 1948 publication *Caste, Class, and Race* where he hypothesized that:

> racial exploitation and race prejudice developed among Europeans with the rise of capitalism and nationalism, and that because of the worldwide ramifications of capitalism, all racial antagonisms can be traced to the policies and attitudes of the leading capitalist people, the white people of Europe and North America. (Cox, p. 322)

Cox supports this hypothesis with evidence of criteria for belonging in various cultures throughout human history. For example, he notes that both the Hellenic Greeks and the Romans maintained cultural, not racial, standards of belonging, and argues that modern race relations began in 1493–94, when Pope Alexander VI's "bull of demarcation" put all the heathen peoples and their resources at the disposal of the first two great colonizing nations, Spain and Portugal.[14] The exploitation of red, black, and yellow labor resulted from European capital's need for labor to continue the process of capital accumulation in the fields, forests, and mines of the world.

> This, then is the beginning of modern race relations. It was not an abstract, natural, immemorial feeling of mutual antipathy between groups but rather a practical exploitive relationship with its socioattitudinal facilitation — at that time only nascent race prejudice . . .but the fact of crucial significance is that racial exploitation is merely one aspect of the problem of the proletarianization of labor, regardless of the color of the laborer. Hence racial antagonism is essentially

> political class conflict . . . the exploitation of native peoples, imperialism, is not a sin, not essentially a problem of morals or vice, it is a problem of production and competition. (Cox, pp. 332, 336)

Cox also notes that "scientific" justifications for racial exploitation began to flourish during Europe's era of colonial expansion and all shared in common arguments for the necessity of white supremacy. Ideologies of racial domination ascended to new levels of social acceptability in the late nineteenth century, well after Europe's superior military might had led to the conquering of many thousands of colored peoples throughout the world.

Unlike Reich, Cox does attribute the rise of modern race relations to the development of imperialism. Although both Cox and Reich analyze racial antagonism in the context of class relations, Cox extends the analysis to an exploration of white labor's historical self-understanding and political action in a capitalist political economy. Cox argues that, insofar as white laborers view themselves as national ethnic groups conscious of a tribal or cultural unity, they will act to protect and reproduce white dominance, but will do so in the context of capitalist social relations. Capitalists certainly benefit from racial divisions within the work force and introduce new colored workers for the same reason that entrenched white workers resist their advance — because they can be paid less for the same amount of labor time. Whereas theories of white superiority legitimate the consignment of colored workers to the most degrading employment within the working class, white workers' rational pursuit of their own self-interest leads them to restrict the occupational opportunities of black workers emerging from the reserve army of labor. Racial income inequality is therefore explained as the product of a process whereby blacks are confined to those spheres of production which accommodate the differential strength of the groups of white workers already in place.

The above analysis offers insights into a variety of historical and contemporary economic phenomena. Thus the Chinese workers of the 19th century, the guestworkers of Western Europe, black strikebreakers in the years between the two World Wars, and Mexico's illegal aliens are/were all correctly perceived as real economic threats to workers already in place in the job hierarchy.

Darity's analysis of the dynamics of materially based and persistent labor market discrimination is worthy of quotation:

> The more established groups within the working class always will seek to protect themselves from being relegated to the reserve army, since that is the most fragile status. The weakest groups — typically the last to be proletarianized — are less able to protect themselves from being hurled in and out of the

> labor market at capital's behest. The real basis for discrimination in the labor market stems from the efforts of groups already in the jobs to guarantee their positions. Someone must be part of the surplus *since there must be a surplus.* The issue then becomes whom. It depends on which groups have won the greatest degree of job security.
>
> The winning can be achieved both within and outside of the workplace. As established groups wield increasing power, they can control the guidelines governing entry into their occupations, adjusting them to preserve the overrepresentation of their own and the underrepresentation of the outsiders. The insiders can control the training of the outsiders. When outsiders can manage to pierce the entry port, as well as control the outsiders' allocation along the job hierarchy. Beyond the workplace, the insiders can affect the credentials and education of the outsiders to prevent them from being qualified to pass through the ports of entry. The insiders also can affect the dissemination of information about new positions on behalf of their own.
>
> As established groups build more protections, it becomes harder for the outside groups to carve a place for themselves in the world of work. . . . As outsideness becomes more persistent, prospects grow increasingly grim for the outsiders. The outsiders themselves take on a growing sense of pessimism and hopelessness, making them increasingly unable to find the motivation and wherewithal to move out of the bottom reaches of the working class. (Darity, 1982b, pp. 133–156)

New groups of workers are therefore in conflict with workers already active in the process of capital accumulation. If the established group can preserve its own position, members of the new group may be thrown back into the reserve army, absorbed into lower-paying jobs from which there is limited access to the privileged positions, or absorbed into altogether new spheres of accumulation. When new groups of workers are ethnically, sexually, or racially different, racist and sexist ideologies legitimate efforts to exclude outsiders. Hence, white men resisted the territorial (occupational) encroachments of blacks and white women, and greeted female and child labor with demands for minimum wages for these new workers. This analysis also contributes to our understanding of two important expansions of the American industrial labor force: both the turn-of-the-century European immigrant and the twentieth century black migrant moving from the South to the North (and from farm to city, in general) who experienced the sort of barriers to entry described herein. Similarly, women were not a threat to men's jobs during the World Wars, but had to be returned to the latent reserve army during peacetime.

We present this theoretical framework because, unlike dualist and traditional theory, the reproduction of ascriptively based inequality is consistent with the Marxist understanding of capital reproduction. Insofar as this line of inquiry aspires to the status of scientific theory, refutable hypotheses must be forthcoming. For example, the older an occupational category or industry, the more likely it is to be male and white. Research along these lines would also gain from close analysis of (1) cases where an outside ethnic group successfully gained access to previously denied positions and (2) mechanisms for intergenerational transfer of occupational status.

Conclusion

Our closing remarks at the end of the second section revealed many methodological failings of modern labor economics as practiced today. We must, nonetheless, recognize the human capital research program's bold commitment to the extension of its "hard core" into areas of economic inquiry (such as the distribution of earnings) where others had previously feared to tread. Yet we did uncover some disturbing tendencies among its practitioners to resort to ad hoc and unfalsifiable hypotheses in the face of empirical challenges, particularly when the contrary evidence threatens an underlying commitment to the view that persistent wage differentials among ascriptively different groups must be rooted in productivity differences between the average members of those groups. We have suggested that a scientific research program is rarely abandoned because a few of its hypotheses are rejected; displacement requires the presence of a comprehensive alternative, which explains much of what the older program explained, plus expanding empirical content.

Neither dualist nor Marxist theory can currently claim to be a major contender for neoclassical/human capital theory's dominant position in labor economics, although the latter may have an upper hand among those concerned with explaining the persistence of ascriptively based labor market discrimination. Notwithstanding these challenges, modern labor economists committed to the neoclassical research program in general and the human capital subprogram more specifically owe themselves and economic science, as now defined, a renewed commitment to the principles of Popperian methodology, which demands the continued generation of falsifiable hypotheses.

Notes

1. See Paul J. McNulty, *The Origins and Development of Labor Economics: A Chapter in the History of Social Thought* (Cambridge: M.I.T. Press, 1980) for a useful discussion of the emergence of today's synthesis.

2. In his excellent 1980 treatise on the methodology of economics, Mark Blaug describes the verificationist approach of nineteenth century theorists (such as John Stuart Mill, John Elliot Cairnes, and Neville Keynes) as follows:

> The great British nineteenth-century economic methodologists focused on the premises of economic theory and continually warned their readers that the verification of economic predictions was at best a hazardous enterprise. The premises were said to be derived from introspection or the casual observation of one's neighbors, and in that sense, constituted a priori truths, known, so to speak, in advance of experience; a purely deductive process led from premises to implications, but implications were true a posteriori only in the absence of disturbing causes. Hence the purpose of verifying implications was to determine the applicability of economic reasoning and not really its validity . . . no grounds, empirical or otherwise, were ever stated in terms of which one might reject a particular economic theory.

See Mark Blaug, *The Methodology of Economics* (Cambridge: Cambridge University Press, 1980), p. 55.

3. See J. Melitz, "Friedman and Machlup on the Significance of Testing Economic Assumptions," *Journal of Political Economy* 1965, pp. 37–60 and E. Nagel, "Assumptions in Economic Theory," in W. Breit and H.M. Hochman (eds.) *Readings in Microeconomics* (New York: Holt, Rinehart, and Winston, 1973) pp. 60–66.

4. R. Harre, *The Principles of Scientific Thinking* (London: Macmillan, 1970), pp. 104–26 and *The Philosophies of Science: An Introductory Survey* (Oxford: Oxford University Press, 1972), pp. 114–132.

5. It should be noted that instrumentalism does not preclude the existence of two or more mutually inconsistent explanations of a given phenomenon which nevertheless yield reasonably accurate predictions.

6. Included among the studies cited are the following: Robert Campbell and Barry N. Siegel, "The Demand for Higher Education in the United States, 1919–1964," *American Economic Review* June 1967, pp. 482–94; Harvey Galper and Rober M. Dunn, Jr., "A Short-Run Demand Function for Higher Education in the United States," *Journal of Political Economy* September/October 1969, pp. 765–77; Sandra Christensen, John Melder, and Burton A. Weisbrod, "Factors Affecting College Attendance," *Journal of Human Resources* Spring 1975, pp. 174–188.

7. See Ruth Klinov-Malull, "Enrollments in Higher Education as Related to Earnings," *British Journal of Industrial Relations* March 1971, pp. 82–91.

8. Thurow's "job competition" model is among the best models developed to date which conceives of the labor market as an allocator of training opportunities. Thurow does not claim to be an advocate of human capital theory. See Lester Thurow, *Generating Inequality* (New York: Basic Books, 1975), chapters 4 and 5.

9. See Lewis Solomon, "Schooling and Subsequent Success," in Lewis Solomon and Paul Taubman (eds) *Does College Matter?* (New York: Academic Press, 1973) for a survey of earnings function literature.

10. In her recursive schooling-earnings model, Datcher models schooling as an endogenous choice variable, as would be consistent with human capital theory.

11. Blaug (1980, chapter 3) presents an informative discussion of economists' role in the history of verificationism.

12. The author (Williams, 1983, section IIIe) has elsewhere discussed Datcher's work at greater length.

13. These conclusions are supported by U.S. Bureau of Labor Statistics data published by the National Urban League in its "Quarterly Economic Report of the Black Worker," table 3.

14. See Oliver Cromwell Cox, *Caste, Class and Race* (New York: Monthly Review Press, 1970, originally published in 1948), pp. 331–332.

References

Andrisani, Paul J. "An Empirical Analysis of the Dual Labor Market Theory" Unpublished doctoral dissertation, Center for Human Resource Research, Ohio State University, 1973.

Becker, Gary. *The Economics of Discrimination.* Chicago: University of Chicago Press, 1957.

______. *Human Capital.* 2d ed. New York: Columbia University Press, (1964), 1975.

Ben-Porath, Yoram. "The Production of Human Capital and the Life Cycle of Earnings," *Journal of Political Economy* (August, 1967), pp. 352–365.

______. "The Production of Human Capital Over Time." In W.L. Hansen (ed.) *Education, Income, and Human Capital.* New York: Columbia University Press, 1970, pp. 129–47.

Blaug, Mark. "Empirical Status of Human Capital Theory: A Slightly Jaundiced Survey," *Journal of Economic Literature* (September 1976), pp. 827–855.

______. *The Methodology of Economics.* Cambridge: Cambridge University Press, 1980.

Cain, Glen. "The Challenge of Dual and Radical Theories of the Labor Market to Orthodox Theory" *American Economics Review* May, 1975.

______. "The Challenge of Segmented Labor Market Theories to Orthodox Theory —A Survey," *Journal of Economic Literature,* December 1976.

Campbell, Robert, and Siegel, Barry. "The Demand for Higher Education in the United States, 1919–1964," *American Economic Review* (June, 1967).

Christensen, Sandra, Melder, John, and Weisbrod, Burton. "Factors Affecting College Attendance," *Journal of Human Resources* Spring, 1975.

Clark, Kim, and Summers, Lawrence H. "Labor Market Dynamics and Unemployment: A Reconsideration," *Brookings Papers on Economic Activity* (1, 1979).

Coleman, James, et al. *Equality of Educational Opportunity.* (United States Office of Education, 1966).

Cox, Oliver C. *Caste, Class, and Race.* New York: Monthly Review Press, 1970.

Darity, William A., Jr. "The Human Capital Approach to Black-White Earnings Inequality — Some Unsettled Questions," *The Journal of Human Resources* (XVII, 1982a), p. 84.

______. "Economists, the Minimum Wage, and the Underclass." In Clement Cottingham (ed.) *Race, Poverty, and the Urban Underclass.* Massachusetts: Lexington Books, 1982(b).

Datcher, Linda. "Effects of Community and Family Background on Achievement," *The Review of Economics and Statistics* (February, 1982).

Doeringer, Peter, and Piore, Michael. *Internal Labor Markets and Manpower Analysis.* Lexington, Mass.: D.C. Heath and Co., 1971.

Freeman, Richard B. *The Market for College-Trained Manpower.* Cambridge: Harvard University Press, 1971.

______. "Changes in the Labor Market for Black Americans, 1948–1972," *Brookings Papers on Economic Activity,* 1973.

______. "Black Economic Process 1964: Who Gained and Why?" *NBER Working Paper No. 282,* Cambridge, Mass., 1978.

Friedman, Alan, and Staaf, Robert J. "Scholastic Choice: An Economic Model of Student Behavior," *Journal of Human Resources* (Summer, 1973).

Friedman, Milton. "The Methodology of Positive Economics." In W. Breit and H. Hochman (eds.) *Readings in Microeconomics.* New York: Holt Rinehart and Winston, 1968 (originally published in 1956).

Galper, Harvey, and Dunn, Robert, Jr. "A Short-Run Demand Function for Higher Education in the United States," *Journal of Political Economy* (June, 1975).

Harre, R. *The Principles of Scientific Thinking.* London: Macmillan, 1970.

______. *The Philosophies of Science: A Introductory Survey.* Oxford: Oxford University Press, 1972.

Hill, Robert, B. *The Illusion of Black Progress.* Washington: National Urban League Research Department, 1978.

______. *The Widening Economic Gap.* Washington: National Urban League Research Department, 1979.

Klinov-Malul, Ruth. "Enrollments in Higher Education as Related to Earnings," *British Journal of Industrial Relations* (March, 1971).

Jencks, Christopher et al. *Inequality: A Reassessment of the Effect of Family and Schooling in America.* New York: Basic Books, 1972.

Kuhn, Thomas. *The Structure of Scientific Revolution.* 2d ed. Chicago: University of Chicago Press, 1970.

Lakatos, Imre. *The Methodology of Scientific Research Programmes. Philosophical Papers.* J. Worrall and G. Currie (eds.) Cambridge: Cambridge University Press, 1978.

Lipsey, Richard, and Steiner, Peter. *Economics,* 6th ed. New York: Harper and Row, 1981.

McNulty, Paul. *The Origins and Development of Modern Labor Economics.* Cambridge: M.I.T. Press, 1980.

Melitz, J. "Friedman and Machlup on the Significance of Testing Economic Assumptions," *Journal of Political Economy* Vol. 73 (1965).

Mincer, Jacob. "Investment in Human Capital and Personal Income Distribution," *Journal of Political Economy* (August, 1958).

______. "On-the-Job Training: Costs, Returns, and Some Implications," *Journal of Political Economy* (supplement, October 1962).

______. *Schooling, Experience, and Earnings.* New York: Columbia University Press and National Bureau of Economic Research, 1974.

Mosteller, Frederick, and Moynihan, Daniel. *On Equality of Educational Opportunity.* New York: Vintage Books, 1972.

Nagel, E. "Assumptions in Economic Theory." In W. Breit and H.M. Hochman (eds.) *Readings in Microeconomics.* New York: Holt, Rinehart, and Winston, 1968.

Oi, Walter. "Labor as a Quasi-Fixed Factor," *Journal of Political Economy* (December 1962), pp. 538–55.

Osterman, Paul. "An Empirical Study of Labor Market Segmentation," *Industrial and Labor Relations Review* (July 1975).

Piore, Michael J. "Notes for a Theory of Labor Market Stratification." In R. Edwards, M. Reich, D. Gordon (eds.) *Labor Market Segmentation*. Lexington, Mass.: D.C. Heath and Co., 1975.

______. (ed.) *Unemployment and Inflation: Institutionalist and Structuralist Views*. White Plains: M. Sharpe, 1979(a).

______. *Birds of Passage: Migrant Labor and Industrial Societies*. Cambridge: Cambridge University Press, 1979(b).

Popper, Karl. *Objective Knowledge: An Evolutionary Approach*. London: Oxford University Press, 1972.

Psacharopoulos, George, and Hinchcliffe, Keith. *Returns to Education: An International Comparison*. Amsterdam: Elsevier Scientific, 1973.

Reich, Michael. *Racial Inequality: A Political Economic Analysis*. Princeton: Princeton University Press, 1981.

Rumberger, Russell, and Carnoy, Martin. "Segmentation in the U.S. Labour Market" — Its Effect on the Mobility and Earnings of Blacks and Whites," *Cambridge Journal of Economics* (June 1980).

Ryan, Paul. "Segmentation, Duality, and the Internal Labour Market" in Frank Wilkinson (ed.) *The Dynamics of Labor Market Segmentation*. London: Academic Press, 1981.

Smith, James, and Finis, Welch. "Black-White Male Wage Ratios: 1960–1970," *American Economic Review* (June 1977).

Solomon, Lewis C. "Schooling and Subsequent Success." In Solomon and Paul Taubman (eds.) *Does College Matter?* New York: Academic Press, 1973.

Thurow, Lester. *Generating Inequality*. New York: Basic Books, 1975.

Wachter, Michael. "Primary and Secondary Labor Markets: A Critique of the Dual Approach," *Brookings Papers on Economic Activity* (3, 1974).

Williams, Rhonda M. "Quantitative Dimensions of Racial Income Inequality: Historical Legacies and Contemporary Trends." In William A. Darity Jr., Julianne Malveaux, and Samuel Myers, Jr. (eds.) *Racial Income Inequality: A Critical Assessment. Forthcoming.*

2 DISCRIMINATION AGAINST WOMEN: THEORY AND EVIDENCE

Francine D. Blau

The post-World War II period has witnessed a rapid growth in female labor force participation and a steady narrowing of sex differences in the extent of participation in work outside the home. In 1950, 86.4 percent of the adult male population participated in the labor force as compared to 33.9 percent of the adult female population.[1] By 1979, 77.6 percent of males and 51.4 percent of females were labor force participants.[2] The large increase in participation rates of married women (husband present), from 21.6 percent in 1950 to 49.4 percent in 1979, was a major factor in the expansion of the female labor force. That these trends were accompanied by an increase in the labor force attachment of women is suggested by the marked rise in the labor force participation rates of married women (husband present) with preschool age children, from 11.9 percent in 1950 to 43.2 percent in 1979.

The author would like to thank Katherine Abraham, Andrea Beller, Barbara Bergmann, Charles Brown, Paula England, Marianne Ferber, Claudia Goldin, Joan Huber, Robert Hutchens, Lawrence Kahn, Michael Reich, Barbara Reskin, and Harvey Rosen for their helpful comments and suggestions. She is indebted to Susan Schwochau for excellent research assistance.

These dramatic shifts in women's work outside the home do not appear to have been accompanied by a noticeable improvement in the relative economic status of women workers. In fact, the median earnings of year-round, full-time women workers as a percentage of men's fell from 63.9 to 58.9 between 1955 and 1977 (Lloyd and Niemi, 1979, p. 152). There have been some differences in these relative earnings trends on the basis of race which we shall consider at a later point. Most of the decline had occurred by the early 1960s, and the earnings ratio has been roughly stable since then. In addition, the occupational distributions of men and women have continued to differ significantly. A small movement toward greater similarity appears to have occurred between 1960 and 1970 based on census data (Blau and Hendricks, 1979). Some estimates suggest that the rate of decline in segregation may have accelerated between 1972 and 1981, although the magnitude of segregation remained substantial (Beller, 1982c).[3] Throughout this period, over 60 percent of the female or male labor force would have had to change jobs to eliminate the overrepresentation of women in certain occupations and their corresponding underrepresentation in others.

The precise role of labor market discrimination in producing these sex differentials in market outcomes has been the subject of considerable debate among economists. In the first section, we consider the explanations that have been offered for sex differentials in earnings and occupations. We focus on the various neoclassical and institutional models of sex and race discrimination and the alternative explanation provided by the human capital model, which emphasizes the voluntary choices of women. In the second section, we evaluate the empirical evidence on the degree of sex discrimination in the labor market and the mechanisms that produce differential outcomes for men and women of equal potential productivity. In the third section, we consider the impact of the federal government's antidiscrimination effort in reducing sex differentials.

Economic Explanations of Sex Differentials in Outcomes

Theories of Discrimination

While most of the discrimination models discussed here were developed to explain — or at least illustrated in terms of — racial differences, we apply them here to sex differences. The foundation for the modern neoclassical analysis of labor market discrimination was laid by Becker (1957). In Becker's model, it is assumed that male and female laborers are perfect substitutes. Discriminatory tastes may be located in employers, coworkers, and/or customers. It may seem odd that males would have tastes for discrimination against women when, in contrast to the case of racial discrimination, men and women live together in families. The issue here may be more one of socially appropriate roles than of the desire to maintain social distance, which Becker emphasized. Employers may have no compunctions about hiring women as secretaries but may be reluctant to employ them as pipefitters. Men may be willing to work with women who are in complementary or subordinate positions, but dislike interacting with women as peers or superiors. Customers may be delighted to purchase nylons from female clerks but eschew women car salespersons or attorneys. In these circumstances, it is not surprising that we observe considerable occupational segregation by sex. These discriminatory tastes may be held independently of beliefs that women would be less productive than men in nontraditional pursuits. This latter possibility is considered under notions of statistical discrimination discussed below.

Employers with "tastes for discrimination" against women will hire women workers only at a wage discount that is sufficiently large to compensate them for the disutility of employing women. This may result in an aggregate pay differential by sex and in some degree of sex segregation of workers by firm, where the latter results from differences among employers in tastes for discrimination.

Becker also showed that even if employers themselves have no tastes for discrimination against women, profit-maximizing behavior by employers may result in sex discrimination if employees or customers have such discriminatory tastes. Male employees with tastes for discrimination against women will work with them only at a wage premium which is sufficient to compensate them for the disutility of female coworkers.[4] In the case of perfect substitutes, complete sex segregation by firm is expected, since sexually integrated work forces are more costly. The necessity for wage differences is obviated by such segregation, however, since men and women do not work together. However, as Arrow (1972a, 1972b, 1973) points out, complete segregation may not be profitable where there exists costs of adjustment (e.g., due to personnel investments in workers).[5] In the case of complementary labor (e.g., supervisors), the existence of sex segregation by occupation might make it difficult to form single-sex work units. Indeed, it is generally assumed that supervisors are all white or all male. Thus, pay differentials combined with tendencies towards segregation may prevail in both cases.

Customers with tastes for discrimination against women will buy products or services produced or sold by women only at a lower price. Intuitively, we would expect this type of discrimination to be more important in sales or service occupations where face-to-face contact with the customer or client occurs. Here, the notion of equally productive male and female labor becomes attenuated since customer discrimination lowers women's marginal revenue product relative to that of men. In any case, a wage differential by sex and tendencies towards segregation may result.

A definition of wage discrimination flows out of Becker's work that has guided much of the empirical analysis of labor market discrimination. Wage discrimination (the market discrimination coefficient) may be defined as the difference between the actual ratio of male to female wages and the ratio that would exist in the absence of discrimination — assuming perfect substitutability, this would be wage parity (Becker, 1957, p. 126). In empirical work, where the wages of heterogeneous male and female labor are compared, this is approximated by the notion of pay differentials that are not accounted for by productivity differentials.

Perhaps the most serious question that has been raised about the Becker analysis, particularly the case of employer discrimination, is the issue of the survival of discrimination in the long run under perfect competition (Arrow, 1973). Assuming that employer tastes for discrimination against women vary, the least discriminatory firms that hire the highest proportion of lower-priced female labor will have lower costs. Capital will flow toward these firms, and, assuming constant returns to scale, only the least discriminatory, lowest-cost firms will survive. The apparent persistence of sex and race discrimination in the labor market over time has given rise to additional analyses of discrimination which we shall consider below. However, this criticism of the Becker model is a double-edged sword in that it creates a skepticism among many economists that labor market discrimination is indeed responsible in whole or part for the observed sex differences in market outcomes. Perhaps the best-developed alternative explanation is the human capital model considered in the next section.

One obvious solution to the problem raised above is that noncompetitive elements are responsible for the persistence of discrimination. Becker (1957) hypothesized that employer discrimination should, on average, be less in competitive industries than in monopolistic ones. In the case of sex discrimination, the focus has tended to be on imperfections in the factor market rather than in the product market. Madden (1973) has developed Robinson's (1933) monopsony model to explain sex differences in wages. A price-discriminating monopsonist will pay less for female labor if it is less elastically supplied to the firm than male labor.

The persuasiveness of this explanation for aggregate pay differentials by sex is unclear, a priori. On the one hand, as Madden (1973, 1976) argues, such factors as occupational segregation and the power of male unions may limit women's options and thus decrease their wage elasticity of supply to the firm, all else equal. Supply-side factors such as the tendency for women to engage in less job search than men or to seek jobs which are closer to home could also contribute to this result. On the other hand, as Blau and Jusenius (1976) argue, the aggregate female labor supply curve is more elastic than the male labor supply curve. This has consequences for the elasticity of supply to the firm in that home work provides a viable alternative for women at the margin of labor force participation.[6] Furthermore, if men are more likely than women to acquire firm-specific training, that would also lower their mobility relative to women. It seems likely that the monopsony explanation is more applicable to specific occupations and labor markets than to the aggregate sex pay differential.[7] An ideal case might be the employed female or male Ph.D. in a one-university town with a spouse who also has a Ph.D.

A second approach to explaining the long-run existence of discrimination is the notion of statistical discrimination (Phelps, 1972; Arrow, 1972a, 1972b, 1973; Aigner and Cain, 1977). Statistical discrimination provides a motivation for discrimination that is compatible with profit-maximizing behavior on the part of employers. It stems from imperfect information and may take one of two forms.

First, employers may discriminate against women because of real or perceived average productivity or productivity-related behavioral differences between men and women. In this case, sex is assumed to provide information regarding expected productivity. Aigner and Cain (1977) argue that economic discrimination does not exist if the employer's perception of the average sex difference is correct — since, on average, each group is paid in proportion to its productivity. However, they acknowledge as disquieting the result that, at each ability level, women will receive lower pay than men.[8] Others have termed this discrimination in that the ". . . individual is judged on the basis of the average characteristics of the group . . . to which he or she belongs rather than upon his or her own characteristics" (Thurow, 1975, p. 172).[9] Implicit in this view seems to be the assumption that other personal characteristics besides sex are readily available and that while the sex difference exists, on average, it would not be present in a ceteris paribus comparison. If so, perhaps this might be more appropriately considered mistaken behavior on the part of employers. But, as Aigner and Cain (1977) point out, discrimination based on employers' mistaken beliefs is as unlikely (or even more unlikely) to persist over time in the face of competitive forces as discrimination based on employer tastes.

Arrow's (1973, 1976) notion of perceptual equilibrium sheds some light on this issue. Arrow's model allows for the endogeneity of qualifications —

workers become qualified by making some type of investment in themselves where the decision to invest depends on the gain from qualifying. In this case, employer's perceptions of sex differences in qualifications may become self-confirming even when there is no intrinsic sex difference in ability or behavior. Multiple equilibria may result. For example, if employers' view of female job instability leads them to give women less training and to assign them to jobs where the cost of turnover is minimized, women may respond by exhibiting the unstable behavior employers expect. This, in turn, confirms employer perceptions. On the other hand, if employers believe women are stable workers, they will hire women for positions which are sufficiently rewarding to inhibit instability (Arrow, 1976).[10] Here pay and productivity differences between potentially equally productive male and female workers which may persist in the long run can result from employers' (in some sense) erroneous beliefs. Viewing the matter somewhat differently, the employers' ex post correct assessment of sex differences in average productivity may be seen to result from their own discriminatory actions.

A second type of statistical discrimination may occur even if the two sexes have equal average abilities or behavior. Risk averse employers may discriminate against women if their ability or behavior is predicted less reliably by some indicator(s) than the ability or behavior of men (Phelps, 1972; Cain and Aigner, 1977). However, Aigner and Cain express doubts that risk aversion could cause discriminatory pay differentials of the magnitude obtained by empirical studies. As they note, dispersion in risk aversion among employers should result in the bidding up of women's wages, just as the existence of less discriminatory firms should erode discriminatory pay differentials in the Becker-type taste for discrimination model. Further, the existence of a large risk discount of women's wages should trigger a market for test instruments or indicators that are equally reliable for them.

At present then, the issue of the persistence of discrimination in the long run does not appear to be satisfactorily resolved at the theoretical level.[11] Perhaps the most promising notion advanced here is Arrow's idea of perceptual equilibrium, a kind of vicious circle or feedback theory of discrimination.[12]

A second major weakness of the Becker model that is particularly relevant to sex differentials is the role accorded to employment segregation. While segregation may occur, it is not a necessary consequence of discrimination. For example, at a sex pay differential that is sufficiently large to compensate discriminating employers for the disutility of hiring women, they will be indifferent in choosing between male and female workers. This makes the high degree of occupational segregation by sex discussed earlier difficult to explain in the face of large ceteris paribus pay differentials by sex (see below), even assuming that discriminatory tastes differ by occupation (Blau and Jusenius, 1976). Further, in the Becker model, discriminatory pay differentials are in some sense the price paid by the discriminated group for associating with the discriminators. In general, differences between the two groups in factor endowments make such association profitable, even in the face of discrimination. However, sufficient opportunities in a segregated context can eliminate the need for pay differentials as we saw in the case of discrimination by perfectly substitutable male labor. From this perspective, one may question why occupational segregation by sex appears to be associated with large discriminatory pay differentials.

Bergmann (1974) has developed an analysis in the Becker tradition which gives a more central role to employment segregation. In Bergmann's "overcrowding" model,[13] discriminatory employer tastes result in the segregation of male and female labor into two sets of occupations. While such segregation need not result in sex pay differentials, differentials will occur if job opportunities (demand) in the female sector are small relative to the supply of female labor. Employers who do hire women will utilize the labor-intensive production techniques that their lower wages make profitable. Thus, in contrast to Becker (1957) and like Arrow (1973), discrimination may cause both pay and productivity differentials between potentially equally productive male and female labor. While the Bergmann model does not shed additional light on the causes of occupational segregation or on the persistence of sex discrimination in the long run, it does suggest that segregation may play a causal role in producing discriminatory pay differentials.

Institutional models, such as the internal labor market analysis or the dual labor market model (Doeringer and Piore, 1971; Piore, 1971),[14] also may shed light on the importance and function of sex segregation in the labor market. Blau and Jusenius (1976) argue that the major contribution of such models is not to suggest new explanations for sex differentials in earnings and employment distributions, but rather to elucidate the linkage between the two: to suggest why the same set of factors that produce earnings differentials are also likely to generate employment segregation. They argue that under the administered system of the internal labor market, the firm attaches wage rates to occupational categories rather than to individuals (see also Thurow, 1975). Under such circumstances, the only way in which the firm can distinguish between men and women in terms of pay is to assign them to different job categories. Within occupational categories, institutional constraints mandate equal pay for equal work, except for relatively small distinctions based on seniority and/or merit considerations. Such group treatment of individuals will be most efficient (result in the discarding of the least information) if occupational categories are as homogenous as possible. Thus, employers are likely to structure female jobs to fit the perceived average characteristics of women workers. This, in turn, influences women's behavior and productivity. Thus, institutional models, like the analyses of Arrow and Bergmann, suggest that discrimination may create productivity differences between initially equally productive male and female workers.

The Human Capital Alternative

Theories of discrimination are concerned with explaining pay differentials between equally productive men and women. The aggregate figures cited earlier, in fact, compare heterogenous male and female labor. Some or all of the observed pay difference may in fact be due to productivity differences between the sexes. The human capital model can provide a consistent explanation for the sex pay differential in terms of the voluntary choices of women, rather than market discrimination against them. It then becomes an empirical question, albeit a difficult one, to determine which view is correct or what portion of the differential is accounted for by each explanation.

As developed by Mincer and Polachek (1974) and others, the human capital analysis calls attention to the traditional division of labor by sex within the family under which women can expect shorter and more discontinuous involvement in market work than can men. This reduces their long-run payoff to human capital investments since they have a shorter work life over which to reap the returns. Similarly, employers will be reluctant to invest in firm-specific training for women workers. Thus, women may earn less than men due both to their lesser amount of labor market experience and to the lower returns to experience they obtain (the latter reflecting their smaller investments per unit of time). Female earnings are further reduced by the depreciation of their stock of human capital during the time they spend out of the labor force.

The human capital model also can provide a theory of occupational choice to explain occupational segregation by sex (Polachek, 1976, 1979, 1981; Zellner, 1975; Landes, 1977). According to this view, women will tend to avoid occupations requiring considerable investments in on-the-job training and having high rates of depreciation for time spent out of the labor force. Thus, we would expect predominantly female jobs to have relatively flat age-earnings profiles.

One problem with this analysis is that the sexual division of labor within the family is in turn determined by the relative market rewards (wage rates) of husband and wife (Becker, 1965, 1973). This implies that labor market discrimination against women could influence their allocation of time between the home and the market and thus the amount and types of their human capital investments. From the standpoint of empirical work, this means that analyses which treat such variables as experience and education as exogenous may underestimate the extent of labor market discrimination (Weiss and Gronau, 1981). Further, women's lower returns to experience may reflect employers' reluctance to provide opportunities for firm-specific training as well as their own voluntary decisions. In the latter case, it would also be important to determine whether the employers' decisions are, in fact, justified by ceteris paribus sex differences in quit propensities.

Empirical Findings

A crude test of the relative merits of the discrimination and human capital explanations for sex differences in earnings is provided by an examination of the time series trends in the sex pay differential. We first briefly consider this time series evidence, then move to a detailed discussion of the more sophisticated cross-sectional analyses of the extent of labor market discrimination. As noted in the introduction, there actually has been some deterioration in the relative earnings position of women since the mid-1950s (Lloyd and Niemi, 1979). It has frequently and incorrectly been assumed that increases in the female labor force participation rate over time are indicative of declines in the average level of experience of women workers due to the impact of new entrants (Economic Report of the President, 1974). In fact, as Mincer (1979) explains, the female labor force grows not only through "widening" (increases in the flow of entrants or reentrants) but also through "deepening" (decreases in the flow of exiters). The impact on the average level of experience of female workers depends on the relative magnitude of these two flows. In addition, since labor force entry tends to be selective of female nonparticipants with higher levels of previous labor force experience and labor force exit tends to be selective of female participants with lower levels of previous labor force experience, labor turnover is not as diluting of average experience levels as it might first appear (Blau, 1975, 1978).

Lloyd and Niemi (1979) present a variety of evidence that the trend has been for women to remain in the labor force longer and more continuously and for entrants to make up a decreasing proportion of the female labor force. They conclude that "it appears . . . the work-experience differential between the sexes has narrowed in the past twenty years" (p. 133). Thus, female participation trends do not seem to be responsible for the widening pay gap. Moreover, they find that "over time, the gap between men's and women's educational attainment has been eliminated and, among young cohorts, it appears that women's propensity to enroll in college is roughly similar to men's" (p. 146). Men and women do continue to diverge sharply in fields of specialization, although some progress has recently been made in this area as well.

While one would like better data, particularly on experience, it seems reasonable to conclude that human capital factors do not account for the widening pay gap between men and women. This provides support for the view that discrimination plays a role in producing the differential. It is unlikely that tastes for discrimination against women have increased during this period. However, as we have seen, little decline occurred in the degree of sex segregation in employment during that time. If increases in the demand for labor in female jobs did not keep pace with increases in the supply of female labor, relative crowding in female jobs may have worsened, exerting a downward pressure on female wages relative to male wages. Increases in the real wages of women over the period could have continued to induce increases in female labor force participation ceteris paribus.

We now turn to a review of studies which attempt to measure explicitly the extent of labor market discrimination. The general practice in empirically estimating the magnitude of labor market discrimination against a particular group (e.g., women) is to ascertain the proportion of the sex differential that is accounted for by differences in the productivity-related characteristics of male and female workers and to allocate the residual to discrimination. Discrimination may be measured by the coefficient on a sex dummy variable in an earnings regression equation, in which case the impact of the other explanatory variables on earnings is constrained to be the same for each sex group. More often, this constraint is relaxed by estimating separate earnings regressions for sex or race-sex groups. In this case, the portion of the pay differential due to sex differences in the returns to a given set of characteristics (i.e., sex differences in coefficients, including the constant term) is attributed to discrimination; the portion of the pay differential that is due to sex differences in endowments of productivity-related characteristics (i.e., sex differences in the means of the independent variables) is attributed to nondiscriminatory factors (Blinder, 1973).

There are a variety of problems with this "residual" approach to measuring labor market discrimination. Perhaps the most serious is the specification problem. On the one hand, conventional data sources do not allow for the measurement of all productivity-related characteristics. The absence of actual labor market experience from the data sets used in the early studies of sex discrimination is a prime example of an important omitted variable. Type of schooling, which varies greatly between men and women, would be another example. If, on average, males are more favorably endowed with the characteristics measured by these omitted variables, the extent of labor market discrimination will be overestimated due to imperfect controls for these omitted factors. On the other hand, group differences with respect to some productivity-related characteristics may reflect the indirect effects of discrimination (Blinder, 1973). For example, as discussed earlier, women may be excluded from high-wage occupations due to their sex. Further, if one takes into account the endogeneity of choice variables, we see that labor market discrimination may discourage women's human capital accumulation or alter its type. Measured labor market discrimination is likely to be underestimated to the extent that such factors representing other dimensions of discrimination are controlled for.

A related problem is the interpretation of sex differences in the coefficients of earnings regressions. For example, a smaller coefficient on labor force experience for women may reflect their decisions to invest in less on-the-job training than men, as proposed by human capital theorists, or discrimination on the part of employers in access to on-the-job training opportunities.[15] Similarly, sex differences in the returns to marital status may reflect unmeasured differences in labor force attachment between married men and women (Polachek, 1975) or sex differences in employer treatment of marital status that is unrelated to productivity (e.g., the view that married men deserve higher salaries because they have families to support).

These problems of specification and interpretation of coefficients reflect a more fundamental problem. We would like to measure the extent of labor market discrimination — a demand-side phenomenon. But wages are influenced by both supply- and demand-side factors. The earnings functions that are typically estimated are essentially reduced-form equations and, thus, their coefficients may reflect the influence of both supply and demand (Butler, 1982; Chiplin, 1981). Ideally, one would like to specify and estimate a structural model with separate supply and demand equations. At present, no one has attempted to specify and estimate such a model on an economy-wide basis.

An additional problem with the earnings regression approach is that, while the theory specifies the measurement of discrimination in terms of pay differences that are not accounted for by productivity differences, the empirical work involves adjustment using proxies for productivity, like education and experience. This gives rise to an errors in variable problem (Hashimoto and Kochin, 1980; Roberts, 1980). For simplicity, let us assume the productivity proxies are measured so that they are positively related to earnings. Then it may be shown that, if women have lower mean values of the productivity proxies than men (as is generally the case), the coefficient on a sex dummy variable (female = 1) in an earnings regression is biased downward, giving an exaggerated estimate of the effect of discrimination (Hashimoto and Kochin, 1980).

Unfortunately, however, there exists no obvious solution to this problem. Roberts (1980) suggests a procedure he terms "reverse regression" in which the independent variable (e.g., education) is regressed on the dependent variable (e.g., earnings) and a sex dummy.[16] Such a procedure will produce unbiased coefficients only if the dependent variable is measured without error. But earnings as measured are only an imperfect indicator of permanent earnings capacity which, one might argue, is the theoretically relevant variable (Hashimoto and Kochin, 1980). Moreover, measured earnings are only a proxy for the total rewards for the job, including fringes and the nonpecuniary benefits of the work (Madden, 1981). Hashimoto and Kochin (1980) suggest performing the analysis on grouped data where the grouping criterion is independent of the measurement errors. But it may not be easy to meet this requirement (or to know whether or not one has met it) and, as they acknowledge, the results can be quite sensitive to one's choice of a criterion. Other classical approaches to the errors-in-variable problem involve prior restrictions on some of the parameters of the model (Madden, 1981). However, the information necessary to formulate such restrictions is likely to be absent.

An additional problem in using conventionally estimated earnings regressions to measure discrimination frequently produce biases in the opposite direction, that is, leads us to underestimate discrimination. Regressions are generally estimated on the selected sample of labor force participants. But Gronau (1974) has argued that it is the wage offers, not the actual wages, of males and females that should be compared. The distribution of actual wages represents only that part of the offer distribution that is acceptable to job seekers.[17] Thus, according to Gronau, mean female wage offers will be overestimated by restriction of the sample to labor force participants.[18] He provides empirical evidence in support of this contention. Since male participation rates (particularly in the prime work ages) are close to one hundred percent, Gronau argues that data on men's wages hardly are affected by selectivity bias.[19] Thus, observed wage differences between men and women will underestimate the "true" male-female wage offer differential.

Bearing these problems in mind, we consider the empirical work on sex discrimination. Most empirical work in this area has focused on the question of whether or not labor market discrimination exists, and has attempted to estimate its magnitude. While a variety of unresolved problems in estimating the extent of labor market discrimination remain, it is not clear from our consideration of them that they result, on net, in over- or underestimates of discriminatory pay differentials. If the evidence suggests that there is labor market discrimination against women, we would like to know the motivation for (e.g., tastes, statistical discrimination) and sources of (e.g., employers, employees, customers), these discriminatory outcomes. We would also like to know the mechanisms that produce the differential outcomes for men and women of equal potential productivity, particularly the role played by employment segregation by sex. Further, a clear understanding of the impact of discrimination on women's labor force and investment behavior would also be important. As yet, these latter questions have received relatively little attention.

Not surprisingly, the estimate of the sex pay differential that is due to discrimination varies considerably depending on the group studied, data set employed, and variables controlled for. We shall focus our discussion upon studies using national samples of individuals across a variety of occupations.[20] For the most part, the earlier studies of male-female pay differentials attibuted a substantial portion of the sex pay differential to discrimination.[21] For example, using 1960 Census data, Fuchs (1971) found that sex differences in individual characteristics could account for only 3 to 15 percent of the differential. Similarly, Oaxaca (1973a,b), using data from the 1967 Survey of Economic Opportunity, found that 80 percent of the pay differential between white men and white women and 94 percent of the differential between black men and black women could not be explained by productivity-related individual characteristics.[22]

As these authors were aware, their lack of data on actual labor force experience created an important omitted variable problem.[23] The general procedure of estimating experience as the years elapsed since school completion, while fairly accurate for males, is much more questionable for females. In addition to their theoretical contributions noted earlier, Mincer and Polachek (1974) were the first to provide empirical estimates of the impact of labor force experience and time spent out of the labor force on the earnings of women using newly available longitudinal data. They analyzed retrospective work history data from the National Longitudinal Survey (NLS) of mature women aged 30 to 44 in 1967. Mincer and Polachek were able to account for 45 percent of the pay gap between white married men and women in that age group on the basis of human capital variables, including actual labor market experience and time spent out of the labor force.

In arriving at this estimate, they were aware of the joint determination of earnings and experience and attempted to adjust for simultaneous equation bias by using a two-stage procedure. While Mincer and Polachek are to be commended for their awareness of the simultaneity problem, their application of the two-stage procedure in their exploratory study is far from thorough. For one thing, their specification of the determinants of lifetime labor supply (the proportion of years the respondent worked 6 months or more since school completion) includes an endogenous variable, number of children. For another, while lifetime experience is treated as endogenous, home time and job tenure (seniority) are entered into the earnings function as exogenous variables (Sandell and Shapiro, 1978; Mincer and Polachek, 1978).

That these problems are serious is suggested by their counterintuitive findings for the two-stage procedure. In the single period context, economic theory would lead one to expect a positive relationship between labor force participation and own wage. An increase in the market wage available to a woman increases the opportunity cost of nonmarket activities for her. This encourages her to substitute market work for time spent on housework and leisure. However, in a multiperiod context, this positive substitution effect could be outweighed by a negative income effect. The negative income effect arises from the fact that the increase in the wage obtained while the woman is working is like an increase in income. At higher income levels she is expected to demand more of all goods from which she derives satisfaction, including leisure. She may thus consume more leisure over the life cycle by supplying less time to the market over the life cycle. Note that she must work some of the time for the income effect to come into play. The evidence suggests, however, that for married women's participation decisions, the substitution effect dominates the income effect, where the latter is indicated by the response to changes in husband's income (Mincer, 1962). Thus, women's labor supply is expected to be positively related to their wages.

This reasoning implies that the positive coefficient on experience in an OLS earnings regression is biased upward. This is because some of the estimated positive impact of labor market experience on wages really is due to a positive effect of wages on experience; at higher wages, women supply more time to the market. Similarly, the negative coefficient on home time is biased upward in absolute value. This is because some of the estimated negative impact of home time on wages really is due to a negative effect of wages on home time; at higher wages, women spend less time out of the labor market. Correction for the simultaneous equation bias should thus reduce the size of both coefficients in absolute value. On the contrary, Mincer and Polachek (1974) find that, if anything, reestimation of the earnings function using two-stage least squares yields "... larger positive coefficients for (total) experience and stronger negative coefficients for home time" (p. S99).

Further, in estimating the proportion of the pay gap explained by the human capital variables, the actual mean levels of the variables are employed. Yet the heart of the endogeneity problem is that wage discrimination may have influenced the amount of human capital women have accumulated. Thus, it is likely that Mincer and Polachek, and analyses modeled on theirs, overestimate the impact of the human capital variables on the sex pay differential. In light of this potential bias, it is notable that Mincer and Polachek found that over half of the pay gap between white married men and women could not be explained by the human capital variables and potentially was due to discrimination.

Another issue that has been raised regarding Mincer and Polachek's (1974) findings is the generalizability of their results for the 30- to 44-year-old age group to the whole female population — as is necessary in order to draw inferences for the aggregate male-female pay gap. The work of Corcoran (1978, 1979) using a full age range from the 1976 Panel Study of Income Dynamics (PSID), suggests that their findings may not, in fact, be generalizable. She found that the wages of women aged 30–44 are much more strongly affected by labor force withdrawals than the broader age range (Corcoran, 1979). Women in this age group are more likely than women in general to have recently reentered the labor market after a prolonged period of nonparticipation. Corcoran suggests that her findings are consistent with the notion that women's wages are temporarily depressed by labor force withdrawals because of misinformation about job opportunities and/or about their own value as workers.[24]

In addition to work histories, the PSID data provide measures of labor force attachment (i.e., absenteeism due to own illness; absenteeism due to illness of others; self-imposed restrictions on work hours and/or job location; voluntary part-time work). For an unrestricted age group of women, Corcoran (1978) found that adjustments for schooling, work history, and labor force attachment accounted for 36 percent of the wage gap between white men and white women and 27 percent of the wage gap between white men and black women. In addition to the difference in age group, some of the difference between Corcoran's and Mincer and Polachek's findings with respect to the importance of the human capital variables may reflect a growing work force attachment of women over the period spanned by the 1967 NLS and the 1976 PSID (Mincer, 1979). These findings of large, unexplained wage gaps for white and black women are impressive in light of Corcoran's detailed controls for productivity-related factors. In addition, since her findings are based on OLS estimates, she has not adjusted for the simultaneous equation bias discussed in reference to the Mincer and Polachek (1974) study. This suggests that, at least with regard to this consideration, she has underestimated the effect of labor market discrimination.

An additional issue raised by the human capital model is the interpretation of sex differences in returns to experience and marital status. For example, Mincer and Polachek (1974) argue that

> . . . the association of lower [female] coefficients with lesser work experience is not fortuitous: a smaller fraction of time and energy is devoted to job advancement (training, learning, getting ahead) per unit of time by persons whose work attachment is lower. Hence, the 45 percent figure in the explantion of the gap by duration-of-work experience alone may be viewed as an understatement. (p. S103)

To what extent do sex differences in returns to experience and marriage reflect employer discrimination and to what extent do they reflect women's choices? While a definitive answer to that question is not available, the evidence suggests that discrimination most likely plays a role.

With respect to returns to experience, a study by Duncan and Hoffman (1979) is particularly interesting. Using direct measures of on-the-job training from the 1976 PSID, they find that men and women receive about the same payoff from on-the-job training. However, "past years of work experience have a high payoff in training for men, especially white men, but have very little effect on the chances that women will receive training" (p. 601). They see their results as consistent with a view that firms have different promotion practices on the basis of sex and race. Thus, the observed lower returns to experience of women may reflect to some extent employer discrimination in providing access to on-the-job training opportunities.

On the other hand, Sandell and Shapiro (1980), analyzing data from the NLS, have found that young white and black women who plan to work at age 35 have experience-wage profiles which ". . . begin at a lower point and have a steeper (initial) slope than those of their 'no-work-plans' counterparts" (p. 343). Thus, some of the sex difference in work experience coefficients may reflect women's own investment decisions based on their work expectations.

However, Sandell and Shapiro also find that the returns to job tenure (seniority), which they take as an indication of investment in firm-specific training, do not differ significantly between those who plan to work at age 35 and those who do not. This, in turn, suggests that part of the differential access to on-the-job training opportunities by sex implied by Duncan and Hoffman's findings may reflect the inability or the unwillingness of employers to distinguish between the committed and uncommitted group. As our previous discussion suggests, there is some difference of opinion as to whether such statistical discrimination would represent economic discrimination or not. However, it is likely to result in committed women getting less training and receiving lower returns to job tenure than committed men.

In evaluating the implications of Sandell and Shapiro's findings for sex differences in earnings, it is instructive to consider Arrow's (1973) notion of perceptual equilibrium. Given the set of market opportunities she can reasonably expect and her expected value of nonmarket time, each young woman determines her work plans for age 35. Since women with given characteristics in the Sandell and Shapiro sample presumably face similar opportunities, the differences in their work plans probably reflect differences in their expected value of nonmarket time (perhaps due to differences in tastes). However, this does not preclude the possibility that, if confronted with a different set of market opportunities, substantially more of the women would be committed to market work. It is even possible that, given the male set of job opportunities (with similar returns to experience and job tenure), they would exhibit the same degree of labor force commitment as males.

With respect to worker and employer firm-specific training investment decisions, it is job, rather than labor force, stability that is the issue. Some evidence in favor of the Arrow notion in this case is provided by the findings of Blau and Kahn (1981) who used data on young men and young women from the NLS to analyze sex differences in quitting. They found that, all else equal (including job-related characteristics), white and black women were no more likely to quit their jobs than men of the same race. They also found that a high proportion of the observed sex differential in quitting was associated with job characteristics rather than personal characteristics.[25] Similar findings were reported by Viscusi (1980) for a larger age range from the PSID.[26] Both Blau and Kahn, and Viscusi found that, all else equal, blacks were less likely to quit their jobs than white workers of the same sex. Blau and Kahn also report some support for one of the models of statistical discrimination presented earlier in that female quits were found to be less accurately predicted than men's by the explanatory variables.[27] No basis for statistical discrimination was found in the case of race.

With respect to the interpretation of sex differences in the returns to marital status, Hill (1979) uses explicit data on experience, human capital investment, and labor force attachment from the 1976 PSID to explore this issue further. She finds that, all else equal, marriage has strong positive wage effects for white and black men, while the effects of marriage on white and black women's wages are not significantly different from zero. Malkiel and Malkiel (1973) and Osterman (1979) report similar findings for the wage effects of marriage from studies of sex differences in the wages of professional workers, also including good controls for work experience and attachment.

A supply-side explanation for these findings cannot be ruled out entirely. Given the traditional division of labor within the home. Married men may be more highly motivated or hard-working than single men with similar measured characteristics, while married women may be less highly motivated or hard-working than their single counterparts. But, as Osterman points out, how do we then explain the absence of a negative effect of marriage on the earnings of women? Moreover, Hill examined the effect of marital status and number of children on wages as more explicit controls for experience, human capital investments, and labor force attachment were added to the wage regressions. She finds that the wage effect of marital status among all race/sex groups remains quite stable and concludes that marital status does not serve as a proxy for these productivity-related factors. If marital status is not serving as a proxy for these obvious and important factors, it seems doubtful that it is serving as a proxy for more subtle traits like motivation. However, Hill does find that number of children to some extent is a proxy for these factors. Both Osterman and Hill feel that employers may believe that married men deserve higher salaries because of their greater financial responsibilities. Given traditional views of men's and women's economic roles, they do not feel the same is true of married women. Such a difference in treatment, if it exists, would have to be classed as discriminatory.

The high degree of employment segregation by sex raises the issue of the relationship of sex differences in occupational distribution to the pay gap. Using data from the 1980 Census, Treiman and Hartmann (1981) found that 35 to 39 percent of the earnings difference between men and women was associated with sex differences in the distribution of their employment among 479 detailed categories.[28] Their calculations indicate, not surprisingly, that the portion of the sex pay gap associated with occupational differences is larger, the finer the occupational categories employed. Occupational differences appear to be a significant factor in explaining the sex pay gap, even when other productivity-related factors are controlled for. For example, Oaxaca (1973b) found that the inclusion of controls for major occupation and industry and class of worker increased the portion of the sex pay gap explained from 20 to 37 percent in the case of whites and 6 to 39 percent in the case of blacks. Using 1950 census data, Sanborn (1964) was able to explain 43 percent of the sex pay gap on the basis of controls for such factors as detailed occupation, age, and education.[29] Further, using data from the 1974 PSID and the 1967 NLS, England (1981, 1982) found that, all else equal, percent female in the occupation has a significant negative relationship with respect to female earnings.[30]

As discussed earlier, the human capital model provides an explanation for occupational segregation by sex in terms of women's optimizing behavior, given the traditional division of labor by sex within the family. Polachek (1979, 1981) provides some support for this view when jobs are categorized according to variants of the Census major occupational groups.

The problem with his approach is that these major occupational categories combine predominantly male and predominantly female jobs (England, 1982). England (1981, 1982) explicitly examines whether women's earnings patterns in predominantly female and predominantly male occupations differ in the way predicted by the human capital model. She finds that the earnings of women in predominantly female occupations do not show lower rates of either depreciation or appreciation than do the earnings of women in occupations containing more males.[31] Further, she finds women who have discontinuous work histories are no more likely to be in a predominantly female occupation than are women who have been employed more continuously. Indeed, since she finds that women earn less in female jobs at all levels of experience, she concludes that "the evidence does not support the contention of human capital theorists that women maximize lifetime earnings by choosing female occupations" (England, 1981, p. 18).

If we provisionally conclude that the human capital analysis of occupational choice discussed above does not explain occupational segregation, at least at the aggregate level, what does? A host of potential candidates remain, ranging from premarket discrimination (e.g., by families through the socialization process or by schools through the actions of teachers, guidance counselors, or admissions committees) to the exclusionary practices of employers (due to their own tastes, statistical discriminations, and/or the tastes of employees or customers). Clearly, considerable additional work needs to be done to narrow the field and/or to attach relative weights to these competing explanations.

The relatively flat earnings profiles of women in female jobs are consistent with the notion advanced in the institutional view that employers would structure female jobs to fit the average perceived characteristics of women workers. However, the finding that women in male jobs also have relatively flat earnings profiles might at first appear inconsistent with the notion that the internal labor market mandates equal pay for equal work by sex. However, it should be noted that the Census categories are aggregated across job levels and firms. Thus, firms may pay women and men in the same job category at roughly the same rate, but promote women more slowly.[32] Further, it may be that women and men in the same Census job category are segregated by firm. Blau (1977) examines the extent of employment segregation by sex within occupational categories and its relationship to intraoccupational pay differentials within the context of an institutional model.

Blau postulates that institutional and market forces determine a wage hierarchy of firms within the local labor market that is consistent across occupational categories. She argues that, while employer tastes for discrimination against women are fairly widespread, the ability to exercise them is constrained by the firm's position in the wage hierarchy. That position is determined by a variety of factors and cannot be altered easily to accommodate employer preferences regarding the sex composition of specific occupational categories. Thus, in each occupational category, male workers are primarily sought by and attracted to the higher-wage establishments, while female workers, for the most part, find employment in the lower-paying firms which, regardless of their preferences, are less able to compete for male labor.

Blau tests this model using unpublished 1970 wage data from the Bureau of Labor Statistics on extremely narrow, white collar occupational categories (e.g., accounting clerk, class A) in three Northeastern cities. She argues that within such narrow categories male and female labor is likely to be fairly homogeneous.[33] Blau finds that within occupations men and women are segregated by establishments to an extent in excess of what would be expected on the basis of chance. Within firms, occupational pay differences are found to be relatively small, and sex pay differentials within occupations are primarily due to differences in pay rates among (rather than within) firms.[34] Further, men tend to earn less when they work with women, which is counter to what we would expect on the basis of the Becker model if discriminatory tastes were located in employees.

Blau finds evidence of a wage hierarchy of firms that is consistent across occupations and sex groups. Controlling for occupational mix, the representation of women in the firm is found to be consistent across occupations and inversely related to the wage standing of the firm. Note that these findings also conflict with the Becker model. In the case of employee preferences, it is not expected that men will earn more when they work with relatively fewer women. In the case of employer preferences, it is not expected that the firms which hire relatively the fewest women (presumably the most discriminatory firms) will pay women the highest wage rates.[35]

We have seen that on a priori grounds the human capital model provides a viable alternative to labor market discrimination as an explanation for sex differences in market outcomes. However, on the basis of our review of the empirical evidence, we conclude that it cannot provide the full explanation and that discrimination most probably plays a role. While pinpointing the exact portion of the sex pay gap due to discrimination is difficult, the findings suggest that over half the differential cannot be explained by sex differences in productivity-related factors. Some considerations (e.g., omitted variables) suggest that this may be an overestimate of the magnitude of discrimination. On the other hand, other considerations (e.g., the impact of labor market discrimination on the incentives to acquire experience, training, etc.) suggest that it may be an underestimate. Thus, we are still left with fairly strong evidence of the importance of discrimination. However, the effort to determine which model of discrimination is most consistent with the data and to determine the mechanisms by which these discriminatory outcomes are produced is still in its early stages. Further, the question of the impact of discrimination on women's labor force participation and human capital investment decision's has received very little attention empirically.

The Federal Government's Antidiscrimination Effort

If we conclude that discrimination has indeed been a factor in the lower earnings of women relative to men, a logical next step is to consider the impact of the government's antidiscrimination effort on the pay gap. At present there exists an impressive array of laws and regulations prohibiting sex discrimination (see Blau, 1977 and Lloyd and Niemi, 1979 for fuller discussions). The Equal Pay Act of 1963 prohibits differential pay rates for men and women who perform substantially equal work in the same establishment. Title VII of the Civil Rights Act of 1964 prohibits employers from discriminating on the basis of sex, race, religion, and ethnic origin in hiring or firing, compensation, terms, conditions or privileges of employment, and employer-provided training. Employment agencies and labor organizations are also covered by Title VII. Initially issued in 1965 to prohibit race discrimination on the part of federal contractors, Executive Order 11246 was extended to cover sex discrimination in 1968. Covered employers are required to take affirmative action to ensure equal employment opportunity. Finally, Title IX of the Education Amendments of 1972 prohibits sex discrimination against employers and students in federally assisted educational programs.

The impact of the federal government's antidiscrimination effort has been examined using two types of data: time series and cross-sectional. In the case of the time series studies, the strategy is to examine trends in the relative earnings of women (minorities) for significant post-1964 (post-Title VII) effects. The problem here is the difficulty of including enough control variables to be confident that post-1964 trends indeed measure the impact of the government's equal employment opportunity (EEO) effort. In the case of cross-sectional studies, the strategy is to compare the relative earnings or employment position of women (minorities) in the sectors in which the laws (regulations) are likely to have their largest effect to their position in other sectors, all else equal. In addition to the problem of adequate controls, such studies face the difficulty of identifying the covered sectors.

For example, the coverage of Title VII is potentially almost economy-wide, with only employers of less than 15 workers officially exempted. Even though the Executive Order is limited to government contractors, its effects may also be difficult to measure. On the one hand, the relative position of women (minorities) employed by noncontractors who hope to obtain government contracts may be positively affected, biasing downward the estimated effect. On the other hand, enforcement of the Executive Order may merely result in a reallocation of discriminatory firms out of, and of nondiscriminatory firms into, the covered sector, biasing upward the estimated effect (Flanagan, 1976). Bearing these problems in mind, we consider both types of evidence.

The unadjusted trends in the earnings ratio between 1955 and 1977 by race-sex group are shown in table 2–1. The focus is on full-time, year-round workers in order to approximate a wage rate. This procedure does, however, exclude the involuntarily unemployed and would have a disproportionate impact upon blacks who have substantially higher unemployment rates. We shall return to this point. The figures in table 2–1 show that the aggregate trends we have noted earlier have been dominated by the experience of white women whose earnings relative to white men declined over the period. After adjustment for sex differences in educational attainment and the impact of the business cycle, Oaxaca (1977) finds that, for the 1955–71 period, the sex pay gap among white full-time, year-round workers widened. As we have seen, it does not appear that adjustment for labor force experience would have altered this finding. However, the evidence suggests a small but discernible reversal in the trend toward increases in the differential in 1966 — about when, according to Oaxaca, the government policy could be expected to start taking effect.

Table 2–1. Ratios of Median Income of Year-Round, Full-Time Workers, by Sex and Race for Selected Years 1955–77

Year	*Female/Male Earnings*		*Nonwhite/White Earnings*		*Nonwhite Females/ White Males*
	Whites	*Nonwhites*	*Males*	*Females*	
1955	65.3	55.1	60.9	51.4	33.5
1959	61.2	67.5	58.4	64.4	39.4
1963	59.0	56.7	64.4	61.8	36.5
1967	58.3	64.3	66.7	76.2	44.4
1971	58.2	74.1	70.8	90.1	52.5
1975	57.5	74.5	76.7	98.2	57.4
1977	57.7	76.5	71.8	95.2	54.9

Source: Calculated from Lloyd and Niemi (1979, p. 171)

Lazear (1979) argues that the improvement in the earnings position of white women is understated when only current wages are considered. He finds that among young men and women, sex differences in the coefficient on experience in OLS wage growth regressions narrowed considerably between 1968 and 1974. He takes this as indicating an equalization in on-the-job training opportunities and presaging a future narrowing of sex pay differentials. However, Kahn (1980) presents evidence that when the coefficient on experience in the wage growth regression is adjusted for simultaneous equation bias, a much higher wage growth return to experience is found for males than for females.

In contrast to the experience of white females, black women have gained relative to all other race-sex groups over the same period (table 2–1). Updating the work of Freeman (1973), Brown (1982) found that after adjusting for relative educational attainment — which increased relative black earnings over the period — and the impact of the business cycle, the median earnings of all black women workers increased relative to white women's throughout the 1950–1977 period, and especially in the post–1964 years. (The former time trend was not significant, however).

This contrasted with Brown's findings for black males. Holding constant relative education and the impact of the business cycle, their median earnings relative to white males exhibited a significantly negative time trend for the period, although the trend for the post–1964 period was significantly positive. Further, the post-1964 trends were greater for black females relative to white females than for black males relative to white males. This continued to be the case after correcting for the selectivity bias of focusing on labor force participants.

By 1977, the median earnings of all black women were 101 percent of those of white women (Brown, 1982). Parity in this figure does not necessarily indicate that racial discrimination has been eliminated among females, however. First, among full-time, year-round workers (table 2–1), the median earnings of black women were 95 percent of those of white women, suggesting that hourly wage rates were still lower for the former than for the latter group. And, in fact, data from the 1976 PSID indicate that the geometric mean wages of black women were 88 percent of those of white women in 1975 (Corcoran, 1978). Thus, the parity in black women's median annual earnings relative to white women's earnings reflects, in part, black women's labor supply behavior. That they are able to compensate for their lower wages by supplying more hours is impressive, particularly in light of their considerably higher unemployment rates — 14.2 percent in comparison to 7.8 percent for white women in March 1977 (U.S. Department of Labor, undated).

Second, given these differences in labor supply behavior, it is possible that, in the absence of racial discrimination, black women's median earnings would exceed those of white women. By March 1977, the educational attainment of black female labor force participants (12.4 years) was only slightly below that of white women (12.6 years) (U.S. Department of Labor, undated). Further, data from the 1976 PSID suggests that in 1975 employed black women averaged two years more work experience than employed white women (Corcoran, 1978).

On the other hand, there are factors which would work in the other direction. For example, a higher proportion of black women reside in the South. According to my own calculations using Corcoran and Duncan's (1979) earnings regression results and sample means for the 1976 PSID, differences in endowments explained only 16 percent of the higher hourly wage rates of white women in 1975. The remainder presumably would reflect racial discrimination against black women. This finding is particularly striking in light of Corcoran and Duncan's detailed controls for experience, training, and attachment to the labor force.

In addition to greater relative gains for black than for white women, some evidence indicates that younger cohorts of women may have exhibited somewhat more progress than older cohorts relative to males. For example, between 1970 and 1977, the ratio of the median earnings of full-time, year-round women workers to those of men fell from 59 to 58 percent for all women, but increased from 65 to 68 percent among 25- to 34-year-olds. Similar small cohort differences were exhibited within the high school and college educated groups (U.S. Department of Commerce, 1980, pp. 74–75). Beller (1982a) presents evidence that, all else equal, the impact of a college education on the probability of a woman obtaining a male job became more favorable between 1971 and 1979, and that these gains were particularly marked for the younger cohort entering the work force. On the other hand, she found that over this period the impact of a high school education on a woman's probability of obtaining a male job became, if anything, less favorable among all age groups.

Thus, an analysis of the time series data suggests relatively little impact of the government's EEO effort on the employment of white women, and considerably larger effects on blacks, particularly black females. One way to view these findings is that government policies have been more effective in reducing race differentials than sex differentials, and that race differentials have declined more rapidly among women than among men. Further, some evidence is found, for women as a whole, that younger cohorts experienced some slight improvement in their relative earnings position, while older cohorts did not. Of course, these changes may or may not be due to the government's EEO effort, but, particularly with respect to the relative progress of blacks, this inference seems reasonable.

Cross-sectional studies of the impact of government enforcement programs seem to raise more questions than they answer when compared to the time series trends. Studies of the enforcement of the Executive Order generally suggests substantial employment gains for black males, but little impact for either black or white women (Lloyd and Niemi, 1979; Brown, 1982). This is consistent with the larger gains for black males than for white females revealed in the time series, but leaves the large gains for black females unexplained (in terms of enforcement of the Executive Order). On the other hand, Smith (1978) cites evidence of increases in the proportion of black women employed directly or indirectly by the government as indicating that black women were the primary beneficiaries of affirmative action programs. Indirect government employment measures employment in industries regulated by either federal or state and local governments and the fraction of industry's sales that go to either the federal or state and local governments. He argues that black women benefit by being able to fill two quotas for the price of one. However, he presents no evidence that black women are doing anything more than moving into typically white female occupations. If so, they do not bolster the firm's representation of women in high-level, typically white male occupations. A recent study by Osterman (1982) found evidence that the Federal Contract Compliance Program lowered the quit rate among women, which he argued was an indication of increased job opportunities. If so, such improvements have not yet been reflected in the aggregate statistics.

As noted earlier, the problems of finding a control group are particularly serious for studies of the enforcement of Title VII. Beller (1979, 1982b) attempts to measure the law's impact through regional differences in the probability of apprehension for violating Title VII and the probability of paying a penalty if a violation is found. She finds that, between 1967 and 1974, enforcement of Title VII narrowed the sex differential in earnings by about seven percentage points and sex differences in the probability of being employed in a male occupation by about six percentage points, all else equal. Beller adjusts for the impact of race on earnings and occupations but does not estimate separate race effects of enforcement.[36] Her findings of the impact of Title VII seem large in comparison to the time series trends which indicate little progress for women as a group during this period. While Killingsworth (1979) argues that the deterrent effects of the EEOC's activities may be more likely to be felt by firms in the same industry rather than in the same region, no alternative explanation has been offered for Beller's findings.

Freeman (1973) suggests that one reason for the more rapid progress of black women relative to white women than of black men relative to white men is the difference in the structure of male and female jobs. The flat age-earnings profiles in female jobs presumably indicate few requirements for experience or on-the-job training, making it possible for black women of all ages to upgrade their occupations and increase their relative earnings. By contrast, older black men made relatively little occupational progress and younger black men made smaller gains than younger black women. This was due, he argues, to the greater experience and training needed for high-paying male jobs.

This reasoning reinforces the view that the greater relative progress of black women reflects a more rapid decline of racial barriers among women than among men, rather than the combined effects of a decline in race and sex discrimination. Similar reasoning could explain why the earnings of the younger cohorts of women have progressed somewhat relative to men's, while the earnings of the older groups have not. Thus far, however, the modest gains of the younger cohorts do not provide overwhelming support for this view. Much will depend on how this group fares in the next few years.[37]

We conclude our review of the effect of government antibias legislation and regulations by noting that this is only one of the ways in which the federal government exercises potential impacts on women's relative economic status. For example, government-subsidized training and employment under the Comprehensive Employment and Training Act (CETA) of 1973 could help to reduce sex differences in wages and occupation.[38] On the other hand, the social security system and the progressive income tax may work to discourage labor force participation of secondary earners who are frequently women, thus lowering their accumulation of human capital and their earnings (Gordon, 1979a, 1979b). From a policy perspective, perhaps the real issue is the net effect of the federal government on women's economic status, taking into account all its various programs, activities, taxes, and expenditures.

Conclusions

A variety of explanations have been offered for the pay and occupational differences between male and female workers. Some emphasize labor market discrimination, while others, most notably the human capital model, focus upon the voluntary choices of women. A review of the empirical literature strongly suggests that, all else equal, including fairly refined measures of work experience and labor force attachment, women do earn less than men. This suggests that labor market discrimination does indeed play a role in producing the lower earnings of women. However, we lack a widely accepted theory of the persistence of sex discrimination in the labor market over time in the face of competitive forces. It is notable that Darity (1982), in a recent review of the literature on black-white earnings inequality, reached a strikingly similar conclusion.

Perhaps it is time now to devote less of our empirical efforts to ascertaining the existence of discrimination and more toward determining which model of discrimination is most consistent with the data and the mechanisms by which these discriminatory outcomes are produced. On the basis of the existing evidence, it appears that sex segregation in employment is an important mechanism for producing sex differences in earnings and that the occupational differences between men and women do not seem to be consistent with optimizing behavior on the part of women. However, considerably more work is needed to understand fully the causes of sex differences in occupational distributions and to determine the role of such occupational differences in producing male-female pay differentials. Finally, the question of the indirect effects of discrimination on the qualifications of women is another area upon which future research could fruitfully be focused.

One of the puzzles in the study of women's economic position is the widening of the male-female pay gap over the past twenty-five years in the face of increasing labor force attachment among women and an impressive array of federal antibias laws and regulations during the post-1964 period. Based on time series data, it appears that government policies have been more effective in reducing race differentials than sex differentials, and that race differentials have declined more rapidly among women than among men. The more rapid progress of black relative to white women than of black relative to white men may be due to the lesser importance of experience and training in most female jobs, making it possible for black women of all ages to upgrade their occupations. Black males may have faced greater experience and training requirements in their efforts to move into high-level male jobs, making it difficult for older cohorts to advance. But such reasoning cannot explain the lack of progress of women as a group relative to men, particularly the only modest gains achieved by the younger cohorts. What does seem clear is that future gains for black as well as for white women depend upon the lowering of sex barriers as well as racial barriers in the labor market.

Notes

1. The labor force participation statistics cited in this paragraph are from U.S. Department of Labor (June, 1980).

2. Black women's participation rates have historically been considerably higher than those of white women, although the differential has declined in recent years. In 1955, the labor force participation rate of black and other nonwhite women was 46.1 percent, in comparison 34.5 percent for whites. By 1979, the participation rates were 53.5 percent and 50.6 percent for nonwhites and whites, respectively. The participation rates of black males have fallen more sharply than those of white males over this period. In 1955, the participation rate of both white and nonwhite males was about 85 percent, by 1979 the participation rates of whites and nonwhites were 78.6 percent and 71.9 percent, respectively (U.S. Dept. of Labor, 1980, pp. 62–3). These differing racial trends in participation rates are an important factor in evaluating the recent gains in black earnings discussed below. See Brown (1981).

3. Lloyd and Niemi (1979) find no change in the degree of segregation using Census data for 1970 and CPS data for 1977. Using comparable CPS data for 1971 and 1977, Beller (1982c) finds that segregation continued to decline over the 1970s. Full resolution of this disparity in results may await the availability of the 1980 Census data. In any case, both studies suggest that the magnitude of segregation remained quite high.

4. The notion of employee discrimination is developed by Bergmann and Darity (1981) in terms of productivity reductions due to employee hostility rather than direct increases in costs due to compensating differentials.

5. Of course, one may wonder why men rather than women are the recipients of these personnel investments. As Arrow (1973) points out, history matters when there are costs to change. Given historically rising female participation rates, women, as relatively new entrants, may find males already in place in many sectors. However, women have always been heavily concentrated in a few female-dominated activities, even when they constituted a small proportion of the labor force. Assuming that discrimination played a role in this segregation, it appears that the notion of personnel investment tends to require both employer and employee discrimination. Further, once we have personnel investments, men and women are no longer in fact equally productive, although they may be potentially equally productive (see below).

6. Women are more likely than men to quit their jobs to exit the labor force (Barnes and Jones, 1974).

7. Some preliminary evidence in support of the monopsony view as an explanation for male-female wage differentials across urban areas, based on data for white males and white, never-married females, is presented by Cardwell and Rosenzweig (1980). Note that in restricting their analysis to never-married females, they focus upon women with the lowest value of nonmarket time.

8. This assumes that the variances of the measurement error and of the productivity indicator are the same for males and females.

9. See also Blau and Jusenius (1976) and Piore (1971). Lewin and England (1982) argue that it is the explicit use of ascriptive characteristics like race or sex in personnel decisions that constitutes the discriminatory aspect of statistical discrimination, even when the employer's perceptions are correct. From a normative perspective, this is certainly correct, but it is not clear that it counters Aigner and Cain's (1977) argument that such behavior does not constitute economic discrimination.

10. See also Spence (1973, 1974).

11. This point is emphasized in Darity (1982)'s consideration of racial pay differentials.

12. A number of other authors have emphasized the importance of feedback effects in analyzing sex pay and occupational differentials. See, for example, Bergmann (1976), Blau (1977), Ferber and Lowry (1976), Strober (1976), Weiss and Gronau (1981).

13. See also Edgeworth (1922) and Fawcett (1918).

14. See also Cain (1976), Gordon, D.M. (1972) and Wachter (1974).

15. Further, one may question the basic premise of the human capital model that upward

sloping experience-earnings profiles are indeed due to on-the-job training. See, for example, Medoff and Abraham (1980, 1981).

16. See also Kamalich and Polachek (1982).

17. See also Heckman (1974).

18. Gronau has argued elsewhere (1973) that the value of time of housewives may be either higher or lower than the market wage of comparable employed women. If the former is true, it is not necessarily the case that restriction of the sample to labor force participants overstates women's wage offers. However, the empirical evidence he presents supports Gronau's (1974) contention. See also Cogan (1980).

19. As noted earlier, black male participation rates are lower than those of whites. Thus, the same type of selectivity problem discussed in the text affects race comparisons among males.

20. For more detailed reviews of the empirical literature, including occupation specific studies, see Kohen (1975), Lloyd and Niemi (1979), and Treiman and Hartmann (1981).

21. The one exception was a study by Sanborn (1964) discussed below.

22. Oaxaca's results including controls for occupational and industrial characteristics are considered below. See also Gwartney and Stroup (1973), Sawhill (1973), and Blinder (1973). On the other hand, Darity and Myers (1981) found that while the structural equations for wages for white males and females were significantly different, they were not so in the case of black males and females.

23. For an exception see Suter and Miller (1973), who restricted their sample to women from the National Longitudinal Surveys in the 30–44 age group who had worked continuously since school completion.

24. Using longitudinal panel data from the NLS on the 30–44 year age group, Mincer and Ofek (1982) find direct evidence of rapid wage growth upon reentry. Unlike Corcoran (1979), however, they attribute it to the "repair" of previously eroded human capital.

25. Job characteristics include current wage, long-run earnings opportunities associated with the job, collective bargaining coverage, and industry and occupation dummy variables.

26. Ragan and Smith (1981) find that sex differences in industry turnover rates explain a substantial portion of the sex difference in earnings among individuals. However, as they acknowledge, since their data refer to the industry's history and not the individual's their findings are consistent with the possibility that women are restricted to low-wage, high-turnover jobs (e.g., those requiring little specific training). Osterman (1979) found no sex differences in absenteeism, all else equal, for a sample of professional workers.

27. While Osterman (1979) reports no basis for statistical discrimination on this ground, Kahn (1981) shows that Osterman does not employ the correct indicator of predictability. When the correct indicator is used, Kahn finds that women's absenteeism is less accurately predicted than men's.

28. See also Chiswick et al. (1974).

29. Including adjustments for even more narrowly defined occupational categories from the BLS, as well as sex differences in turnover, absenteeism, and work experience, Sanborn (1964) was able to explain 71 percent of the pay gap. The problem with this portion of his analysis is that he most probably engaged in double-counting. He assumed that the sex differences in age and education which prevailed within the census categories also prevailed within the more detailed BLS categories. Further, he adjusted within occupations for estimates of aggregate sex differences in turnover, absenteeism, and work experience. Leaving aside the issue of endogeneity, labor quality differences between men and women are likely to be considerably smaller within occupations than in the aggregate, since it is these traits that sort people into occupations. Indeed, in the presence of discrimination, women may be more qualified than men

in specific occupations. See Hamilton (1973) for some evidence consistent with the latter possibility.

30. See also Roos (1981), Ferber and Lowry (1976), Cabral et al. (1981), Stevenson (1975), Jusenius (1977).

31. See also Beller (1982c). She finds that when one examines detailed (3-digit) census occupations, the evidence for the human capital model is mixed, in that the expected signs on the labor supply variables are not always obtained. King (1977) finds little evidence of flatter age earnings profiles for women in female as compared to male professions.

32. Note that such a sex difference by job level would not support the human capital view, in that it would not be economically rational for women to opt to take the lower-paid training positions but not to reap the gains of moving up the job ladder. For findings suggesting that women have lower promotion probabilities, see Duncan and Hoffman (1979), Cabral et al. (1981), and Malkiel and Malkiel (1973).

33. See note 29.

34. For other studies reporting differences in the distribution of men and women by firm that are associated with pay differentials, see Buckley (1971), McNulty (1967), Bridges and Berk (1974), Talbert and Bose (1977), Allison (1976), Dussault and Rose-Lizée (1980).

35. Note that the comparisons made in the text between the results expected on the basis of the Becker and institutional models rest somewhat heavily on the assumption that labor is fairly homogeneous within these detailed occupations. Otherwise, variations in labor quality might account for these interfirm differences in pay rates.

36. In Beller (1977), separate race effects of enforcement on female earnings are estimated. She found larger effects of Title VII for black than for white females. This is consistent with the race differences in time-series trends among women discussed above.

37. Much attention is now focused upon the comparable worth approach to narrowing the sex differential in earnings, see Livernash (1980), Treiman and Hartmann (1981), Ferber (1982), Newman and Vonhof (1981), and Bergmann and Gray (1982).

38. For a study of the impact of CETA on women's economic status, see Waite and Berryman (1982).

References

Aigner, D.J., and Cain, G.C. "Statistical Theories of Discrimination in Labor Markets." *Industrial and Labor Relations Review* (January 1977), 175–187.

Allison, E.K. "Sex Linked Earnings Differentials in the Beauty Industry." *Journal of Human Resources* (Summer 1976), 383–390.

Arrow, K. "Economic Dimensions of Occupational Segregation: Comment I." *Signs* Part 2, (Spring 1976), 233–237.

______ . "Models of Job Discrimination." In A.H. Pascal (ed.) *Racial Discrimination in Economic Life.* Lexington, Mass.: D.C. Heath and Co., 1972a, 83–102.

______ . "Some Mathematical Models of Race in the Labor Market." In A.H. Pascal (ed.) *Racial Discrimination in Economic Life.* Lexington, Mass.: D.C. Heath and Co., 1972b, 187–204.

______ . "The Theory of Discrimination." In O. Ashenfelter, and A. Rees (eds.) *Discrimination in Labor Markets.* Princeton, New Jersey: Princeton University Press, 1973, 3–33.

Barnes, W.F., and Jones, E. "Differences in Male and Female Quitting." *Journal of Human Resources* (Fall 1974), 439–51.

Becker, G. "A Theory of Marriage." *Journal of Political Economy* (July/August), 813–846.

______ . "A Theory of the Allocation of Time." *Economic Journal* (Sept. 1965), 493–517.

______ . *The Economics of Discrimination.* Chicago: University of Chicago Press, 1957.

Beller, A.H. "EEO Laws and the Earnings of Women." *Proceedings of the Twenty-Ninth Annual Meeting of the Industrial Relations Research Association.* University of Wisconsin, Madison, 1977, 190–98.

______ . "The Impact of Equal Employment Opportunity Laws on the Male/Female Earnings Differential." In C.B. Lloyd, E. Andrews, and C.L. Gilroy (eds.) *Women in the Labor Market.* New York: Columbia University Press, 1979.

______ . "The Impact of Equal Opportunity Policy on Sex Differentials in Earnings and Occupations." *American Economic Review* (May 1982a), 171–5.

______ . "Occupational Segregation by Sex: Determinants and Changes." *Journal of Human Resources* (Summer 1982b), 371–92.

______ . "Trends in Occupational Segregation by Sex: 1960–1990." mimeographed (July 1982c).

Bergmann, B.R. "Occupational Segregation, Wages and Profits When Employers Discriminate by Race or Sex." *Eastern Economic Journal* (April–July 1974), 103–10.

______ . "Reducing the Pervasiveness of Discrimination." In E. Ginzberg (ed.) *Jobs for Americans.* Englewood Cliffs, N.J.: Prentice Hall, 1976, 120–41.

Bergmann, B.R., and Darity, Jr., W. "Social Relations in the Workplace and Employer Discrimination." *Proceedings of the Thirty-Third Annual Meeting of the Industrial Relations Research Association.* University of Wisconsin, Madison, 1981, 155–62.

Bergmann, B.R., and Gray, M.W. "The Economics of Compensation Claims Under Title VII." mimeographed (May 1982).

Blau, F.D. *Equal Pay in the Office.* Lexington, Mass.: D.C. Heath and Co., 1977.

______ . "Longitudinal Patterns of Female Labor Force Participation." In H.S. Parnes et al. *Dual Careers: A Longitudinal Analysis of the Labor Market Experience of Women* V. 4. Columbus, Ohio: Center for Human Resource Research, Ohio State University, December 1975, 27–55.

______ . "The Impact of the Unemployment Rate on Labor Force Entries and Exits." In *Women's Changing Roles at Home and on the Job.* A special report of the National Commission for Manpower Policy, Report No. 26 (Sept. 1978), 263–286.

Blau, F.D., and Hendricks, W.E. "Occupational Segregation by Sex: Trends and Prospects." *Journal of Human Resources* (Spring 1979), 197–210.

Blau, F.D., and Jusenius, C.L. "Economists' Approaches to Sex Segregation in the Labor Market: An Appraisal." *Signs* Part 2, (Spring 1976), 181–199.

Blau, F.D., and Kahn, L.M. "Race and Sex Differences in Quits by Young Workers." *Industrial and Labor Relations Review* (July 1981), 563–577.

Blinder, A.S. "Wage Discrimination: Reduced Form and Structural Estimates." *Journal of Human Resources* (Fall, 1973), 436–55.

Bridges, W.P., and Berk, R.A. "Determinants of White-Collar Income: An Evaluation of Equal Pay for Equal Work." *Social Science Research* (Sept. 1974), 211–34.

Brown, C. "Black/White Earnings Ratios Since the Civil Rights Act of 1964: The Importance of Labor Market Drop-outs." *NBER Working Paper No. 617* (January 1981).

______. "The Federal Attack on Labor Market Discrimination: The Mouse That Roared?" in Ronald Ehrenberg (ed.) *Research in Labor Economics Vol. 5* Greenwich, Conn.: JAI Press, 1982, 33–68.

Buckley, J.E. "Pay Differences Between Men and Women in the Same Job" *Monthly Labor Review* (November 1971), 36–39.

Butler, R.J. "Estimating Wage Discrimination in the Labor Market." *Journal of Human Resources* (Fall 1982), 606–21.

Cabral, R., Ferber, M.A., and Green, C.A. "Men and Women in Fiduciary Institutions: A Study of Sex Differences in Career Development." *Review of Economics and Statistics* (November 1981), 573–80.

Cain, G. "The Challenge of Segmented Labor Market Theories to Orthodox Theory: A Survey." *Journal of Economic Literature* (December 1976), 1215–1257.

Cardwell, L.A., and Rosenzweig, M.R. "Economic Mobility, Monopsonistic Discrimination and Sex Differences in Wages." *Southern Economic Journal* (April 1980), 1102–17.

Chiplin, B. "An Alternative Approach to the Measurement of Sex Discrimination: An Illustration From University Entrance." *The Economic Journal* (December 1981), 988–997.

Chiswick, B.R., O'Neill, J.A., Fackler, J., and Polachek, S.W. "The Effect of Occupation on Race and Sex Differences in Hourly Earnings." *Business and Economic Statistics Section Proceedings of the American Statistical Society* 1974, 219–28.

Cogan, J. "Married Women's Labor Supply: A Comparison of Alternative Estimation Procedures," In J.P. Smith (ed.) *Female Labor Supply: Theory and Estimation.* (Princeton, N.J.: Princeton University Press, 1980), 90–118.

Corcoran, M. "The Structure of Female Wages." *American Economic Review.* Papers and proceedings (May 1978), 165–170.

______. "Work Experience, Labor Force Withdrawals and Women's Earnings: Empirical Results Using the 1976 Panel Study of Income Dynamics." In C.B. Lloyd, E. Andrews, and C.L. Gilroy, (eds.) *Women in the Labor Market.* New York: Columbia University Press, 1979.

Corcoran, M., and Duncan, G.J. "Work History, Labor Force Attachment, and Earnings Differences Between the Races and Sexes," *Journal of Human Resources* (Winter 1979), 3–20.

Darity, W.A., Jr. "The Human Capital Approach to Black-White Earnings Inequality: Some Unsettled Questions," *Journal of Human Resources* (Winter 1982), 72–93.

Darity, W.A., Jr., and Myers, S. "Changes in Black-White Income Inequality, 1968–1978: A Decade of Progress?" *Review of Black Political Economy* (Summer 1980), 354–79.

Doeringer, P.B., and Piore, M.J. *Internal Labor Markets and Manpower Analysis.* Lexington, Mass.: D.C. Heath and Co., 1971.

Duncan, G.J., and Hoffman, S. "On-the-Job Training and Earnings Differences by Race and Sex," *Review of Economics and Statistics.* (November 1979), 594–603.

Dussault, G., and Rose-Lizée, R. "La Discrimination À L'Égard Des Femmes Et La Ségrégation Sur les Marchés Du Travail: Le Cas Des Employés De Bureau À Montréal." In *La Discrimination À L'Égard Des Femmes Sur Le Marché Du Travail,* Collection Tirés A Part, No. 25. Québec: Université Laval, 1980, 475–504.

Economic Report of the President. Washington, D.C.: U.S. Government Printing Office, February 1974.

Edgeworth, F.Y. "Equal Pay to Men and Women for Equal Work." *Economic Journal* (Sept. 1922), 431–57.

England, P. "Wage Appreciation and Depreciation: A Test of Neoclassical Economic Explanations of Occupational Sex Segregation." mimeographed (December 1981).

______. "The Failure of Human Capital Theory to Explain Occupational Sex Segregation." *Journal of Human Resources* (Summer 1982), 358–70.

Fawcett, M.G. "Equal Pay for Equal Work." *Economic Journal* (March 1918), 1–6.

Ferber, M.A. "Women and Work: Issues of the Eighties," *Signs* (Winter 1982), 273–95.

Ferber, M.A., and Lowry, H.M. "The Sex Differential in Earnings: A Reappraisal," *Industrial and Labor Relations Review* (April 1976), 377–87.

Flanagan, R.J. "Actual Versus Potential Impact of Government Anti-Discrimination Programs." *Industrial and Labor Relations Review* (July 1976), 486–507.

Freeman, R.B. "Changes in the Labor Market for Black Americans, 1948–1972." *Brookings Papers on Economic Activity* 1973, 67–131.

Fuchs, V.R. "Differences in Hourly Earnings Between Men and Women." *Monthly Labor Review* (May 1971), 9–15.

Gordon, D.M. *Theories of Poverty and Underemployment.* Lexington, Mass.: D.C. Heath and Co., 1972.

Gordon, N.M. "Institutional Responses: The Federal Income Tax System." In R. Smith (ed.) *The Subtle Revolution.* Washington, D.C.: The Urban Institute, 1979a, 201–21.

______. "Institutional Responses: The Social Security System." In R. Smith (ed.) *The Subtle Revolution.* Washington, D.C.: The Urban Institute, 1979b, 223–55.

Gronau, R. "The Intrafamily Allocation of Time: The Value of Housewives' Time." *American Economic Review* (September 1973), 634–51.

______. "Wage Comparisons — A Selectivity Bias." *Journal of Political Economy* (November/December 1974), 1119–43.

Gwartney, J.D., and Stroup, R. "Measurement of Employment Discrimination According to Sex." *Southern Economic Journal* (April 1973), 575–87.

Hamilton, M.T. "Sex and Income Inequality Among the Employed." *The Annals of The American Academy of Political and Social Sciences* (Sept. 1973), 42–52.

Hashimoto, M., and Kochin, L. "A Bias in the Statistical Estimation of the Effects of Discrimination." *Economic Inquiry* (July 1980), 478–486.

Heckman, J.J. "Shadow Prices, Market Wages and Labor Supply." *Econometrica* (July 1974), 679–94.

Hill, M.S. "The Wage Effects of Marital Status and Children." *Journal of Human Resources* (Fall 1979), 579–594.

Jusenius, C.L. "The Influence of Work Experience, Skill Requirement, and Occupational Segregation on Women's Earnings." *Journal of Economics and Business* (Winter 1977), 107–115.

Kahn, L.M. "Sex Discrimination in Professional Employment: A Case Study — Comment." *Industrial and Labor Relations Review* (January 1981), 273–75.

______. "Wage Growth and Endogenous Experience." *Industrial Relations* (Winter 1980), 50–63.

Kamalich, R.F., and Polachek, S.W. "Discrimination: Fact or Fiction? An Examination Using an Alternative Approach." *Southern Economic Journal* (October 1982).

Killingsworth, M.R. "EEO: Training and Affirmative Action: Comment." In C.B. Lloyd, E.S. Andrews, and C.L. Gilroy (eds.) *Women in the Labor Market.* New York: Columbia University Press, 1979.

King, A.G. "Is Occupational Segregation the Cause of the Flatter-Experience-Earnings Profiles of Women?" *Journal of Human Resources* (Fall 1977), 541–49.

Kohen, A.I., with Breinich, S.C., and Shields, P. "Women and The Economy: A Bibliography and a Review of the Literature on Sex Differentiation in the Labor Market." Center for Human Resource Research, College of Administrative Science, Ohio State University, 1975.

Landes, E.M. "Sex Differences in Wages and Employment: A Test of the Specific Capital Hypothesis." *Economic Inquiry* (October 1977), 523–38.

Lazear, E. "Male-Female Wage Differentials: Has the Government Had Any Effect?" In C.B. Lloyd, E. Andrews, C.L. Gilroy (eds.) *Women in the Labor Market.* New York: Columbia University Press, 1979.

Lewin, P., and England, P. "Reconceptualizing Statistical Discrimination." Paper presented at the Annual Meetings of the Southwest Social Science Association, San Antonio, Texas (March 1982).

Livernash, R.E. (ed.) *Comparable Worth: Issues and Alternatives.* Washington, D.C.: Equal Employment Opportunity Council, 1980.

Lloyd, C.B., and Niemi, B.T. *The Economics of Sex Differentials.* New York: Columbia University Press, 1979.

Madden, J.F. "Economic Dimensions of Occupational Segregation: Comment III." *Signs* Part 2 (Spring 1976), 245–250.

______. *The Economics of Sex Discrimination.* Lexington, Mass.: D.C. Heath and Co., 1973.

______. "A Potpourri of Current Theoretical and Empirical Issues in Measuring Employment Discrimination." Paper presented to the Seventeenth North American Peace Science Conference, Philadelphia, November 11, 1981.

Malkiel, B.G., and Malkiel, J.A. "Male-Female Pay Differentials in Professional Employment." *American Economic Review* (September 1973), 693–705.

McNulty, D.J. "Differences in Pay Between Men and Women Workers." *Monthly Labor Review* (December 1967), 40–43.

Medoff, J.L. and Abraham, K.G. "Are Those Paid More Really More Productive? The Case of Experience." *Journal of Human Resources* (Spring 1981), 186–216.

Medoff, J.L., and Abraham, K.G. "Experience, Performance, and Earnings." *Quarterly Journal of Economics* (December 1980), 703–36.

Mincer, J. "Wage Differentials: Comment." In C.B. Lloyd, E.S. Andrews and C.L. Gilroy (eds.) *Women in the Labor Market*. New York: Columbia University Press, 1979, 278–285.

______. "Labor Force Participation of Married Women." In *NBER Aspects of Labor Economics*. Princeton: Princeton University Press, 1962, 63–97.

Mincer, J., and Ofek, H. "Interrupted Work Careers: Depreciation and Restoration of Human Capital." *Journal of Human Resources* (Winter 1982), 3–24.

Mincer, J., and Polachek, S. "An Exchange: Theory of Human Capital and the Earnings of Women: Women's Earnings Reexamined." *Journal of Human Resources* (Winter 1978), 118–134.

______. "Family Investments in Human Capital: Earnings of Women." *Journal of Political Economy* Part 2 (March/April 1974), S76–S108.

Newman, W., and Vonhof, J.M. "Separate But Equal — Job Segregation and Pay Equity in the Wake of Gunther." *University of Illinois Law Review* (1981), 269–331.

Oaxaca, R. "Male-Female Wage Differentials in Urban Labor Markets." *International Economics Review* (October 1973a), 693–709.

______. "The Persistence of Male-Female Earnings Differentials." In F.T. Juster (ed.) *The Distribution of Economic Well-Being*. (Cambridge, Mass.: Ballinger Publishing Co., 1977), 303–344.

______. "Sex Discrimination in Wages." In O. Ashenfelter, and A. Rees (eds.) *Discrimination in Labor Markets*. Princeton, New Jersey: Princeton University Press, 1973b, 124–151.

Osterman, P. "Affirmative Action and Opportunity: A Study of Female Quit Rates," *Review of Economics and Statistics* (November 1982), 604–12.

______. "Sex Discrimination in Professional Employment: A Case Study." *Industrial and Labor Relations Review* (July 1979), 451–64.

Phelps, E.S. "The Statistical Theory of Racism and Sexism." *American Economic Review* (September 1972), 659–661.

Piore, M.J. "The Dual Labor Market: Theory and Implications." In D.M. Gordon (ed.) *Problems in Political Economy: An Urban Perspective*. Lexington, Mass.: D.C. Heath and Co., 1971), 90–94.

Polachek, S.W. "Occupational Segregation Among Women: Theory, Evidence, and a Prognosis." In C.B. Lloyd, E.S. Andrews, and C.L. Gilroy (eds.) *Women in the Labor Market*. New York: Columbia University Press, 1979, 137–157.

______. "Occupational Segregation: An Alternative Hypothesis." *Journal of Contemporary Business* (Winter 1976), 1–12.

______. "Occupational Self-Selection: A Human Capital Approach to Sex Differences in Occupational Structure." *The Review of Economics and Statistics* (February 1981), 60–69.

______. "Potential Biases in Measuring Male-Female Discrimination." *Journal of Human Resources* (Spring 1975), 205–229.

Ragan, J.F., Jr., and Smith, S.P. "The Impact of Differences in Turnover Rates on Male/Female Pay Differentials." *Journal of Human Resources* (Summer 1981), 343–365.

Roberts, H.V. "Statistical Biases in the Measurement of Employment Discrimination." In E.R. Livernash (ed.) *Comparable Worth: Issues and Alternatives.* Washington, D.C.: Equal Employment Advisory Council, 1980, 173–196.

Robinson, J. *The Economics of Imperfect Competition.* London: MacMillan and Co., Ltd., 1933.

Roos, P.A. "Sexual Stratification in the Workplace: Male-Female Differences in Economic Returns to Occupation." *Social Science Research* (September 1981), 195–224.

Sanborn, H. "Pay Differences Between Men and Women." *Industrial and Labor Relations Review* (July 1964), 534–50.

Sandell, S.H., and Shapiro, D. "An Exchange: Theory of Human Capital and the Earnings of Women: A Reexamination of the Evidence." *Journal of Human Resources* (Winter 1978), 103–117.

______. "Work Expectations, Human Capital Accumulation, and the Wages of Young Women." *Journal of Human Resources* (Summer 1980), 335–353.

Sawhill, I.V. "The Economics of Discrimination Against Women: Some New Findings." *Journal of Human Resources* (Summer 1973), 383–96.

Smith, J.P. "The Improving Status of Black Americans." *American Economic Review* (May 1978, 171–78.

Spence, A.M. "Job Market Signaling." *Quarterly Journal of Economics* (August 1973), 355–74.

______. *Market Signaling.* Cambridge, Mass.: Harvard University Press, 1974.

Stevenson, M.H. "Relative Wages and Sex Segregation by Occupation." In C. Lloyd (ed.) *Sex, Discrimination, and the Division of Labor.* New York: Columbia University Press, 1975.

Strober, M.H. "Toward Dimorphics: A Summary Statement to the Conference on Occupational Segregation." *Signs* Part 2 (Spring 1976), 293–302.

Suter, L., and Miller, H. "Income Differences Between Men and Career Women." *American Journal of Sociology* (January 1973), 962–74.

Talbert, J., and Bose, C.E. "Wage Attainment Processes: The Retail Clerk Case." *American Journal of Sociology* (September 1977), 403–424.

Thurow, L.C. *Generating Inequality.* New York: Basic Books, Inc., 1975.

Treiman, D.J., and Hartmann, H.I. (eds.) *Women, Work, and Wages: Equal Pay for Jobs of Equal Value.* Washington, D.C.: National Academy Press, 1981.

U.S. Department of Commerce, Bureau of the Census. *A Statistical Portrait of Women in the United States: 1978.* Current Population Reports, Special Studies, Series P-23, No. 100 (February 1980).

U.S. Department of Labor, Bureau of Labor Statistics. "Educational Attainment of Workers, March 1977." *Special Labor Force Report No. 209,* (undated).

U.S. Department of Labor, Bureau of Labor Statistics. "Perspectives on Working Women." (June 1980).

Viscusi, W.K. "Sex Differences in Worker Quitting." *Review of Economics and Statistics* (August 1980), 388–398.

Wachter, M. "Primary and Secondary Labor Markets: A Critique of the Dual Approach." *Brookings Papers on Economic Activity,* No. 3. (1974), 637–694.

Waite, L.J., and Berryman, S.E. "Occupational Desegregation in CETA Programs: The Record for Female and Male Hispanic, White, and Black Participants." Paper presented at The Workshop on Job Segregation by Sex, National Research Council, Washington, D.C., May 1982.

Weiss, Y., and Gronau, R. "Expected Interruptions in Labour Force Participation and Sex-Related Differences in Earnings Growth." *Review of Economic Studies* (October 1981), 607–619.

Zellner, H. "The Determinants of Occupational Segregation." In C.B. Lloyd (ed.) *Sex, Discrimination and the Division of Labor.* New York: Columbia University Press, 1975, 125–145.

3 THEORETICAL EXPLANATIONS OF THE PERSISTENCE OF RACIAL UNEMPLOYMENT DIFFERENTIALS

Julianne Malveaux

Despite significant occupational advances among blacks between 1960 and 1980, the racial unemployment differential has not improved and, in some cases (especially for young blacks), has worsened over time. Table 3-1 shows the oscillation of male unemployment ratios to be around two prior to 1975, with a temporal worsening among most age groups after that. Except for women under 25, the female ratios oscillate around a point slightly below two. There is no clear indication of a change in unemployment ratios — instead, the relative differences between black and white female unemployment seem somewhat stable.

This chapter is concerned with the way that labor market theorists explain the peristence of racial unemployment differentials. Several approaches are reviewed, including human capital theory, job search/turnover theory explanations, institutional labor market theories, crowding hypotheses, dual labor market theories, theories of labor market stratification, discrimination theories, and cyclical and demographic explanations. This writer concludes that existing theories only partially explain the persistence of racial unemployment differentials and suggests other ways of viewing the labor market and racial differences in unemployment.

Table 3–1. Unemployment Rates and Ratios for Selected Years

	1960	*1965*	*1968*	*1970*	*1973*	*1975*	*1977*	*1979*	*1981*
Black Males									
16 and over	10.7	7.4	5.6	7.3	7.6	13.7	12.4	10.3	14.1
16–17	22.7	27.1	26.6	27.8	34.4	39.4	38.7	39.4	40.0
18–19	25.1	20.2	19.0	23.1	22.1	32.9	36.1	29.6	36.0
25–34	10.5	6.2	3.8	6.1	5.8	11.9	10.6	8.6	12.6
35–44	8.2	5.1	2.9	3.9	4.0	8.3	6.1	5.8	18.3
Black Females									
16 and over	9.4	9.2	8.3	9.3	10.5	14.0	14.0	12.3	14.3
16–17	25.7	37.8	33.7	36.9	36.5	38.9	44.7	39.4	41.4
18–19	24.5	27.8	26.2	32.9	33.3	38.3	37.4	33.4	36.5
25–34	9.1	8.4	8.4	7.9	9.7	12.9	12.9	11.0	13.9
35–44	8.6	7.6	5.0	4.8	5.3	8.6	8.5	7.0	18.9
White Males									
16 and over	4.8	3.6	2.6	4.0	3.7	7.2	5.5	4.4	6.5
16–17	14.6	14.7	12.3	15.7	15.1	19.7	17.6	16.1	19.9
18–19	13.5	11.4	8.2	12.0	10.0	17.2	12.0	12.3	16.4
25–34	4.1	2.6	1.7	3.1	3.0	6.3	5.0	3.6	6.1
35–44	3.3	2.3	1.4	2.3	1.8	4.5	3.1	2.5	4.0
White Females									
16 and over	5.3	5.0	4.3	4.5	5.3	8.6	7.3	5.9	6.9
16–17	14.5	15.0	13.9	15.3	15.7	19.2	18.2	15.9	18.4
18–19	11.5	13.4	11.0	11.9	10.9	16.1	14.2	12.5	15.3
25–34	5.7	4.8	3.9	5.3	5.1	8.5	6.7	5.6	6.6
35–44	4.2	4.1	3.1	4.3	3.7	6.6	5.3	4.2	4.0
Male Unemployment Ratios									
16 and over	2.2	2.0	2.1	1.8	2.0	1.9	2.2	2.3	2.2
16–17	1.5	1.8	2.2	1.8	2.3	2.0	2.2	2.1	2.0
18–19	1.8	1.8	2.3	1.9	2.2	1.9	2.8	2.4	2.2
25–34	2.6	2.4	2.2	2.0	1.9	1.8	2.1	2.4	2.1
35–44	2.5	2.2	2.1	1.7	2.2	1.8	2.0	2.3	4.6
Female Unemployment Ratios									
16 and over	1.8	1.8	1.9	1.7	2.0	1.6	1.9	2.1	2.1
16–17	1.8	2.5	2.6	2.4	2.3	2.0	2.5	2.5	2.3
18–19	2.1	2.1	2.4	2.8	3.0	2.4	2.6	2.7	2.4
25–34	1.6	1.8	2.1	1.5	1.9	1.5	1.9	2.0	2.1
35–44	2.0	1.8	1.6	1.1	1.4	1.3	1.6	1.7	3.7

Source: Employment and Earnings Report of the President, 1982

A Human Capital Theory of Racial Unemployment Differentials

The central purpose of human capital theory, as explained by Becker (1964) in his pioneering work, is to explain wage differentials between various segments of the labor force. Becker departed from the theory of a perfect labor market with a homogeneous labor force by developing a notion of heterogeneous labor, and focused on the heterogeneity in education and training as the explanation for different marginal products among workers.

The key explanatory factor for wage differentials, then, is captured by equation 3.1

$$E = E_0 + rs \tag{3.1}$$

where E = earnings,
r = rate of return, and
s = years of schooling/training.

Human capital theory distinguishes between general training, or education that is neither occupation- nor firm-specific and specific training, or training that can be used only in a certain job or with a certain firm. According to the theory, workers would pay for general training, since it would increase their marginal product regardless of the firm that they worked for; employers would pay for specific training, since it would increase productivity, and thus profits for the firm.

The notion of specific training bridges the gap between human capital theory as an explanation of wage differentials and human capital theory as an explanation of unemployment differentials. Since firms pay the cost of specific training, they have made an investment in the worker not unlike the capital investment they make on a piece of machinery. As Gilroy (1975) notes

> The firm which paid for the training of a worker who quit for another job has part of its capital expenditure wasted; a worker laid off after having paid for specific training would likewise suffer a capital loss . . . Turnover should be least, then for more specifically trained workers and greatest for those with little or general training.

This is consistent with Walter Oi's (1962) view of labor as a "quasi-fixed" factor of production. Where there are no specific skills that a worker possesses, this worker becomes a variable factor of production, hired and fired with few transaction costs. But when workers possess specific training, there are costs associated with turnover. These costs include items such as recruitment, screening and testing, and may be higher for more skilled employees. Further costs are accrued when the employer pays for specific training. Thus, skilled workers become a "quasi-fixed" factor of production since heavy transactions costs may be involved in hiring and retraining.

The layoff of an individual represents not only the loss of the investment embodied in his or her training but also the cost of hiring him or her. Thus, human capital theory suggests that when layoffs must take place, those workers with little or no training will be laid off before those workers with specific training who represent an investment for the employer. This is true even where less skilled workers earn lower wages, since transaction costs differ substantially across skill range.

In a job competition model of the labor force, Lester Thurow (1972) develops the concept of a job queue where skills are not important in the ordering of the queue (although education is). The notion that most skills are acquired on the job is supported by actual patterns, since sixty percent of all workers are trained through on-the-job training. This is as true, if not more so, for college graduates as it is for other workers. In such a job competition model, the cost-effective employer will hire individuals who can be trained at the lowest cost.

While general education may not be correlated with skill, it may be considered positively correlated with ability to perform. When education is used to determine the "trainability" of an individual, it serves as a screen. It will determine, when layoffs take place, the extent to which some workers will be unemployed and others will not. It should be noted that the connection between education and unemployment is not direct here. If an individual with less education than others is somehow chosen to undergo a training program (for example, because the market is tight and there is competition for qualified trainees), there is no indication that, after completing training, this person would be laid off sooner than any other trained worker. However, to the extent that education was used to screen individuals for training, there is an inverse connection between education and unemployment.

How do these aspects of human capital theory relate to high black unemployment rates? If education is used to screen individuals for training, the fact that blacks have less education than whites means that fewer blacks will be employed in jobs where employers consider their training as an investment and, therefore, are cautious about whom they lay off. Further, blacks may hold fewer jobs where on-the-job training was acquired because employers may screen workers not only by the ease with which they can be trained, but also by the probability that they will remain on the job. An employer who notes high black turnover rates may then screen out black applicants as less likely to complete training or to remain on the job long enough to recoup training costs. This phenomenon is called statistical discrimination.

If statistical facts or screens suggest that blacks are not easily trained, less likely to complete training, and likely to leave jobs more frequently, employers have the choice of either hiring blacks less frequently, placing them in lower-skilled jobs, or paying them less. Aggregate data suggest that a combination of the three occurs: less frequent hiring yields higher unemployment rates; less skilled hiring yields an occupational distribution where blacks are overrepresented in lower-skilled jobs; lower pay is implied in the black-white wage gap (although a discussion of wage rigidity late in this chapter explains that at the bottom of the wage hierarchy, minimum wage laws prevent lower payments in the legal labor market).

It is important to note that because of statistical discrimination as well as other factors, the training opportunity, not education, is the key to minimizing racial unemployment differentials. Even where blacks are highly educated, their unemployment rates are higher than those for whites with similar education profiles, even in the same occupation. Moreover, when educational differences are taken into account, the black unemployment rate dropped by less than 20 percent in 1975 (Malveaux, 1980), a much smaller drop than the 45 percent drop attributable to educational differences in 1960 (Gilroy, 1973).

Thus, human capital theory contributes to the notion that education and training are important in explaining the racial unemployment differential. The link between education and training is critical in such an approach. Consequently, observers have a tendency to wonder why blacks do not get more education. Further, a decade of public policy with respect to minorities was based firmly on the premise that increased educational opportunities would favorably impact economic outcomes for the disadvantaged.

However, an individual investment in education is based on the presumption of reasonable future returns. To the extent that some black workers expect, often realistically, that they will experience lower or minimal returns to education, they will be less likely than white workers to invest in it. Thus, where education is used merely as a screen, it may have no inherent value except to exclude some workers from consideration for jobs. On the other hand, since education is but one of several screening devices that firms utilize, the attainment of a certain level of education certainly does not guarantee a worker a job or even consideration. Thus, the decision of black workers to forego educational investment may be a function of stark realism and not misinformation.

In firms where there are only limited ports of entry to a training hierarchy, the term "internal labor market" describes the situation well. While theories of wages and employment are related to both a human capital theory and a theory of dual labor markets, this writer mentions the concept at this point since specific training (though perhaps as nebulous as "knowledge of the firm") is important in explaining longevity in these firms.

Most entry into internal markets takes place at an initial hiring point. Performance at this entry port is part of the screening that takes place when a decision is made about an individual's training prospects and eventual upward mobility in an internal market. An internal labor market may be somewhat more rigid than other markets described in human capital theory since individuals may have other opportunities to demonstrate their trainability in human capital markets, such as in jobs lateral to training jobs. On the other hand, they may have fewer opportunities to do so in an internal market where only one entry port exists.

A view of internal labor markets is important in understanding unemployment differentials because the presence of either pro forma or statistical discrimination during any hiring period would limit the chance of black workers to hold entry level jobs, as would differential rates of educational attainment if education were used as a screen. Over time, black workers would have fewer opportunities in fairly protected jobs where turnover is low, but would instead find work in jobs with higher turnover and unemployment rates. Even in the absence of current discriminatory practices, an internal labor market theory would suggest that unemployment rates would be higher for blacks than for whites, especially for older blacks who did not compete successfully for entry-level jobs.

Job Search/Turnover Theories and Unemployment Differentials

Job search/turnover theories of the labor market can be seen as related to human capital theories in that both theories focus on heterogeneity of individuals in labor markets. In a job search/turnover world, differences are not necessarily in the investment in education, but in investment in search time for finding employment. This is especially important from a wage perspective when longer search may result in a broader spectrum of wage offers for a worker to choose from.

A good way to start a discussion of job search/turnover theories of the labor market is by noting that the unemployment rate here is viewed as the product of average duration and turnover. Equation 3.2 shows such a relationship as formulated by Barret and Morgenstern (1974) where N is the number of individuals experiencing unemployment, S is the number of weekly spells of unemployment, DUR is the duration in weeks of unemployment per spell, and L is the size of the labor force.

$$\frac{U}{L} = \frac{N \times S \times DUR}{52L} \tag{3.2}$$

Dividing the unemployment rate into components enables us to focus on the different explanations of each part of the rate. It is also conceivable that the size of the components will vary by demographic group.

The duration of unemployment will be related to (1) the availability of job vacancies, (2) the cost of search, and (3) the individual's reservation wage. In terms of job vacancies, it is clear that in tight job markets there will be relatively more vacancies and search will be much easier than it might be in a slack market. Search costs include such things as foregone wages, as well as the costs of physical search (such as travel interviews). However, search costs are often partially or fully subsidized if an individual collects unemployment insurance, and the presence of financial resources may also enable some individuals to search longer than they would have had these resources not been available. The individual's reservation wage and its relationship to the actual range of wage offers a person will receive is a factor in determining the duration of unemployment. If market knowledge is imperfect and reservation wages are unrealistic, it may take some time for expectations to converge with the actual wage distribution. Therefore, the duration of unemployment will lengthen.

When viewing unemployment rates by race, we must wonder if the entire range of job vacancies is available to the entire labor force. If there are occupational barriers to entry in some cases, then the set of vacancies available to black workers is relatively smaller than the set of vacancies available to white workers. One would expect a higher duration of unemployment. Flanagan (1976) notes that unemployment differentials would arise if blacks expect the same offers from the same wage distribution as whites but, in fact, face a lower distribution of wage offers.

Empirically, Barret, Gerardi, and Morgenstern (1975) found that the average duration of unemployment was not substantially different by race. Duration of unemployment in 1969 was about 20 percent higher for black males than for white males and 15 percent higher for black females than white females. However, those things that statistically explained duration differed somewhat by race. Age was most important in explaining duration for whites, while education was most important for blacks. Also, occupation and industry factors were not at all significant for blacks, although there were some effects for whites, which means that while whites improved their employment experience when occupation or industry improved, this was less likely to occur for blacks.

Osterman (1978), in viewing unemployment differences among youth by race, noted that gaps in the duration of unemployment were likely if black youth had reservation wages that either were too high or did not converge to the actual wage distribution as rapidly as did the reservation wages of white youth.

While the differences in the duration of unemployment reported by Barret et al. (1975) may not be applicable in a slack labor market, data developed by Marston (1976) from monthly averages from 1967–73, a period which included diverse market conditions, shows that racial differences in the duration of unemployment are minimal for workers over 25 (see table 3–2). Since differences in racial unemployment differentials cannot be fully attributed to differences in the duration of unemployment, a discussion of the determinants of turnover is in order here.

Turnover in the labor market can take place either because workers quit or because they are laid off. Clearly, the factors that determine quits and those that determine layoffs may differ significantly. Also, while turnover is a component in an unemployed equation, not all quits and layoffs result in unemployment. Especially with quits, although possibly also with layoffs, job-leaving can be immediately followed by the acquisition of another job.

Quitting, or voluntary turnover, can be considered a form of job search. Burdett (1978) differentiates dynamic quits, which result from changes in the wage distribution, from equilibrium quits, which are part of an individual's overall job search strategy, where the wage distribution is constant. Quitting will depend on the individual's wage in relation to his or her perception of the wage distribution, search costs, and the attractiveness of the individual's present job. Unless an individual miscalculates the variables that determine his or her decision to quit, the returns to quitting should be positive (Rosen, 1972).

What does a theory of voluntary job-leaving have to say about high black unemployment rates? Flanagan (1978) notes that when an individual's wage is

Table 3–2. Average Duration of Unemployment (in weeks) 1967–1973

	16–19	*20–24*	*25–59*
Black Females	8.14	9.59	7.63
White Females	6.68	7.65	7.58
B/W	1.22	1.25	1.01
Black Males	7.82	12.04	9.73
White Males	6.81	7.94	9.41
B/W	1.15	1.51	1.03

Source: Marston (1976)

low in relation to the wage distribution, she or he will be likely to quit. To the extent that the individual has misjudged the size of the range of the wage distribution, quitting may not lead to a higher wage. In particular, when black workers do not distinguish between the set of wage offers made to blacks and those made to whites, their quitting is often the result of the expectation of a wage offer in the white wage distribution. In relation to this behavior, however, Flanagan (1976) suggests that as blacks learn through search that the distribution of their wage offers differs by race, their wage expectations will adjust and quitting based on misperception will fall. Thus, it is expected that younger blacks will have higher quit rates than older blacks, and thus higher unemployment rates.

A key aspect of Flanagan's discussion of unemployment differentials deals with the assumption that blacks may face a different wage distribution than whites. It is important to note that this assumption assumes an aspect of discrimination that the model goes on to explain. It assumes that while whites face the entire wage distribution, blacks face a smaller distribution with a lower average wage. Flanagan's model further assumes that blacks are naive about their wage prospects being different from those of whites.

Considering search costs as part of the decision to quit also favors a higher quit rate for black than white. Phelps (1970) noted that where black wages are lower than white wages, the cost of search is lower for blacks than it is for whites. This should be balanced, though, with some notion of financial ability to engage in search. Despite lower wages, if blacks have fewer nonearnings income options than do whites, they may be reluctant to quit. However, Piore (1975) suggests that the availability of nonmarket income-generating options may positively influence the quit rate, especially for young blacks.

One aspect of explaining higher black quit rates and higher rates of black unemployment is the notion that blacks may have false expectations about the labor market. For example, if they believe they will be treated identically with whites, and thus follow an indentical path of human capital acquisition, search behavior, and occupational choice, then the existence of discrimination will force a different outcome between black and white labor market experience, especially in terms of level of employment. On the other hand, if blacks believe they will be treated differently than whites in the labor market, then it is rational that their behavior will differ substantially from that of whites. Then, for example, blacks will have different patterns of human capital acquisition, search behavior, and occupational choice. These differences will lead to differences in employment experience.

Whether blacks have accurate or inaccurate perceptions of the labor market, the existence of discrimination suggests that blacks will have higher unemployment rates, regardless of expectation. Either they will adjust behavior (and risk higher unemployment) based on the accurate perception that discrimination will prevent equal job attainment; or, as Flanagan suggests, the inaccurate expectation of equal labor market experience will cause blacks to search furtively for an identical wage and occupational distribution. Lengthy search will cause higher black unemployment rates. Thus, regardless of expectation, the outcome for black workers is similar. This suggests that a key way to close the gap between black and white unemployment rates is to minimize the discrimination that blacks experience in the labor market. Alternatively, the gap might close if black expectations more accurately reflect their labor market options.

Table 3–3 shows the frequency of turnover as calculated by Marston (1976) from monthly data from 1967–73. It is clear that black turnover rates are higher than those of whites. Unlike the duration of unemployment, racial differences in these rates are substantial.

In an empirical effort to analyze turnover, Barret et al. (1975) find that the occupational composition of the labor force is important in explaining high black turnover rates. Turnover declined with age and education, which is important since there are proportionately more black than white youth, and since the educational profile of the black population displays somewhat less education than the white population. Barret et al. (1975) also found that married persons with spouses present had lower turnover rates for both races. The presence of children was associated with low turnover for whites but not for blacks. Finally, the theoretical assertion that low-paying, low-status jobs have higher turnover was confirmed in this research since the relationship between turnover and income was negative.

Some of the Barret et al. findings are corroborated in recent research by Blau and Kahn (1978). They found that racial differences in occupations

Table 3–3. Frequency of Unemployment (Percent of the Labor Force per Month) 1967–1973

	16–19	*20–24*	*25–34*
Black Females	16.75	6.37	3.38
White Females	8.31	3.82	2.10
B/W	2.02	1.67	1.61
Black Males	13.58	4.14	1.77
White Males	7.51	3.41	1.05
B/W	1.81	1.21	1.69

Source: Marston (1976)

held raise the quit rates of blacks relative to those of whites. However, Blau and Kahn also noted that if blacks were given jobs comparable to those of whites their quit rates would be lower than white quit rates.

Flanagan (1978) found in his estimates of turnover that for older (45–59) black males, the probability of quitting is positively related to previous employment instability. Given a certain number of job changes, the probability of a quit is three times as high for blacks as it is for whites. On the other hand, job changing was more profitable, in terms of wage-rate increases, for older blacks than for older whites. Among the young males (14–24) that Flanagan studied, job instability was a reliable predictor of quitting only for whites. Further, job instability was not associated with wage advances for either blacks or whites.

Another aspect of the turnover process is layoffs which are involuntary. There is no search theory explanation for racial differences in layoffs because search theories focus on the voluntary aspects of turnover. Still, a queue theory would suggest that those workers with the lowest marginal products would be the first to be laid off. This is consistent with the human capital notion (Oi, 1962) of labor as a "quasi-fixed" factor of production. In some cases, however, despite investment in a training program, the layoff determinants may be institutional. For example, seniority usually determines the order of layoffs in firms that have collective bargaining agreements. Thus, Osterman's (1978) finding that the length of employment is negatively associated with layoffs for both blacks and whites — although the coefficient of the tenure variable is twice as large for whites as for blacks — is consistent with expectations about the dynamics of employer layoff decisions.

Search theory highlights important differences in the behavior of black workers, especially with respect to voluntary turnover. Since our interest here is in intraoccupational variations, we speculate that differential black quit behavior within occupations may be related to variations in institutional arrangements for an occupation across industries. As in Flanagan's (1978) hypothesis about misperceptions in the shape of the wage offer distribution, blacks may be frustrated in their attempt to obtain jobs in highly sheltered industries that provide higher wages and better benefits than do jobs in more competitive industries. To the extent that they quit to search for such jobs, their unemployment rates will be higher than those of whites.

Institutional Explanations of Unemployment Differentials

The development of the theory that wages are equal to marginal product embodies the assumptions that markets are perfect and labor homogenous. Human capital theory maintains the assumption of perfect markets while focusing on the heterogeneity of the labor force in explaining wage and employment differentials. Institutional theory, on the other hand, rejects the assumption of perfect labor markets.

Institutional theories of the labor market are concerned primarily with the relative wages of groups over time. These theories study and explain the impact of institutional factors on wages and employment, institutional factors including unionization, political power, ability of firms to pay wages, barriers to geographic mobility, legislative constraints to free markets (such as minimum wage), and other factors that make markets imperfect. Clark Kerr's (1954) theory of balkanization in labor markets is considered an early example of institutionalist labor market theory. He postulated that organization was evolving from an unstructured competitive market system to a more structured, highly organized noncompetitive system. In structured markets, a system of the market determination is less operative than are sets of complex rules, such as government regulations and collective bargaining agreements. Kerr's theory also noted the distinction between the union role in raising wages by restricting the supply of workers.

Institutional theories describe the benefits of unionization, the process of union ownership of a communal resource (labor), and the ownership benefits that accrue to some because of exclusionary practices. It is useful to view explanations for the historical exclusion of blacks from highly sheltered, highly paid work, since such exclusion is clearly a factor in the existence of high black unemployment rates.

Marxian theories of the labor market are similar in approach to institutional theories in that they focus on those institutions that define a capitalist system of production and class relations in such productive systems. Marxian theories explain the dominance of capital and are useful in explaining the exclusion of blacks in unions over time. The presence of blacks in the labor market, according to Marxists, is a cyclical buffer for the labor needs of capitalists. By encouraging black migration to the north, manufacturers developed a reserve army of the unemployed and a large, readily available labor pool which became a visible threat to the organizing efforts of white workers.

The secondary status of blacks both enhanced the status of working whites and generated white resentment and race hatred of blacks. The role of blacks as a reserve army forced white workers to be moderate in wage demands, thus linking capitalist gains to the promotion of racism. Cox (1948) comments lucidly on this linkage

> Race prejudice . . . developed gradually in Western society as capitalism and nationalism developed. It is a divisive attitude seeking to alienate dominant group sympathy from an "inferior" race, a whole people, for the purpose of facilitating its exploitation.

The exploitation of black labor was rooted in development of its role as reserve army. Labor history is rich with examples of this role. Weaver (1946), for example, notes the role blacks played as strikebreakers in the iron, steel, and meat-packing industries. This role limited gains that labor was able to make, except in the case of the United Mineworkers, who often organized strikebreaking blacks in their units (Green, 1978). The nature of mine work may have played a role in the organizational effort of the UMW.

Clearly, an organized labor force poses a threat to employers. Thus, when racism can be used as a wedge to separate black and white workers, it is clearly advantageous to employers. While the polarity that a strikebreaking role generated between blacks and whites may no longer exist, the reality of high black unemployment rates makes the concept of a reserve army a compelling explanation for them, at least historically.

On the other hand, the maintenance of a reserve army may be technologically unncessary as labor force needs change. Wilhelm (1974) suggests that a reserve army was only necessary for menial and unskilled work — jobs for which there is currently a declining market. The structural mismatch between the skills of black workers and the needs of employers is evidenced both by high unemployment rates and by falling rates of black labor force participation.

Still, the tension and conflict caused by the maintenance of a reserve army remains between black and white workers. The backlash from affirmative action policies represents one example of white resistance to black labor market gains. The backlash from costs accrued by maintaining a reserve army is another. As the income maintenance programs that allow the reserve army to subsist become subject to political whim, it is clear that concern about preserving work incentives is used as a wedge between black and white workers in the same way that strikebreakers were used in the past. As Piven and Cloward (1982) point out, though, questions about work incentives raise further issues about the sufficiency of work rewards. If the choice between subsistence and working is a close one, there are some intuitive conclusions to be drawn about the adequacy of wage levels. In an alarming historical parallel, worker solidarity is undermined as the racist wedge separates blacks and whites with identical between-worker concerns.

Unemployment Differentials and the "Crowding Hypothesis"

The "crowding hypothesis" of labor markets is one of the developments in labor market theory that seems quite harmonious with institutional notions of labor markets. In its most simple form, this hypothesis assumes that there are two labor markets with entry restricted in one case but not in the other case. If we assume (fig. 3-1) that market A is restricted to include only E_a persons, then the remaining E_b persons in the labor force will be crowded into labor market B where wages will be lower. Further, if minimum wage laws limit the paying of certain wages, unemployment will be high in labor market B. In any case, workers in labor market A will not be threatened by the lower wages in the other sectors, as they would in a competitive market, because there are barriers to entry. Further, the entry of new workers in the labor market will cause, almost exclusively, downward pressure in labor market B.

The scenario described here is called "simple" crowding. More involved types of crowding can be developed where there are differences in the characteristics of the two markets causing the slopes of the marginal revenue product line to be different. These variations on a "simple" crowding model are called "complex crowding" (Bluestone, 1974). Bergmann (1974) developed much of the crowding hypothesis to illustrate the ways the interests of the "in" group of protected workers are maintained when others are excluded from markets.

The crowding hypothesis is clearly relevant in explaining the extent of occupational segregation in the labor market. The practice of having male and female titles for similar work jobs is an example of this. In a discussion of sexism in the publishing industry, for example, a writer notes that entry jobs for women were researcher jobs, while male entry jobs were for

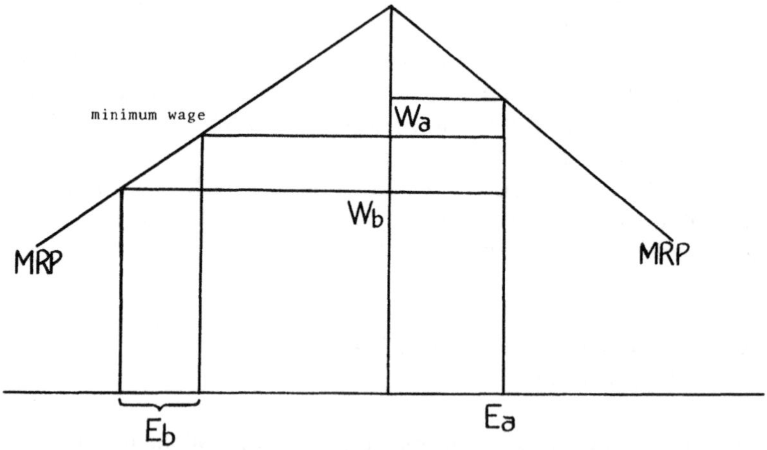

Figure 3-1. Labor Market Crowding

writers. Although educational qualifications were the same, the writer jobs were higher paying than the researcher jobs (Korda, 1973). Similar separate hiring tracks existed in plants between blacks and whites, and occupational segregation prior to the Civil Rights Act was so pronounced that there were separate racial units and seniority lists for blacks and whites. As blacks attempted to move from their traditional production units to those that required more skill after the Civil Rights Act was passed, the determination of their seniority rights became a major judicial issue (Wallace, 1976).

Racial unemployment differentials are consistent with a crowding hypothesis of the labor market. If the restricted labor market uses race as a barrier, and unlimited job opportunities do not exist in the unrestricted labor market, then blacks will have a higher probability of unemployment than whites. This is especially true where institutional constraints, such as the minimum wage, prevent the indefinite expansion of the unrestricted sector of the labor market.

Occupational segregation is not as pronounced as it has been in the past; thus, previously established crowding patterns may be determinants in the occupational choice of new labor market entrants. While the black occupational distribution has a broader range than it did in 1960, there is still disproportionate representation in some menial jobs. Even intraoccupationally, there may be crowding effects, although these are less pronounced than effects across the entire occupational spectrum.

Among operatives, for example, one observes a high concentration of blacks and women in nondurable goods industries but a significantly lower concentration in the more sheltered (because of higher concentration ratios among firms) durable goods industries. Similarly, one observes while the representation of black women in the clerical occupations has increased, their presence in the most skilled of secretarial jobs, legal and medical secretaries, is far below their proportion of secretaries as a whole.

The crowding hypothesis describes an "in" group sheltering the most preferred job opportunities and passing the remaining opportunities to others. High unemployment occurs because the number of jobs in noncrowded sectors may be lower than the number of workers competing for those jobs. One of the gaps in this theory, however, is a notion of how the "in" group gained its position and how it is sustained over time, even as new occupations and industries are created.

Myra Strober (1982) has been developing a theory of how occupational segregation is sustained. While her theory applies most directly to women, she mentions "constraints laid down by race and sex" in her discussion. Strober suggests that

> the decision concerning the gender assignment of jobs is made by men. . . . Male workers decide which occupations they will inhabit; . . . Remaining jobs are offered to women . . .; if sufficient numbers of women don't wish to work in the job, then the employer recruits workers from abroad, i.e., immigrants.

Strober further suggests that, as new jobs develop, men maximize their economic gains by deciding whether the new job should be claimed by them, perhaps by vacating a currently held job to be opened up for women, or whether it should become "women's work".

It requires no major alteration of Strober's concept to suggest that the decision makers do not include black males, but only white males. Other workers, including black and white women and black men, are given first choice on jobs that white men want less. Strober describes a tension between the male pursuit of profit and maintenance of male privilege.

Again, extending her theory, the tension is between the white male pursuit of profit and maintenance of privilege. In fact, adding the racial dimension to Strober's concept explains the clear tension between maintenance of privilege (thus advancing other, albeit black, males) and of maximizing profits (thus advancing white women) which may be viewed in the context of comparing populations in jobs that are predominantly white male. Ninety percent of all engineers were white men, five and a half percent were black men, about four percent were white women, and fewer than a scant half percent were black women. If we apply Strober's theory here, the maintenance of male privilege is less important than the maintenance of power and profit among whites.

Strober's analysis of occupational segregation and her historical analysis of how elementary and secondary school teaching jobs became predominantly female adds a dimension to our discussion of crowding. For as the educational profiles of blacks have changed, new occupational ghettoes have been created. Or, as Strober suggests, new jobs are being developed that white males do not want to hold. Consider, for example, the company "urban affairs specialist," the "affirmative action specialist," or the "minority recruiter." Although classified as management-level jobs, these newly created positions are generally held by blacks and tend to be only loosely connected to a corporate hierarchy, with few chances of upward mobility. Samuel Yette (1971) suggests this is a consequence of white male design instead of white male choice in the labor market when he mentions the creation of poverty program jobs coincident with the increased entry of black college graduates into the labor market.

How do white males maintain their monopoly position in the process of job allocation? Strober's historical argument suggests that the cumulative power of the white male paternalist position is a factor in current occupational segregation and job allocation.

As antidiscrimination laws prevent the rigid occupational segregation that took place in the past, the effects of the crowding hypothesis on new labor market entrants may be lessened somewhat. According to the discussion above, the conditions of the trade-off between profit and privilege change when new legal conditions are added. But if the effects of occupational segregation have lessened, if only slightly, for younger cohorts, its impact on older cohorts may have produced lock-in effects that continue to have an impact on racial unemployment differentials. Furthermore, while rigid crowding may not exist, the perception of male, female, black, or white jobs may shape both the occupational preference of employees and the hiring preferences of employers. To that extent, the crowding hypothesis will remain important in explaining racial differences in unemployment.

Theories of Dual Labor Markets and Labor Market Stratification

Like institutional market theory, dual labor market theory deals with critical imperfections in the labor market. However, while institutional theory is concerned with a wide range of market imperfections, dual labor market theory develops the notion of one key barrier: a lack of mobility between two separate labor markets termed primary and secondary. The two labor markets have different types of jobs and require different types of market behavior. Dual labor market theories bear some resemblance to the crowding hypothesis. The difference lies in the characteristics of the markets and the people who work in them.

Secondary labor markets are characterized by low pay, poor working conditions, low status, instability, little chance of advancement, the need for little or no education, little training or skill investment, lack of formalized grievance procedures or any other formal structures, and the personalized relationship between the employee and the employer (Gordon, 1973). Primary jobs, on the other hand, feature better pay and working conditions, a system of upward mobility, the possibility of training embodied into the job situation, formalized grievance procedures, formal procedures for hiring and advancement, and other clearly defined work rules.

Because there is so little skill required in secondary jobs, employers are indifferent about who performs the work tasks. Thus, jobs are almost casual, and workers may or may not show up for work on a given day. When there are shortages of labor, employers recruit through an informal system of word-of-mouth. In a study of low-wage industries in Boston, for example, Piore (1973) noted a recruitment system of sending a worker to Puerto Rico to get others who would work at low-paying jobs. This is important for many reasons: workers willing to work for low wages may see the job as temporary, planning a return to Puerto Rico. Thus the structure of a primary labor market may not be necessary in this case. The secondary market usually is located in industries where there is a low concentration ratio, a high amount of price competition, and a labor-intensive production technique. The sector is dominated by blacks, Hispanics, women, and youth.

For some workers, there is no mobility between the primary and secondary labor market. Furthermore, since there are loosely structured work rules in the secondary labor market, participants in that market tend to develop a set of work habits that are unacceptable in primary labor markets, even if they could gain access there. These habits include lateness and absenteeism that are not penalized in the secondary labor market. However, the delineation of the direction of causality in the development of work habits is often unclear, and researchers who describe the secondary labor market often view job characteristics and individual characteristics interchangeably.

For workers in the secondary labor market, there seems to be little payoff to acquiring training or skill. First of all, their probability of finding a job where they could use this skill is low. Second, there is little return to additional education in the secondary labor market.

Dual labor market theory was developed to explain the high black unemployment rates that existed in the 1960s, especially in the face of very tight labor markets. Clearly, if blacks are disproportionately represented in the secondary sector, then their turnover will be higher as they move from job to job, since neither skill nor longevity has any payoff. However, in order for dual labor market theory to explain why white youths can leave secondary labor markets with relative ease compared with black youths requires the notion of a lock-in effect that differs by social strata.

To this end, it seems that theories of labor market stratification are useful in explaining high black unemployment rates (Piore, 1975). However, discussion of such theories quickly moves one out of the realm of considering only jobs and into the realm of discussing individuals as well. It is interesting to note, however, that notions of labor market stratification have a strong parallel to John Stuart Mill's concept of noncompeting groups. In a different era, Mill noted the balkanization of labor markets even within family units, where the roles for sons, depending on order of birth, were clearly delineated.

In a theory of stratification in the labor market, it is argued that market stratification merely mirrors societal stratification. Linkages are made between classes, types of school attended, and type of family structure. Bowles (1971, 1972) for example, discussed the role that the educational system plays in socializing the population for their role in the labor market. Factors such as whether or not a family migrated also are considered in terms of the employment outcome for individuals, where migration is seen as an indicator of family instability.

While the basic structure of the dual labor market (with primary and secondary sectors) is maintained, the primary sector is divided into "self-directed" and "subordinate" sectors. The path, then, from a lower class background through possible migration and certainly poor schooling, leads to a secondary labor market job. For the working-class person, the path leads to a subordinate primary job. These jobs include employment in internal labor markets where hierarchies are clearly defined and work rules are clearly structured. Finally, middle-class identity leads to an "innovative" education and to a job in the self-directed section of the primary labor market. These jobs are primarily professional and managerial.

In this characterization of the labor market there seems to be little interaction between the supply and demand for labor. Instead, supply for labor is rooted in the dynamics of the class subcultures while demand is a function of technology. The role that migration, both from the rural South and Puerto Rico, and illegally, from Mexico, plays in replenishing the secondary labor market should be noted also.

Again, theories of labor market stratification are consistent with high black unemployment rates. To the extent that historical discrimination has disproportionately placed blacks in the lower tier of the class distribution and adversely affected influencing factors such as family stability, blacks are tracked to secondary labor market jobs which have high turnover, lower chances for advancement, and so on. The lock-in effects discussed in a secondary labor market theory also indicate that the implications of a head of household holding a secondary market job are multi-generational.

Empirically, the rigidity implied in stratification theories is not as absolute as theory would suggest. Blau and Duncan (1966), in viewing the 1950s and 1960s, noted that while most intergenerational occupational mobility is small, this small mobility exhibits a clear upward trend. Furthermore, given the magnitude of societal changes, the meaning of some of the parameters in a stratification model are unclear. For example, family stability has seemed an interesting variable to include as an index of labor market stability. But as the incidence of white separation, divorce, and female headship increase, poor proxies such as these for racial differences may need to be revised to reflect reality. It will be interesting, in a decade or so, to consider the impact that these trends will have on theories of stratification.

Discrimination Theories and Unemployment Differentials

The existence of discrimination has been implicit in the discussion of all of the labor market theories above. While various unemployment theories make the link between low-paying jobs and high unemployment clear, discussion of the historical impact of discrimination clarifies the disproportionate representation of blacks in these low-paying jobs. We will discuss two views of the impact of present discrimination on racial differentials.

These arguments indicate that racial wage differentials that are attributable to discrimination have a positive impact on racial unemployment differentials both through the demand-side actions of employers and supply-side reactions of employees.

Gilman (1965) discusses present discrimination and unemployment rates in terms of what he calls a "differential wage rigidity" hypothesis. In the absence of discrimination, employers will hire blacks and whites until the traditional equilibrium condition is attained, and relative wages are equal to relative marginal products.

$$\frac{W_w}{W_b} = \frac{MRP_w}{MRP_b} \tag{3.3}$$

However, when there is discrimination, the equilibrium condition is altered to account for the presence of a discrimination coefficient (Becker, 1957). The new equilibrium condition is shown in equation (4).

$$\frac{W_w}{W_b} = \frac{MRP_w(Hd)}{MRP_b} \tag{3.4}$$

The effect of the presence of discrimination will be to decrease black wages relative to white wages or to decrease black employment relative to white employment, or some combination of the two. Gilman's wage rigidity hypothesis indicates that since there are legislative barriers to flexible wages, such as minimum wage laws and union regulations, adjustment will take place as black employment is reduced relative to white employment. This will increase black unemployment rates. Gilroy (1975) further suggests that differential wage rigidity pushes black workers into nonunionized, low-paying occupations and sectors.

Recent discussions of soaring black youth unemployment rates apply the concept of differential wage rigidity to suggest that black youth are not worth the minimum wage to employers. Those who suggest that minimum wage laws be relaxed to provide more employment opportunities for youth argue that the marginal product of black youth is lower than that of white youth because young blacks have received a lower quality educational experience than young whites of the same age. Is there any evidence for this assertion? When white youth who live in inner cities (and thus have the same poor educational experience as do young blacks) experience half the unemployment that blacks in those same areas do, it is clear that the quality of education does not pose barriers for white youth employment (Malveaux, 1981). Thus, the relevant issue in exploited racial unemployment differentials among youth may be the size of the discrimination coefficient instead of the differences in marginal product.

The Gilman/Gilroy point of view looks at the demand side of the labor equation exclusively. Flanagan (1978) views supply-side effects of wage discrimination among blacks by analyzing the quit behavior of blacks. His findings indicate (1) that racial wage discrimination raises the black quit rate, especially among youth, and (2) that racial wage differentials probably increase the duration of unemployment for blacks by providing an incentive for search activity.

Cyclical and Demographic Explanations of Racial Unemployment Differentials

A discussion of discrimination and unemployment differentials should note the effect of discrimination on the placement of blacks in a queue of workers to be hired. Thus the "last hired, first fired" hypothesis explains the greatest market vulnerability of blacks as a function of their low position on the queue. The "last hired, first fired" phenomenon is not always the result of present discrimination. In occupations that were traditionally closed to blacks, their recent entry has placed them, by virtue of seniority, at the bottom of an employment queue. With less seniority, these blacks are most susceptible to layoffs.

Harry Gilman (1965) did not agree that the "last hired, first fired" phenomenon was operable. He felt that racial unemployment differentials are independent of the position of the business cycle and that, instead, the disproportionate increase in black unemployment rates during the trough of the business cycle is due to the unfavorable occupational distribution of blacks. However, whatever the reason, it is clear that blacks fare worse than whites in recessionary periods. The incremental ratio shown in table 3-4 tracks the cyclical changes in the unemployment rate over time. An incremental ratio of 1.0 suggests that the same proportion of blacks as whites either enter unemployment in recession or leave unemployment in recovery.

There has been some improvement in the historically adverse affect that recessions have had on black workers. In the 1958–59 downturn, twice the proportion of black workers were added to unemployment than were whites. This incremental ratio dropped to 1.44 in the 1973–75 recession, but has risen somewhat in the two most recent recession periods. Of course, the measurement of unemployment may mask the decline in black male labor

Table 3-4. The Incremental Ratio of Black-White Unemployment Based on Changes in Jobless Rates During Recession and Recovery Periods (Quarterly Averages, 1957-1982, seasonally adjusted)

Recession and Recovery Periods	*Beginning Unemployment Rates*		*Ending Unemployment Rates*		*Absolute Percentage Point Change*		*Incremental Ratio*
	Black and Other	*White*	*Black and Other*	*White*	*Black and Other*	*White*	
Recession periods							
1957 I-1958 II	7.4	3.6	13.4	6.6	6.0	3.0	2.00
1960 II-1961 II	9.9	4.7	12.9	6.3	3.0	1.6	1.88
1969 IV-1971 IV	6.2	3.3	10.1	5.5	3.9	2.2	1.77
1973 IV-1975 II	8.6	4.3	14.2	8.2	5.6	3.9	1.44
1980 I-1980 IV	11.8	5.5	13.9	6.7	2.1	1.2	1.75
1981 II-1982 II*	14.6	6.2	18.5	8.4	3.9	2.2	1.77
Recovery periods							
1958 II-1960 II	13.4	6.6	9.9	4.7	3.5	1.9	1.84
1961 II-1969 IV	12.9	6.3	6.2	3.3	6.7	3.0	2.23
1971 IV-1973 IV	10.1	5.5	8.6	4.3	1.5	1.2	1.25
1975 II-1980 I	14.2	8.2	11.8	5.5	2.4	2.7	.89
1980 III-1981 II	13.9	6.7	14.6	6.2	-0.7	0.5	-1.40**

Source: Job (1978)

Note: This table updates work done by Job (1978) on the 1957-78 period.

*The second quarter of 1982 is not a turning point in either black or white unemployment rates but represents the latest available data to mark the 1981-82 recession.

**Since unemployment rates of the races moved in opposite directions here, the incremental ratio means that blacks entered unemployment at 1.4 times the rate whites left unemployment.

force participation. The fact that black men have experienced less unemployment over time does not speak to their increased representation among discouraged workers and also outside of the labor force.

Gilroy noted that the disproportionate employment burden that blacks bear in recession was balanced by proportionately greater employment experienced in recovery periods (1974). Table 3–4 shows the proportion of blacks leaving unemployment exceeded that of whites during the last three recovery periods. Further, the impact of recovery was greatest in the 1961–69 period when the proportion of blacks leaving unemployment was twice that of whites. However, recovery periods have not had so favorable an effect recently on blacks. In the 1971–73 recovery period, blacks were employed at only 1.25 the rate of whites. Between 1975 and 1978, proportionately fewer blacks left unemployment than did whites. Finally, in the most recent recovery, blacks experienced more unemployment, while whites slowly left unemployed status.

Job (1978) suggests part of the reason for the lower strength of recovery for blacks is the increase in black labor force participation rates that took place between 1975 and 1978. But labor force participation of blacks, especially black males, recently has declined somewhat. While the black female labor force participation rate remained constant at 59.8 percent between 1980 and 1981, black male labor force participation declined slightly from 74 percent to 73.2 percent.

Thus, recent cyclical trends show that, while recessions produce relatively more black unemployment, recoveries have been relatively beneficial to blacks. This may lend credence to a "last hired, first fired" hypothesis, especially if recent recoveries have been too short to be of benefit to "last hired" blacks. It also is interesting to note that the improvement in black occupational status has been accompanied by a more adverse impact from recession and a weaker effect from recovery. This contradicts Gilman's argument that cyclical effects on unemployment must be considered in light of the occupational distribution.

Again, theories of stratification are consistent with high black unemployment rates. To the extent that a history of discrimination has placed blacks disproportionately in the lower tier of the class distribution, there is a tracking to secondary jobs which have higher turnover, lower chances for advancement, etc.

Further recent trends, albeit in the face of alleged black progress, confirm the existence of a Marxian "reserve army" of the unemployed, where black unemployment grows, even in a recovery, as long as white employment needs are unmet.

Changes in the demographic composition of the labor force also are often considered a factor in explaining both races' unemployment rates that were observed in the 1970s. The 1978 *Economic Report of the President* weighed the composition of the labor force by age and sex and reported that the 4.9 percent benchmark unemployment rate would have been 4.0 percent if the labor force looked like it did in 1955. Cain (1979) shows, however, that changes in demographic composition have not contributed significantly to increases in the rate of unemployment.

Similarly, one might look at the differential distribution of labor force advances in the black community to suggest that a black "underclass," like the one described by Wilson (1978) experiences most of the black unemployment. If this is true, it suggests that persistent racial unemployment differentials mask what progress has been made. The discussion of an underclass often further suggests that black unemployment rates may be overstated because of unmeasured employment in an underground or peripheral economy, characterized by cash transactions and the existence of illegal activities such as drug sales or numbers running.

These demographic discussions seem to minimize the magnitude of racial unemployment differentials and the implications of these differentials. These discussions fail to integrate the effects of racism in several sectors of the economy. It seems pointless to suggest that if blacks were distributed differently by occupation unemployment rates might drop, when it is clear that discrimination prevents full occupational access for all blacks. A discussion of black progress masks the persistence of poverty for a segment of the black population. It seems meaningless to note that demographic changes partly explain high unemployment differentials, since there is little that can be done to restore the composition of the labor force to its former state. Finally, the existence of the underclass and the possible participation of this group in an underground economy should be seen as symptomatic of persistent racial unemployment differentials instead of as an explanation for why these differentials exist. Further, the underground economy is not a substitute for legitimate labor market activity. Instead, this activity depletes the black male population both by death and imprisonment far beyond the proportion of blacks in the total population.

Conclusion

A review of the labor market theories that attempt to explain racial unemployment differentials is a frustrating task for the writer who is interested in using theory to form public policy. This is especially true since, except for some institutional theories, they are poor explanations for the persistence of racial unemployment differentials, unless the sheer pervasiveness of racism in America is considered a decisive explanation. In fact, theorists commonly seem to model supply-side decisions to show that racial differences in education, quit behavior, or even family background explain differences in unemployment. But there is inherent endogeneity in such explanations since these supply-side decisions are made in the context of the realities of a racist society (or the demand side). Further, the models that test these theories seem to explain statistically only a small portion of racial unemployment differentials. Thus our theories represent efforts similar to those of blind men describing an elephant alternatively as a snake and a tree.

Like the blind men who failed to recognize the elephant, our theories fail to recognize the full reality of black labor market participation and the impact that racism has on every aspect of this. The disproportionate unemployment of blacks in the recent recession, the decline in black labor force participation, and the pessimistic prospect for leaving unemployment unless a recovery is of sufficient length especially seem indicative of the effects of racism. The prescription for these ills has been occupational diversity and more education; both took place in the 1960–1980 period, but seemingly were only slightly successful.

It seems that part of the problem is the way that economists have chosen to model the labor market. Our concepts of rational decision making, of occupational choice, of the linkage between employment and the quantity and quality of education seems reflective of the labor market experiences that we as economists have ourselves. However, the labor market experiences of economists, which include structured training, a proscribed and rational method of job search, market signalling through quality of education, etc., are atypical of the labor market experiences of other workers, especially nonacademics.

A more realistic theory of the labor market might note that most workers choose jobs by occupational accident, not by deliberate occupational choice. Initial job search often is not exhaustive but begins as one questions friends, colleagues, and exploits accessible resources. If these sources fail to yield job opportunities, then other sources might be used, but, clearly, differences in the resource set might explain differences in racial employment experiences. Further, given differences in the resource set, different signals might be appropriate to indicate job suitability. Thus, a white youth might signal suitability via parental connection, while a black youth's sole availability signal might be participation in a training program.

These thoughts on how labor markets, and thus black unemployment, might be explained more realistically are clearly preliminary. However, this review of the range of existing labor market theories suggests that the inability to explain fully racial unemployment differentials is as persistent as the differentials themselves.

References

Barret, Nancy, and Morgenstern, Richard. "Why Do Blacks and Women Have High Unemployment Rates?" *Journal of Human Resources* (May 1974), 452–464.

Barret, Nancy, Gerardi, Geraldine, and Morgenstern, Richard. "The Determinants of Unemployment Among Blacks and Women: A Cross Section Analysis." Mimeographed 1975.

Becker, Gary. *The Economics of Discrimination.* Chicago: Chicago University Press, 1957.

Becker, Gary. *Human Capital.* New York: Columbia University Press, 1964.

Bergmann, Barbara. "Occupational Segregation, Wages and Profits When Employers Discriminate by Race or Sex." *Eastern Economic Journal* (April/July, 1974), 103–110.

Blau, Peter, and Duncan, Otis Dudley. *The American Occupational Structure.* New York: Wiley, 1966.

Blau, Francine, and Kahn, Laurence M. "Race and Sex Differences in the Probability and Consequences of Voluntary Turnover." Mimeographed (September 1978).

Bluestone, Barry. *The Personal Earnings Distribution: Individual and Institutional Determinants.* Chestnut Hill, Mass.: Social Welfare Regional Research Institute (SWRRI), Publication No. 20, November 1974.

Bowles, Sam. "Unequal Education and the Reproduction of the Social Division of Labor." *Review of Radical Political Economics* (Fall-Winter, 1971).

Bowles, Sam. "Schooling and Inequality from Generation to Generation." *Journal of Political Economy* (May 1972).

Burdett, Kenneth. "The Theory of Employee Job Search and Quit Rates." *American Economic Review* (March 1978).

Cain, Glen J. "The Unemployment Rate as an Economic Indicator." *Monthly Labor Review* (March 1979).

Cox, Oliver, C. *Caste, Class, and Race.* New York: Doubleday, 1948.

Flanagan, Robert J. "On the Stability of the Racial Unemployment Differential." *American Economic Review* (May 1976), 302–308.

Flanagan, Robert J. "Discrimination Theory, Labor Turnover, and Racial Unemployment Differentials." *Journal of Human Resources* 1978.

Freedman, Marcia K. *Labor Markets: Segments and Shelters.* New York: Universe Books, 1976.

Freeman, Richard B. "Changes in the Labor Market for Black Americans, 1948–72." *Brookings Papers on Economic Activity* (Summer 1973).

Freeman, Richard B. *The Black Elite.* (New York: McGraw Hill, 1977).

Freeman, Richard. "Black Economic Progress Since 1964." *The Public Interest* (Summer 1978).

Freeman, Richard, and Medoff, James. "New Estimates of Private Sector Unionism in the U.S." *Industrial and Labor Relations Review* (January 1970).

Gilman, Harry. "The White/Nonwhite Unemployment Differential." In Mark Perlman (ed.) *Human Resources in the Urban Economy.* Washington, D.C.: Resources of the Future, 1963.

Gilman, Harry. "Economic Discrimination and Unemployment." *American Economic Review* (December 1965), 1077–1096.

Gilroy, Curtis L. Investment in Human Capital and the Nonwhite/White Unemployment Differential." Unpublished Ph.D. dissertation, State University of New York at Binghamton, 1973.

Gilroy, Curtis L. "Black and White Unemployment: The Dynamics of the Differential." *Monthly Labor Review* (July 1975).

Gordon, David. *Theories of Poverty and Underemployment.* Lexington, Mass.: D.C. Heath, 1973.

Green, James. *Grass Roots Socialism: Radicalism in the Southwest 1895–1943.* Baton Rouge: Louisiana State University Press, 1978.

Hall, Robert, and Kasten, Richard. "The Relative Success of Blacks and Whites." *Brookings Papers on Economic Activity* (Fall, 1973).

Hall, Robert. "Why Is There So Much Unemployment at Full Employment?" *Brookings Papers on Economic Activity* (1970).

Job, Barbara. "The Black Labor Force During the 1975–78 Recovery." *Monthly Labor Review* (May 1978).

Kerr, Clark. "The Balkanization of Labor Markets. In E. Wight Bakke (ed.) Labor Mobility and Economic Opportunity. Cambridge: New Technology Press, 1954.

Korda, Michael. *Male Chauvinism.* New York: Random House, 1973.

Malveaux, Julianne. *Unemployment Differentials by Race and Occupation.* Unpublished Ph.D. dissertation, M.I.T., 1980.

Malveaux, Julianne. *Shifts in the Occupational and Employment Status of Black Women: Current Trends and Future Implications.* Presented at The Women's Center, University of California at Berkeley, 1981.

Marston, Stephen. "Employment Instability and High Unemployment Rates." *Brookings Papers on Economic Activity* (1976).

Oi, Walter. "Labor as Quasi-Fixed Factor of Production." *Journal of Political Economy* (October 1962), 538–55.

Osterman, Paul. "Racial Differentials in Male Youth Unemployment." Mimeographed (1978).

Phelps, Edmund, et al. *Microeconomic Foundations of Employment and Inflation Theory.* New York: 1970.

Piore, Michael J. *The Role of Immigration in Industrial Growth: A Case Study of the Origins and Characters of Puerto Ricans Migrating to Boston.* Cambridge, Mass.: M.I.T. Working Paper 112A, May, 1973.

Piore, Michael J. "Notes for a Theory of Labor Market Stratification." In Richard Edwards, David Gordon, and Michael Reich (eds.) *Labor Market Segmentation.* Lexington, Mass.: D.C. Heath, 1975.

Piven, Frances F., and Cloward, Richard A. *The New Class War.* New York: Pantheon Books, 1982).

Reich, Michael, Gordon, David, and Edwards, Richard C. "A Theory of Labor Market Segmentation." *American Economic Review* (May 1973), 359–365.

Rosen, Sherwin. "Learning and Experience in the Labor Market." *Journal of Human Resources* (1972), 326–342.

Smith, Ralph E., and Holt, Charles C. "A Job Search Turnover Analysis of the

Black-White Unemployment Ratio." In *Industrial Relations Research Association,* Proceedings of the 23rd Annual Meeting, 1970.

Strober, Myra. "Segregation by Gender in Public School Teaching Toward a General Theory of Occupational Segregation in the Labor Market." Unpublished paper, May 1982.

Thurow, Lester. "Education and Economic Equality." *The Public Interest* (Summer 1972).

U.S. Department of Labor. *Employment and Training Report of the President.* Washington, D.C.: Government Printing Office, 1982.

Wallace, Phyllis. *Affirmative Action and Seniority.* Washington, D.C.: National Urban Coalition, June 1976.

Wallace, Phyllis, and Lamond, Annette (eds.) *Women, Minorities and Employment Discrimination.* Lexington, Mass.: Lexington Books, 1977.

Weaver, Robert. *Negro Labor: A National Problem.* New York, 1946.

Wilhelm, Sidney. *Who Needs the Negro?* New York: Doubleday, 1974.

Wilson, William Julius. *The Declining Significance of Race.* New York: University of Chicago Press, 1978.

Yette, Samuel. *The Choice.* New York: Pantheon Books, 1971.

4 THE EFFECT OF RACIAL DIFFERENCES IN BACKGROUND ON SCHOOLING: A SURVEY

Linda P. Datcher

Introduction

For many years, schooling has been considered one of the main avenues for overcoming the effects of the long history of racial discrimination and exclusion in the United States. This view is based on the notion that, independent of other considerations, schooling increases one's value in the labor market and thereby raises earnings. A prerequisite for education to be successful in this role of equalizing opportunities is that blacks must, on average, attain at least as much schooling as similarly endowed whites.[1]

While this criterion seems reasonably straightforward, it is subject to many interpretations. A weak version defines endowment broadly to include social origins and ability. It is satisfied when, if there were no racial differences in average background characteristics and ability, blacks would obtain as much schooling as whites. A strong version defines endowment only in terms of ability, and is, therefore, not satisfied until the social origins of blacks do not handicap their educational achievement.

The main purpose of this chapter is to review empirical evidence on how well education satisfies these weak and strong criteria and to identify the sources of impediments to successful performance. First, it briefly reviews theoretical work that discusses the potential barriers. It then considers the results of studies which use a relatively limited set of background measures. Next, it investigates how the conclusions of these studies are altered when a wider array of indicators are available. Finally, it summarizes the implications of the reviewed work.

Theoretical Framework

This section will summarize a subset of the theories which help to explain why weak and strong versions of the criterion for equal educational opportunities may not be met. These include human capital theory, social capital notions, and radical analysis.

According to the human capital approach, individuals make decisions about their amount of personal investment in schooling so as to maximize their net earnings power (see Becker, 1975). Their marginal rate of return or demand for schooling depends on production costs and increases in earnings associated with each additional unit of investment, while their marginal cost or supply of schooling depends on the costs of financing such investment. The optimal choice occurs at the level where the supply equals the demand.

Background affects schooling mainly through altering the marginal cost of financing the investment. Parents will invest more in their children if the price of the investment is lower, if they have more financial resources, and/or if their preferences for investment are higher. The greater the amount of investment that parents make, the lower is the marginal cost to offspring of financing additional investment and the greater the level of investment and earnings obtained. The human capital approach, therefore, implies that a weak version of the criterion will be met when equally able blacks and whites with the same background face identical marginal rates of return and marginal cost curves. The strong version, however, will not be satisfied until blacks with a given ability have the same marginal cost curves as their white counterparts, even though their backgrounds are poorer.

Loury's social capital (1977) extension of this approach emphasizes the importance of the neighborhood of origin. When there is social stratification by income, the amount of schooling that individuals acquire will vary by the type of community environment they face. Positive externalities in the form of peer values and aspirations, school quality, information about educational and career opportunities, and explicit help from neighborhood associates in pursuing such opportunities will be more available to those in high stratus, high income communities than to others.

When there also is stratification by race, the community environment of an individual will depend on his or her racial group as well as on family income. The history of discrimination against blacks would, therefore, imply that whites systematically have more positive community externalities available than blacks, and that blacks and whites with the same rate of return curve and parental investment will not face the same marginal cost curve. Racial differences in community quality would, therefore, be an important barrier to meeting the strong criterion of equal educational opportunity or the weak criterion which holds family, but not neighborhood, background constant.

According to the radical point of view (see Bowles and Gintis, 1976), socioeconomic origins are important because occupation roles are grouped largely by the degree of control and self-direction exercised by the jobholder. Such personality traits are developed at an early age by the family and school environment. Children of parents high in the occupational hierarchy are exposed to greater freedom and independence compared to the authoritarian relations that dominate the working-class environment. Thus, upper- and middle-class children tend to develop the personality characteristics that are required for positions high in the job hierarchy, while working-class children generally do not.

Instead of being the great equalizer and the path by which individuals can overcome background handicaps, schooling serves to reinforce class distinctions. Working-class children with a given number of years of schooling have received a much different type of instruction than middle-class children with the same educational attainment. As a result, the latter tend to remain in school longer. Thus, the radical approach emphasizes the role of attitudes and personality, independent of ability, as barriers to satisfying the criterion for equal educational opportunity.

Studies Using a Limited Set of Background Measures

The rest of this chapter will review the empirical studies that discuss how well education satisfies these criteria and will uncover the evidence of the impediments identified in the previous section. Many of these studies consider only a small number of background items based on retrospective reports of parental status by offspring. These include Featherman and Hauser (1976), Freeman (1981), and Datcher (1982a).

Using the 1962 and 1973 surveys of Occupational Changes in a Generation (OCG) carried out in conjunction with the Current Population Survey, Featherman and Hauser regressed total years of schooling on father's education, father's occupation, number of siblings, broken family, farm background, and southern origin, first by five-year age cohorts and later separately for blacks and whites in four different ten-year age cohorts. Their racial differences findings were generally supportive of the role of education as an effective means of equalizing opportunities between individuals with different social backgrounds.

For example, they found that the coefficient of the dummy variable for whether black in the five-year age cohort regressions changed from a strong negative impact for older cohorts to essentially no effect for young men. This implies that, holding background constant, the disparity between the levels of schooling obtained by blacks and whites has completely eroded over time, thus satisfying the weak criterion of equalizing educational opportunity. Featherman and Hauser also found that the variance in schooling attributable to social background declined absolutely by nearly half for both blacks and whites between old and young cohorts. This suggests that, while background disadvantages may still prevent blacks with a given level of ability from acquiring the same schooling as their white counterparts, the importance of this consideration has declined. Thus, education also has moved toward satisfying the strong criterion of equalizing educational opportunities.

While these findings begin to illuminate the degree and nature of black/white differences in the effects of background, they do not fully exploit the regression results obtained from the analysis. For example, rather than relying on the size of a dummy variable for race, a more accurate measure of whether blacks achieve the same level of schooling, ceteris paribus, can be obtained from the separate black regression coefficients.[2] Using these values, it is possible to determine how much of the racial gap in mean years of schooling would be eliminated if blacks had the same mean level of background characteristics as whites.

Columns 1, 3, and 5 of table 4–1 show the hypothetical change in years of schooling for black men if the mean of black background variables changed from those of young blacks to those of young whites. Columns 2, 4, and 6 show similar figures using racial differences in background between older men. Table 4–1 indicates that 1.2 of the 1.4 years racial gap in mean schooling of young men can be accounted for by differences in background characteristics compared to 2.6 of the 3.4 years disparity for older men. These findings indicate that poorer social origins account for 1.4 fewer years of the racial difference in schooling for the young cohort compared to the older cohort. The results also imply that there has been a significant decline in the degree to which blacks achieve lower levels of schooling, holding background constant. With the same mean background characteristics as whites in their age group, young black men would obtain only .2 fewer years of schooling, while older black men would acquire .8 fewer years.

Table 4–1 also can be used to identify the source of the reduction in the impact of poorer black social origins. Comparison of columns 1 and 2 shows

Table 4–1. Effects of Racial Differences in Mean Background Characteristics on Years of Schooling by Age

	Total Difference	*Total Effect Using Racial Differences in Means for:*		*Family Effect Using Racial Differences in Means for:*		*Place of Origin Effect Using Racial Differences in Means for:*	
		Young	*Old*	*Young*	*Old*	*Young*	*Old*
OCG: 1973							
Using coefficients of:							
Black men 27–36	1.4	1.20	1.23	1.01	.90	.19	.33
Black men 57–66	3.4	2.22	2.58	1.14	1.02	1.08	1.56
NLS: 1969							
Using coefficients of:							
Black men 17–27	1.6			1.39	1.61		
Black men 48–62	3.7			1.20	1.33		

that racial differences in mean background characteristics for the young cohort have almost as much effect as those for the older group. Similarly, comparing rows 1 and 2 of columns 3 and 4 indicates that there was only a small reduction in the influence of family background factors over time. Thus, virtually all of the decline in the impact of poorer black social origins results from the dramatic drop in the effects of farm and southern origins as seen by rows 1 and 2 of columns 5 and 6.

Other studies using a similar set of background variables to examine the effects of social origin on schooling include Freeman (1981) and Datcher (1982a). Freeman (1981) uses a sample of black and white men ages 17 to 27 and 48 to 62 in 1969 taken from the National Longitudinal Studies (NLS). He first regresses years of schooling on parental years of schooling, parental occupational status, presence of male head of household at age 14, and a variety of types of place of origin variables by age and race. He then estimates a logit equation on the probability of going to college using the same variables. These results strongly support the conclusion that most of the weakening of the overall impact of background is not the result of a narrowing of racial differences in mean family background characteristics or a reduction in the impact of given family differences. They instead suggest, once again, that the decline originates from a fall in the influence of southern and rural origins.

Freeman's logit estimates of the probability of attending college are largely consistent with the findings of the total years of school regressions. The impact of parental occupation is much closer for the young cohort, but the effects of parental education have diverged somewhat. The effects of broken home and place of origin variables are not reported.

The data for the Datcher (1982a) analysis comes from a sample of black and white men ages 25–34 and 45–64 taken from the University of Michigan Panel Study of Income Dynamics. Using tobit analysis, Datcher separately estimates the effects of father's education, mother's education, father's occupation, number of siblings, rural origin, and southern origin on years of precollege and years of college schooling. For both the young and old cohorts, racial differences in mean family background characteristics account for about 21 percent of the racial difference in years of college schooling. The gap in precollege schooling for the young cohort would be eliminated if blacks had the same social origins as whites, but about .4 of the 2.2 years gap among the older group would still remain.

Datcher's results also suggest that the impact of family background on the old cohort is approximately the same as for the younger group. Using the difference in mean black/white characteristics among the younger cohort as a measure of background effects shows that the larger impact on years of college for younger blacks compared to the older group (.27 versus .06 years, respectively) is almost exactly outweighed by the greater effect on years of precollege education for the older group (.25 years for younger blacks versus .47 years for older blacks). Although Datcher does not calculate the effects of rural and southern origin on years of precollege and college schooling using the estimated tobit coefficients, the differences in the coefficient sizes between the old and young black cohorts suggests that their impact has substantially eroded. For years of precollege schooling, the tobit coefficients of southern origin and rural origin moved from −2.54 to −.05 and −1.04 to .03 respectively between cohorts. The changes for years of college were less dramatic but were in the same direction.

The main problems with these three studies result from omitted variables and measurement error. The general problem with omitted variables is as follows: Suppose that schooling depends on family income, neighborhood income, and parental attitudes but that the analyst only considers the effect of the first item. The resulting estimate of the impact of family income will be a biased indicator of both its separate influence and the total impact of background. Assuming that family income is correlated with the left-out variables, its coefficient will pick up some but not all of their effects. As a result, it is not possible to isolate the role of family financial resources noted prominently (but not exclusively) in human capital theory. Nor is it possible to distinguish that effect from the impact of (1) neighborhood features pointed to by Loury or (2) attitudes and personality emphasized by the radical view.

Also because of the limitations of the data used, these studies do not have proxies for innate ability. To the extent that ability and social origins are positively correlated, the estimated background effects will be biased upward.

The problem of omitted variables may be compounded by measurement error. In a simple one explanatory variable model, measurement error will bias downward the coefficient estimate (see Johnston, pp. 281–2). However, in more complicated models with other explanatory variables, its impact is uncertain. Measurement error is likely to be important in models such as the ones presented thus far because reports of parents' education and occupation are given retrospectively by offspring.

Studies Using More Elaborate Background Measures

Other studies of the effects of social origins on schooling attempt to reduce omitted variables and measurement problems by including a wider array of background and other variables and/or obtaining more reliable reports of social origins. Many of the findings of these studies are consistent with the general conclusions drawn from the Featherman and Hauser, Datcher, and Freeman analyses mentioned earlier. The following discussion will highlight, therefore, the unique contributions of these efforts. These include Morgenstern (1973) and Akin and Garfinkel (1977) who investigated the influence of per capita educational expenditures on the level of schooling achieved; Datcher (1982b) and Freeman (1981) who examined the effects of other community and family factors; and Bielby, Hauser, and Featherman (1977) who estimated the bias due to response errors.

The data for the Morgenstern study came from the 1968 Urban Problems Survey conducted at the University of Michigan. The sample included black and white men from 15 northeast and midwest cities. In addition to measures of parental education, Morgenstern included the level of per pupil expenditures in the state and decade that the individual attended primary school in his education regressions. His analysis indicated that black/white differences in mean father's education account for .4 of the 1.3 years racial difference in school and that differences in per pupil expenditures explain .6 years.

Although the Featherman and Hauser, Freeman, and Datcher studies did not include measures of school quality, they may have captured part of this effect in the coefficients of southern origin. However, such variables are, at best, very crude proxies for per pupil expenditures. This implies that, relative to the Morgenstern findings, the previously mentioned studies may understate the similarity between blacks and whites with the same background characteristics, and understate the importance of poorer social origins of blacks relative to whites.

Akin and Garfinkel used a sample of men ages 30 to 55 in 1972 taken from the University of Michigan Panel Study of Income Dynamics. The background variables available from this data set included father's years of schooling, father's occupation, parents' income class (poor, middle-income, or upper-income), respondent's number of siblings, the state in which the individual grew up, the degree of urbanization of the area in which he grew up, the individual's score on an achievement orientation test, and the score on a 13-sentence completion verbal "ability" test. In addition, each individual in the sample was assigned the per pupil school expenditure and per capita income for the state in which he lived.

The Akin and Garfinkel results indicated that racial differences in the mean of family background characteristics account for 0.72 years of the 3.2 years' gap in education between blacks and whites; racial differences in schooling expenditures explain 0.61 years; achievement motivation, 0.08 years; and verbal ability, 0.72 years. Thus, their findings largely echo those of Morgenstern. In both cases, family background differences alone explain less than one-third of the black/white gap in schooling, and the effect of schooling expenditures is large relative to effect of family background alone.

One distinction between the Akin and Garfinkel and Morgenstern studies is that the former attempted to control for ability. Its potential importance is suggested by the size of its effect on racial differences in years of schooling. If the sentence completion test truly measures ability and if the correlation between ability and family background is large and positive, the failure to include such a measure may produce a large upward bias in the impact of social origins.

The Morgenstern and Akin and Garfinkel studies are aimed at reducing the omitted variables problem of analyses with more limited background variables, but they are also subject to data difficulties. For example, the verbal "ability" test used in the Akin and Garfinkel study was administered at the time of the rest of the survey in 1972. It may, therefore, reflect the impact of schooling, family background, and all other items that affect an individual's vocabulary and knowledge of word use independent of innate ability. As such, it would largely measure achievement and would be an endogenous variable in the schooling equation. Since no instrumental variables or other technique is used to eliminate correlation with the error term, the coefficient of the score on the verbal "ability" test would not be consistent. The same problem arises for achievement motivation if it depends on success in schooling.

Morgenstern's problem with omitted variables may be more serious because the only family background variables in his study were dummy variables for father's education less than 8 years, mother's education less than 8 years, father's education 12 or more years, and mother's education 12 or more years. Therefore, comparisons between the relative effects of family background factors and per pupil schooling expenditures certainly underestimate the former.

Furthermore, as Akin and Garfinkel point out, an additional problem with the Morgenstern study is that the sample was restricted to 15 northeast and midwest cities. Individuals with the lowest per pupil expenditures are likely to be those who migrated from the South. If those who migrated are more able, ambitious, or otherwise resourceful than those who were born in the Northeast or Midwest, then ability will be negatively correlated with school expenditures, and the absence of a measure of ability will bias downward the school-expenditure coefficient.

A problem common to Morgenstern and Akin and Garfinkel is the interpretation of the coefficient of schooling expenditures. Given the degree of intrastate variation in per capita schooling outlays, the statewide measure used in both studies is only a crude approximation of the desired variable. In addition, statewide per capita school expenditures may be correlated with other characteristics that affect years of schooling through other channels.

Akin and Garfinkel noted that per capita school expenditures may reflect the effect of community income through peer group influences or variations in permanent parental family income not captured by the father's occupation or family income measures used. In order to test whether per capita school expenditures simply act as proxies for nonschooling variables related to local income, Akin and Garfinkel included in their education regressions a measure of per capita income in the state in which the respondent grew up. Although both the black and white school expenditure coefficients became insignificant, their size was only reduced by about 20 percent. This suggests that most of their effect is unrelated to per capita state income. However, the high degree of colinearity between the two variables prevent a definitive test with the available data.

One of the principal objectives of the study by Datcher (1982b) was to separate the effects of family background from those of the neighborhood of origin. A unique feature of the study was that community data on average family income and racial composition were available by five-digit zip code areas. This is far more disaggregated than the usual statewide or SMSA-wide proxies for community quality. Furthermore, in order to limit the extent to which these community variables simply act as proxies for unobserved family characteristics, the Datcher study used a broader and more accurate array of family background variables. In addition to father's education, mother's education, and number of siblings, they included parental family income, whether the parents expected their children to go to college, and whether the head of the family felt that it was important to make his own decisions on the job. Furthermore, reports of these items were obtained directly from the parents rather than from retrospective accounts by the offspring.

Datcher's results showed that differences in family background for blacks at the top quartile of the family income distribution compared to those at the bottom quartile account for .42 out of the .74 (57 percent) difference in years of schooling. Differences in community characteristics explain .25 years, or 34 percent. Thus, although differences in family background are the principal sources of the effects of social origins, community effects are also significant as they are about 60 percent as large as family effects. Datcher's results also showed that half of the total .53 years racial difference in schooling due to background results from differences in the means of family characteristics and half from differences in neighborhood quality.[3] The findings therefore, validate the importance of Loury's social capital notions as embodied in neighborhood of origin.

Estimates of family effects include the impact of parental attitudes, namely educational aspirations for children and whether the head of the family reported that it was important to make his own decision on the job. The influence of these attitudinal items were almost two-thirds as large as that for parents' education and number of siblings combined. To the extent that these measures pick up the impact of attitudes alone, they provide some evidence for the radical emphasis on personality development as a determinant of level of schooling and subsequent economic success.

As in the case of the Akin and Garfinkel and Morgenstern studies, a major shortcoming with the Datcher study is that the source of the neighborhood effects cannot be identified definitively. This omission is particularly important in examining the role of education as the principal channel for social reform. If community effects result from differences in school expenditures, then background handicaps can be overcome through compensatory spending on education. If, on the other hand, they result from peer influences, local information and resource networks, and neighborhood values and aspirations, then community effects exacerbate family background differences when there is segregation by income class and race.

In addition to the analysis mentioned earlier, the Freeman paper includes a set of regressions for the younger NLS cohort which estimates the impact of a wider set of background variables, i.e., presence of magazines, presence of newspapers, and presence of a library card in the home. He assumes that these items are proxies for home educational resources and concludes that their absence reflects the lack of home reading material available to children. His main finding was that these variables significantly influence years of school and are substantial intervening variables in the background-education relationship. Over 40 percent of the difference between average years of schooling of black and white men can be accounted for by these variables. This compares to 31 percent for parental occupation, 25 percent for parental years of education, and 6 percent for presence of father. Overall, then, differences in the mean levels of these family background characteristics account for all of the difference in average schooling between blacks and whites.

While the size of the effect of the home educational resources implies that they are proxies for important background effects, it is not clear that the direct interpretation that Freeman applies is accurate. Rather than denoting the presence or absence of home reading material, these items may reflect the impact of a wide array of other family and/or neighborhood influences. These include parental feelings of efficacy, parental attitudes toward education, school quality, etc. It seems implausible that racial differences in the availability of home reading material alone would account for 40 percent of the difference in mean schooling between blacks and whites.

Bielby, Hauser, and Featherman (1977) estimated the biases in background effects due to inaccurate reports of background variables. They specified a model of patterns of response error that depends on obtaining multiple indicators of background variables. In such models, the covariation among the indicators is generated by unobserved "true scores." Specifically, they assumed that the true model of offspring educational attainment is given by

$$S_i = \beta_1 T_{i1} + \beta_2 T_{i2} + u_1 \tag{4.1}$$

but that respondents' report of T_{ik} at time j equals X_{ikj}, where

$$X_{ikj} = \lambda_{ikj} T_{ik} + e_{ikj}. \tag{4.2}$$

Three types of covariation among response errors are considered. First, response errors may depend on the respondent's true score of the variable, i.e., λ_{kj} may not be equal to one. Second, respondents may overstate the consistency between different variables ascertained on a single occasion. Third, respondents' errors in reporting a given variable may be correlated across time.

The data necessary to distinguish such errors come from the 1973 OCG study mentioned earlier, along with second reports of background variables that were obtained from a random subsample interviewed about three weeks after the original survey. These two reports, along with certain restrictions on the covariance between the u_i, are sufficient to identify models with within-variable and within-occasion error covariances. Bielby, Hauser, and Featherman found that the most appropriate model for blacks includes both within-variable and within-occasion correlated response errors. The failure to correct for response errors for blacks has no effect on father's occupation and education. However, the impact of parental income is biased downward by about 40 percent.

Summary

A summary of the findings of the studies examined in this chapter indicates that there has been substantial progress made in satisfying the weak criterion of equalizing educational opportunities. While older blacks attain much less schooling than whites in the same age group, holding background constant, this gap has been almost completely eliminated for the younger groups. This conclusion could be supported even if the analysis were restricted to examining the studies which include only a limited set of background measures. However, it is strengthened by the results of studies which consider more accurate and/or extensive indicators of social origins. These studies uniformly point toward further narrowing of the gap in black/white schooling in the absence of racial differences in mean background variables.

Overall, there also has been progress in satisfying the strong criterion of equalizing educational opportunity. The percentage of the variance in years of schooling due to background characteristics and the racial difference in schooling due to poorer black social origins declined between the old and young black cohorts.

A conclusion of impending success in satisfying the strong criterion of equalizing education opportunities should be tempered by two important qualifications. First, virtually all of the change in the impact of background between old and young blacks resulted from a reduction in the effects of farm and southern origins. The decline in the influence of family factors is, at best, marginal and there is some evidence that such items have been more, rather than less, important. Second, studies which include more accurate and extensive measures of social origins indicate that the effects are more important and pervasive than implied by the usually limited set of family and type of place of origin variables available in many data sets.

In general, the studies reviewed here provide little evidence useful in distinguishing between the different theories of impediments facing blacks in obtaining equal educational opportunity. However, the Datcher work does suggest that neighborhood characteristics as well as parental attitudes have important effects on schooling, independent of other family considerations. Moreover, the Akin and Garfinkel and Morgenstern studies imply that, whatever the sources of the barriers, compensatory expenditures on schooling for blacks can be significant in overcoming the effect of poorer black social origins on years of schooling.

Notes

1. Other prerequisites not discussed in this paper include the conditions that (1) schooling does, in fact, raise earnings, (2) the payoff to schooling is as high for blacks as for whites, and (3) blacks obtain the same quality of schooling as whites.

2. The dummy variable approach constrains the coefficients of the explanatory variables to be the same for whites and blacks, allowing only the intercept term to differ.

3. This is a lower bound estimate of the effects of neighborhood of origin because the hypothetical value is the level for blacks in the upper quartile of the family income distribution and not complete integration.

References

Akin, John S., and Garfinkel, Irwin. "School Expenditures and the Economic Returns to Schooling." *Journal of Human Resources* (Fall 1977), 460–81.

Becker, Gary. *Human Capital.* New York: Columbia University Press, 1975.

Bielby, William I., Hauser, Robert M., and Featherman, David L. "Response Errors of Black and Nonblack Males in Models of the Intergenerational Transmission of Socioeconomic Status." *American Journal of Sociology* (May 1977), 1242–88.

Bowles, Samuel, and Gintis, Herbert. *Schooling in Capitalist America.* New York: Basic Books, 1976.

Datcher, Linda. "Effects of Community and Family Background on Achievement." *The Review of Economics and Statistics* (February 1982a), 32–41.

Datcher, Linda. "Racial Differences in the Effects of Background on Achievement." Unpublished paper, 1982b.

Freeman, Richard. "Black Economic Progress Since 1964: Who Has Gained and Why?" In Sherwin Rosen (ed.) *Studies in the Labor Market.* Chicago: The University of Chicago Press, 1981.

Hauser, Robert M., and Featherman, David L. "Equality of Schooling: Trends and Prospects." *Sociology of Education* (April 1976), 99–120.

Johnston, J. *Econometric Methods.* New York: McGraw-Hill Book Co., 1972.

Loury, Glenn. "A Dynamic Theory of Racial Income Differences." In P.A. Wallace, and A. LaMond, (eds.) Lexington, Mass.: D.C. Heath, 1977.

Morgenstern, Richard. "Direct and Indirect Effects on Earnings of Schooling and Socioeconomic Background." *The Review of Economics and Statistics* (May 1973), 225–33.

5 OCCUPATIONAL SAFETY AND HEALTH REGULATION AND ECONOMIC THEORY

William T. Dickens

Introduction

From the point of view of someone engaged in the formulation of policy, a good theory is one which has clear implications for the effects of the actions being considered and is supported by evidence.[1] In order for a theory to be well supported, the key assumptions which yield the policy recommendations must have strong, observable implications which have been demonstrated by empirical research. If we accept these two criteria then, for the purpose of occupational safety and health (OSH) policy formation, there is considerable room for improvement in our current theories of labor market behavior.

Existing theory gives us a very clear picture of what constitutes good policy when labor markets are characterized by perfect competition. How-

I would like to acknowledge the able research assistance of Daniel Hagen, Kathy Marshall, and Paula Mizelle. I would also like to thank Allen Berger, Shulamit Kahn, Kevin Lang, Mike Riordan, and Jamie Robinson for the helpful comments on earlier versions of the ideas presented here. Finally, the Institute of Business and Economic Research and the Institute of Industrial Relations at Berkeley provided generous research support.

ever, the assumptions of the perfect competition model are quite strict. Few economists would be willing to argue that it should be our primary guide in making OSH policy. To formulate good policy we need to know how the market will behave if those assumptions do not hold. Unfortunately, with few exceptions, we do not know. First, although it is widely believed that many of the assumptions of the pure competition model are violated, we do not know what the implications of these failures are for the efficacy of the major policy alternatives. Second, we do not know how to test these assumptions. We may know some implications of these assumptions but we do not know what the implications are of the failure of the assumptions.

This problem suggests the need for analysis of how the labor market will behave with respect to the provision of OSH when these assumptions do not hold. We need to develop a theory which allows us to evaluate alternative policies and to test the important assumptions. This paper focuses on the first task.

The presentation proceeds in three sections. In the second section, a critical review of current theory is presented. It begins with a description of the competitive model and its important assumptions. The assumptions are then reviewed and the relevant literature on how the labor market will behave when each assumption is violated is explored. Areas in which more work is needed are identified. The section concludes with a discussion of the direction future work should take. In the third section, some preliminary work elaborating current theory is presented. The importance of additional work is made evident by the number of surprising results this investigation turns up. For instance, it is shown that even if monopsonists provide an optimal amount of safety given the level of employment they choose, forcing them to provide more may improve welfare. It is also shown that providing workers with additional information about their job hazards may make them worse off. Finally, under some circumstances there may be reasons to prefer standards which require all firms to provide the same level of safety, to an injury tax which allows firms to differ in the level of safety they provide. The final section is a conclusion which summarizes the major findings of the literature review and new theoretical work and suggests where more work is needed.

Literature Survey

Two features of OSH distinguish it from most other economic commodities and cause it to require special analysis. The first of these is that OSH is always produced in conjunction with other commodities. In particular, OSH is produced only as labor is consumed. As a result, one cannot buy OSH separately — it is bundled as part of the worker-employer transaction. Second, the sale of this bundle takes place in the labor market, a market which has a large number of institutional peculiarities that make standard economic analysis difficult to apply. Thus a literature treating the market for OSH has been developed.

In the simplest pure competiton model of the provision of OSH, workers are utility maximizers and firms maximize profits. Each worker's utility depends on the amount of income received and the safety of his or her job.[2] On the firm's side, costs are dependent on the level of safety that is provided. This is the basic outline of the model. In addition, the pure competition model specifies several very strong assumptions about the market environment and how agents behave:

1. Markets Are Competitive: Workers are free to choose any job that is offered. Firms are able to set wages and safety levels to maximize profits, but there are a large enough number of workers and firms so that, given the safety level the firm chooses to offer, the firm can hire all the labor it desires at or above a certain wage and can hire no labor for a lower wage.
2. Perfect Information: Both firms and workers know with certainty all wage and safety levels of all jobs in the economy.
3. No External Economies: The agents making employment decisions bear all the costs and reap all the benefits of their actions.
4. Rationality: Both workers and firms use all available information as efficiently as possible to maximize utility or profit.

Sufficient conditions for an equilibrium to exist and to have the most common properties may also include some restrictions on the technology and on people's tastes. The standard assumptions about the convexity of preferences and production technology are sufficient.

If the above conditions are met then an equilibrium can be characterized as follows: First, if firms have different costs of producing safety or if workers have different preferences for levels of money income and safety, then it is most likely that all jobs will not offer the same combination of wages and safety. Given otherwise identical workers and jobs, some jobs will be safer than others and will pay less. This is the first important implication of the pure competition model. It was first observed by Adam Smith (1776, p. 89) in *The Wealth of Nations* when he discussed the source of wage differentials. Since then the result has been more formally developed; first in the product quality literature (Rosen, 1974) and then specifically for the case of OSH (Thaler and Rosen, 1976). Second, competiton guarantees that the worker's total compensation — wages plus the marginal cost of safety per worker — will be equal to the value of the worker's marginal product. Finally, the first-order conditions for profit and utility maximization require that the marginal cost of safety per worker be equal to the marginal rate of substitution of money income for safety in the worker's utility function in each job.

The last two conditions imply that the market outcome is Pareto efficient. No change in the level of safety can make anyone better off without imposing a cost on someone else that would be larger than what the benefited person would be willing to pay. If there is perfect competition in the insurance market there will also be an efficient amount of risk sharing. For this reason, any government interference in this market can only produce Pareto inefficient results. A government interested in income distribution might still want to intervene. However, trying to redistribute income through the labor market will have efficiency costs which might be greater than the costs of redistribution using other methods.[3]

All this is well understood by economists working in this area. Most discussions of OSH policy begin with a review of these results.[4] In addition, there is a large and growing literature on empirical studies of the labor market which attempt to identify the size of the wage differentials paid workers in more dangerous jobs.[5] What is not discussed extensively in the literature is what happens if the assumptions mentioned above do not hold. We do not have a good idea of what policy implications are in that case. We also do not have practical tests of these crucial assumptions. What follows is a summary of what we do and do not know about how markets behave when each of the four assumptions of pure competition discussed above are violated.

Competitive Markets

In the literature, six deviations from competitive conditions have been considered: noncompeting groups of workers, monopsony power, minimum wages, unions, disequilibrium, and regulation. We will consider each in turn.

Noncompeting groups. Perhaps the most famous objection to Adam Smith's hypothesis of compensating wage differentials was made by John Stuart Mill, who pointed out something that remains, for the most part, true today — the worst jobs also receive the lowest pay. Mill explained this in part by suggesting that workers were divided by class background into noncompeting groups (Mill, 1909, p. 388). Today, differences in workers' productive characteristics are often taken as the explanation for why some workers have both better jobs and higher wages. However, theories of discrimination[6] and labor market segmentation[7] are modern heirs to Mill's reasoning.

It is clear that this particular market failure can have a substantial impact on the distribution of income between the different groups. However, if within each submarket the assumptions of perfect competition hold, then given that distribution of income, the market result will be Pareto efficient. Any changes in the level of safety of one group will cost more than that group would be willing to pay for those changes. More efficient methods of redistributing income would almost certainly exist. It is unlikely that there would be any more of a role for OSH regulation in this world than in the perfectly competitive world.

Monopsony power. Monopsony power exists if a firm does not face an infinitely elastic supply of labor. This will be the case if a firm is large relative to its market or if workers cannot choose costlessly between firms.[8] It is well known that in this circumstance firms will hire a suboptimal amount of labor and that workers will be paid less than their marginal revenue products.

Consideration of OSH introduces another complication. In the case of pure competition, worker mobility between jobs insures that each job will have the property that the worker's marginal rate of substitution will equal the firm's marginal cost of providing safety. However, in the absence of such mobility, the job a worker chooses will not necessarily have that property. This has been pointed out by Robert Smith (1976, p. 31) and formalized by Viscusi (1980a).

For example, take the case of the company town. A worker's only choice is whether or not to work for the one firm in the town. If we assume that the firm must set the same wage and safety levels for each worker,[9] then the firm will choose them so that the marginal cost of labor is equal to marginal revenue and will set the marginal cost of safety per worker equal to the marginal rate of substitution between money income and the level of safety for the marginal worker. Thus it is the tastes of the marginal worker that determine the amount of safety that is provided. This is no problem if marginal workers have the same preferences for safety as other workers. However, Smith (1976), Freeman (1981), and Viscusi (1980a)[10] have all suggested that the marginal worker may not be typical of all workers. All three believe that younger workers are most likely to be less attached to the labor market and to particular firms and are, therefore, the most likely to be the workers firms are trying to attract. Smith and Viscusi also believe that younger workers are more likely to take dangerous jobs.

This is mostly speculation. Besides younger workers, older workers with more portable skills or women with less attachment to the labor market might also be marginal workers. In a rural area, agricultural workers employed in factories to supplement their income might be marginal workers. It is also not clear a priori whether younger workers would prefer more hazardous jobs or less hazardous jobs. On the one hand, a health capital argument would lead one to conclude that they would probably be more interested in avoiding hazards than older workers. The explanation given by Viscusi and Smith is that older workers, because of their family obligations, can afford less the interruption in their income that an accident or disease might entail. Smith suggests that younger workers may know less about job hazards. These authors go on to point out that OSH may be underprovided as a result.

Shulamit Kahn (1980) has argued that OSH will not be underprovided if young workers are rational and foresee that they will one day be older and desirous of greater safety. Further, Kahn shows that long-term employment contracts, either implicit or explicit, that are made in competitive markets which are in long-run equilibrium must be Pareto efficient. Thus, any monopsony power that arises from costs to changing jobs will not result in inefficiency.

If Smith and Viscusi are right, and younger workers do not foresee that their changing life situation will lead them to desire more safety in the future, then this sort of imperfection might provide justification for safety regulation. However, there is still one important theoretical issue and several empirical issues that would need to be addressed first. To begin with, the work of the authors cited examines the question of whether job safety is optimal given the level of employment or wages chosen by the monopsonist. It is possible that safety could be optimal given that level but that a minimum safety standard could still improve or worsen welfare by causing the monopsonist to change the wage and the level of employment.

There are also three empirical issues: Do marginal workers have tastes which are different from the average worker? Must all or most jobs in a plant have the same safety level? Is monopsony power prevalent? Kahn (1982) has research under way which aims to identify which workers' tastes determine the level of safety. Her preliminary results would seem to support Viscusi and Smith's position. However, some puzzling results — negative weights for middle-aged workers' preferences — raise questions about the methodology. Viscusi (1979d, 1980a) presents evidence that unionized workers receive larger compensating wage differentials than nonunion workers. He finds this to be consistent with the monopsony-young worker hypothesis.[11] However, such evidence is indirect and there are other hypotheses which could account for this difference.[12]

Minimum wages. One case in which it is clear that OSH will be under-provided is if a job is subject to a binding minimum wage and there are costs to providing an optimal level of safety. In the presence of a binding minimum wage, employers will reduce safety expenditures until they are zero or until the market is in equilibrium. In this case the employee would gladly accept a lower wage in exchange for safer working conditions but that is prevented by the minimum wage law.

That this condition may exist in some workplaces has been pointed out by Dunn (1977) in a study of people's preferences for job attributes. Workers in a Southern textile firm were asked how much pay they would be willing to give up for a number of different improvements in their working conditions. Interestingly, the workers sampled had a strong desire for air conditioning — strong enough that they would collectively be willing to pay more to have it installed than the employer would have to pay. Despite this, there was no air conditioning nor did the study prompt the employer to install it. The author's explanation was that many workers in the plant earned the minimum wage or near it. Consequently the firm maintained working conditions which were inferior to those it would have had in the absence of the minimum wage.

How important is this result for policy? Probably it is not very important. In 1980, 6.2 percent of the work force earned the minimum wage (Minimum Wage Study Commission).[13] However, if minimum wage legislation is to be maintained, these observations do suggest that it should be accompanied by minimum OSH standards to insure that the intent of the law is not undermined by adjustments to this important dimension of job quality.

Unions. The effects of unions on OSH have been considered in two articles. First, Zeckhauser and Nichol (1978) have pointed out that if unions negotiate only wages there will be incentives for firms, just as with minimum wages, to allow working conditions to deteriorate. However, there is evidence that many collective bargaining agreements do specify working conditions as well as wages;[14] so the question becomes how do unionized firms go about choosing the trade-off between OSH and money income?

Viscusi (1980a) examines the effects of labor unions by assuming that they will seek to maximize the total surplus of all members. He claims that if unions act as monopolies in what would otherwise be a competitive market, their effect on job safety is indeterminate — they may demand more or less than is socially optimal. Unions will choose the optimal level of safety if the marginal cost of providing safety of the marginal firm is equal to the marginal cost to the average firm. Viscusi (1980a, p. 183) does not believe that this necessarily will be the case. But, if it is not, then there will be potential gains for both employers and unions from market segmentation or negotiation, which results in different wages and safety levels for different jobs.[15] Allowing such differences will tend to equalize the incremental costs of safety of the marginal and average firms. However, as with the monopsonist, the union's choice of the optimal level of safety, given the level of wages or employment, does not mean that a safety standard could not improve welfare by changing the level of wages or employment chosen.

As Viscusi notes, the surplus maximization model of union behavior has been subject to criticism. Several other models have been proposed but no one method has gained acceptance as the best way to model union behavior.[16] Viscusi's efforts represent a very worthwhile beginning, but taking a different approach to modeling union behavior and bargaining may lead to different results.

For example, a common criticism of the surplus maximization model is that the elected officers of a union cannot be viewed simply as representatives of the workers but must be viewed as independent agents with their own interests — primarily keeping their jobs.[17] Taking this approach may give very different results. Recent work by Lawrence Root (1982, pp. 179–182) on pension bargaining suggests that when a company's market conditions are bad the union leadership may be willing to make concessions that the workers would not be willing to make. In that case, it has been suggested that rather than accept lower wages, provisions of pension plans (particularly funding standards) may be manipulated so that the concessions are made in ways which workers may not be able to discern. Given the obscurity of the costs and benefits of certain aspects of OSH, unions may well be led to do similar things with safety provisions in contracts.

Beyond this particular consideration, much work could be done on the effects of different regulatory tactics on outcomes under different assumptions about the nature of the bargaining process and the union political structure. Case study work on how unions bargain OSH issues would be a valuable first step toward developing this type of analysis.

Disequilibrium. Those with experience teaching the pure competition model of OSH choice find that the two most common objections students have to it are that workers do not have much information about job hazards and even if they did they almost always face a labor market where their choice is to take any job that is offered or be unemployed. We will deal with the first of these objections in the next section. It has received attention in the literature. However, the second objection is almost never mentioned.[18]

If we were to rephrase the students' objection into the language of economists, what they are suggesting is that wages do not adjust to clear labor markets. As a result, getting a job is a matter of being in the right place at the right time. Once a worker is employed, he or she is in no position to complain about working conditions since there are many other people who would be happy to take the job.

It is easy to see why economists have ignored this objection. Up until recently most economists have been of the opinion that disequilibrium in labor markets was a relatively transitory thing. While it may take time for wages to adjust to shocks to the market, it seems unlikely that wages would adjust slower than safety conditions. Wage changes may require a new contract, but changes in safety conditions often require changes in plant and equipment.

However, some economists recently have been turning to a different view of wage stickiness which opens the door for a further examination of this objection. While the predominant view in the profession is that wage stickiness — if it is important at all — is due to such things as contracts and adjustment costs, there is a growing literature which suggests that there may be sociological explanations.[19] For example, Akerlof (1982) has argued that people may adjust their work effort if they feel that they are being paid less than some customary wage for their job. This may lead employers to pay wages which are too high to clear markets.

Just as the differences in observability between wages and OSH conditions may lead to different treatment in bargaining, they may also lead to differences in the social customs which determine them. Unfortunately, the economic investigation of this topic is in its infancy. Besides anecdotal evidence from the industrial relations literature, little is known about the extent and the nature of this phenomenon. A compilation of anecdotal evidence, augmented perhaps by interviews, would be a good first step towards a formal theory of these processes. This could allow the working out of the implications — not only for OSH regulation but also for macropolicy — and suggest how the phenomenon could be verified empirically and its extent and importance gauged.

Regulation. Almost every economic analysis of OSH regulation begins by noting that in the absence of other market failures safety regulation can make everybody worse off. The purpose of doing this is usually not to argue against regulation but rather to point out the dangers of too much regulation and that the market mechanism may already provide some incentives to employers to protect workers' safety.[20] Smith (1976, p. 20) invents a fable to make this point. In his fable, people's lives are made less safe by OSH regulation which makes marketed goods so expensive that they replace them with nonmarket activities which are far less safe.

What has received less attention than the effects of regulation on otherwise perfectly competitive markets are the effects of regulation in the presence of other imperfections. Articles by Diamond (1979) and Rea (1981), discussed below, examine the impact of laws requiring increased insurance coverage of occupational injuries when workers and insurance companies have imperfect information about the danger of jobs and firms and have imperfect information about workers' self-protection efforts. Rea also briefly considers the effects of safety standards. Beyond this, authors analyzing regulation only assume that, for any of a number of reasons, the market provides too little safety and then propose different methods of getting it to provide more.

Smith (1976) proposes an injury tax to create incentives for firms to make work safer. Under Smith's proposal, employers would have to pay a penalty every time a worker was injured. To rationalize regulation of health hazards, Smith proposed that new OSHA standards be subjected to cost-benefit analysis. Zeckhauser and Nichol (1978) propose making firms' workers' compensation premiums dependent on their safety records.[21]

Viscusi (1979b) and Viscusi and Zeckhauser (1979) examine the effect of standards when enforcement is less than complete. They show that setting too high a standard can lead to a deterioration of OSH as more firms decide to violate the law. They argue that cost-benefit analysis, which assumes complete enforcement, would not be a good guide to setting standards. Viscusi shows that the optimal standard with incomplete enforcement necessarily will be more lenient than complete enforcement.

The major problem with all this work is that, in not specifying the reason for the underprovision of safety, the authors leave open the question of how the market will respond to particular programs. For instance, if the reason for the underprovision is that firms lack information about the true safety of the jobs they offer or about alternative (and safer) techniques, an injury tax or experience rating will not produce the desired effects. Other problems with this approach are pointed out in the discussion of imperfect information later in this chapter.

Perfect Information

Imperfect information is probably the most often cited justification for OSH regulation. It is surprising, therefore, that so few authors writing on the subject have given much consideration to how markets will behave in the presence of imperfect information.[22] Many do not go further than to observe that if workers are completely ignorant of job hazards, there will be no incentive for employers to provide safety, and workers will not be compensated for the risks they do face.

Walter Oi (1973) examines a market where workers have different assessments of the safety of a hazardous job. He notes that the existence of workers who underestimate the hazards of jobs is not a sufficient condition for there to be a greater number of workers in dangerous jobs than is socially optimal. Overemployment in dangerous occupations will take place only if the marginal workers in dangerous jobs underestimate the danger. Assuming otherwise identical jobs and workers, the marginal worker will be the one with the least favorable view of a job's safety. Oi concludes from this that there is no reason to believe a priori that imperfect information will lead to overemployment in dangerous jobs. However, if the pool of workers that a firm is drawing from is relatively large, all those who take jobs at a firm, including the marginal worker, may have considerably more favorable impressions of the safety than the average person in the work force. Thus even if workers, on average, overestimate the danger of all jobs, if the errors in each individual's estimate of the safety of each job are not highly correlated it is still likely that overemployment could occur. Oi also examines the provision of safety in a market where workers uniformly underestimate the danger of all jobs and shows that employers will provide too little safety.

Chelius (1977, p. 37) analyzes the effect of imperfect information on the incentives to employers to provide adequate safety. He notes, as did Oi, that compensating wage differentials will be inadequate only if all workers in a job underestimate its dangers.[23] Chelius goes on to argue that if wage premiums are inadequate, firms will not have an incentive to provide an optimal amount of safety. Strictly speaking, this is not true. What matters is not the perception of overall risk but the perception of the effects of marginal changes in safety precautions or risk. Workers could overestimate the safety of their jobs and receive inadequate compensating differentials but if they could perceive correctly the effects of marginal changes in safety precautions, employers would have the proper incentives to provide an optimal amount of safety. This result is developed more formally in the third section.

Viscusi, in a number of publications, has considered a variety of models of worker and firm behavior when either or both have imperfect information about job quality or how likely different workers are to have accidents. In particular, Viscusi has analyzed the optimal dynamic behavior of workers who face markets where job safety is not known with certainty.

One result derived from this analysis is that, all other things held equal, young workers will prefer jobs about which they know less. The result obtains because of the value of the information one gets by taking such a job. Viscusi also shows that optimal behavior involves learning from experience and switching jobs if one observes a sufficient number of unfavorable outcomes.

These results suggest two hypotheses which Viscusi examines empirically. The first is that quit rates, particularly those of younger workers who are just learning about the job market, should be higher on more dangerous jobs. This is borne out by the data. The second is that older workers' quit rates should be less affected by job safety since they should have sorted themselves out and should be through their learning phase. This latter hypothesis is not borne out (Viscusi, 1979d).

Viscusi also has examined the optimal wage policy for firms facing labor markets where workers have different and unknown propensities to have accidents or have prior beliefs about the safety of firms, which are held with different degrees of sharpness.

Finally, he has examined the incentives for firms to provide information to workers about the dangers of their jobs and has introduced a new consideration into the discussion of the likelihood of lack of information being a serious problem. His analysis of dynamic worker choice suggests that even if workers enter the labor market with imperfect information they may learn about jobs from their search experience. The result that workers will prefer jobs about which they have less information suggests a reason why firms may want to conceal the true safety level of the jobs they offer.

Viscusi also examines unraveling models of information provision. In such models, workers assume firms have the average safety level unless they are told otherwise. Firms which are safer than average have incentives to publicize this information but may not since it is also assumed that disseminating such information would be costly. If the safest firms do publicize their records, the average safety of the unknown firms drops and it may become worthwhile for the safer of the remaining unknown firms to publicize their safety. Viscusi suggests that this sort of process may lead firms to provide information voluntarily on the safety of their jobs. He also suggests that it might be beneficial for government information provision to begin with the safest firms rather than the least safe in the hopes that doing so would set off an unraveling.

Of course, publicizing information about the safest firms might not cause people to revise their assessments of the safety of the remaining firms downward. Depending on how people use the information, it might have a "halo" effect and cause them to believe that other firms are safer. In this case there would be no unraveling.

Viscusi's work provides many interesting insights into how labor markets will function when job quality is uncertain. His analysis of dynamic worker choice is of particular importance. However, besides his observations on the need for and the effects of the provision of information, his analysis is not directly relevant to policy since he does not investigate the effects of information problems on the provision of safety.

One author who has analyzed the effects of policy in the presence of imperfect information is Samuel Rea. As Diamond (1979) and Oi (1973, p. 68) pointed out before him, if workers underestimate the probability of injury they will prefer too little insurance. Rea finds that if workers or firms may vary the effort they put into preventing accidents, then requiring firms to provide more insurance than they provide in competitive equilibrium may lead workers and firms to put less effort into safety precautions. This lowered safety level may or may not offset the gain in utility from the increased insurance, so that workers may be worse off as a result of the increase. He showed that mandatory safety standards may lead to a reduction in insurance and that also may make workers worse off.

Rea's work suggests the importance of examining the impact of different policies when workers' information is imperfect. We cannot simply assume that regulation will compensate for market failures. However, his research is only a beginning. Rea assumes all firms face the same costs for providing safety and that all workers have the same tastes and incorrect estimate of the safety of their job. He assumes that workers' perceptions of the safety of their jobs are a function only of their protective efforts and those of their employers. This assumption is not motivated by any description of how workers form their expectations. Analysis which allows for a richer description of the nature of labor markets and the way workers form their expectations about job safety can produce different results, as the work presented in the third section shows.

Thus the implications of even the most often cited failure of the assumptions of the perfect competition model have not been analyzed thoroughly — or at least not in the literature on OSH. Various types of information failures have been investigated in the literature on product quality and product price. Although a review of the product quality literature is beyond the scope of this paper, it is clear that our thinking about the appropriateness of different types of OSH regulation would be aided by a reading of this literature with an eye toward which models are most relevant for the problem of labor markets with uncertain job quality. The analysis presented in the third section draws on some of this literature.

Beyond a review of the product quality literature, what sort of analysis is needed? First, since workers are certainly aware that jobs may be dangerous, they must consider this when deciding to take or switch jobs. A worker has many possible sources of information about a job. What is necessary is a better understanding of how workers use (or do not use) information in forming expectations of job safety. What are the likely characteristics of workers' beliefs? Under what circumstances would we expect workers to be uncertain about job quality? If they are uncertain, will their best estimates be unbiased? Will there be differences among workers in their estimates of the safety of jobs? Once the process by which workers form their expectations is understood, the next questions are how will employers behave and what market outcomes will result? Next, it would be important to identify the effects of different types of policies. Finally, if the effects of policies depend on assumptions about the nature of information or how workers use the information, it would be important to be able to test those key assumptions.

External Economies

Three sources of external economies have been considered in the literature. The first is that workers may take toxic chemicals with them on their clothes or bodies, when they leave the workplace and then expose others to those hazards. It generally seems to be agreed that this is not likely to be an important consideration (Zeckhauser and Nichol, 1978, p. 180). This is because those most likely to be affected are family members. For the purpose of work decisions, it seems appropriate to treat the family as the decision unit, so that the costs of bringing dangerous chemicals home would not be viewed as external.

The second source is that more accident-prone workers or workers who care less about their personal safety may choose dangerous jobs and endanger their coworkers. This also seems unlikely to be an important consideration since coworkers are likely to be friends. If they are, the costs of carelessness are to some degree internalized. Even if coworkers are not friends, the social sanctions and employer sanctions for carelessness are likely to be sufficient to minimize this problem.

The third source is insurance when premiums are not adjusted to reflect the risks involved in each case. If a worker's health and/or life insurance is not adjusted to take into account the conditions of the plant in which he or she works, or if the workers' compensation carried by firms is not adjusted on a plant-by-plant basis, then there will be less of an incentive for firms to provide safety and for workers to seek safe jobs. This argument has been suggested by Smith (1976, p. 29), Oi (1973, p. 68), and Zeckhauser and Nichol (1978, p. 181). Viscusi (1979c) discusses the problem in a dynamic context. Zeckhauser and Nichol argue that this externality is the strongest rationale for OSH regulation.

The need for intervention in the presence of this type of problem is clear. What is less clear is the degree of distortion actually created by the lack of complete differentiation in insurance policies. Three considerations argue against it being very important. First, most workers' compensation is now experience rated.[24]

Second, Coase (1960) has pointed out, externalities can only exist in the presence of transaction costs. In this case, the relevant costs are those of experience rating firms' workmens' compensation and individuals' health insurance. While such costs are not trivial, they are far from overwhelming. Currently many life insurance policies are adjusted for a host of health and life-style factors. If the incentives provided by the failure to differentiate insurance policies were strong enough to create large behavioral changes then there would also be strong incentives for insurance companies to engage in more examination and differentiation.

Third, the insurance payments involved are small and generally do not even cover all the pecuniary costs of an accident or replace the earnings of a dead head of household. It seems reasonable to believe that the nonpecuniary costs in these cases far outweigh the pecuniary costs so that the effect of the lack of incentives is likely to be marginal at best. The two empirical studies that have been done on experience rating found no evidence of any effect (Chelius and Smith, 1981 and Russell, 1974).

Rationality

The existing literature considers two deviations from rationality. The first is mentioned by Zeckhauser and Nichol (1978, p. 178). It has been shown in laboratory settings (Tversky and Kahneman, 1974) that people behave as if they systematically underestimate true probabilities when the probabilities are very small. This observation has been suggested as an explanation for why people fail to purchase actuarially advantageous insurance (Kunreuther, 1976; Kunreuther and Slovic, 1978). Since the risks most people face in their jobs involve very low probability events, they may make faulty employment decisions. The result could be an underprovision of safety if workers do not respond to small decreases in the probability of death or serious injury.[25]

The second deviation from rationality that has been explored in the literature is cognitive dissonance (Akerlof and Dickens, 1982). The argument here is that workers do not want to believe that their jobs are dangerous. This is because if they do they will feel anxious about the danger.

They may also feel that it reflects badly on them as a person — that they were stupid/desperate/careless to take such a job. As a result, workers will have a tendency to change their beliefs about their job so that they will underestimate its true danger. This may lead them to make incorrect decisions in the future, such as failing to take adequate safety precautions or failing to change jobs if a better alternative becomes available.

Where does this leave the policy-maker? With respect to the tendency for people to underestimate the importance of low probability events, the major questions are: First, what is the extent of these low probability hazards and second, what is the practical importance of them being underestimated? Finally, is the laboratory evidence, where the outcomes that people are evaluating are hypothetical or trivial, extendible to real-life situations where people have considerably more at stake? Two economists, Grether and Plott (1979), have attempted to examine this last question and conclude that the evidence probably can be taken as indicative of how people will behave outside the laboratory. Kunreuther (1976) and Kunreuther and Slovic (1978) discuss a number of real life situations where they believe people make irrational decisions about buying insurance because they behave as if they believed that certain low probability events were less likely than they were in actuality. It therefore seems that (1) the supposition should be that the behavior does extend beyond the laboratory and (2) its relevance to policy depends on the first two questions.

The economic model of cognitive dissonance behavior specified by Akerlof and Dickens is highly stylized. For instance, it is assumed that workers can choose to have or not to have a cognitive dissonance reaction. In reality the process is almost certainly unconscious. The authors have developed a typescript to accompany the paper where market outcomes for a wide range of other possible specifications of the nature of the cognitive dissonance phenomena are worked out. However, this taxonomical approach also leaves something to be desired — policy-makers would like to know which specification to choose. It is also not clear how important it is to the functioning of labor markets that workers have correct perceptions of the danger of their current job after they have chosen it. If the marginal worker really does determine the level of safety for all the other workers, and the marginal worker is a new worker, cognitive dissonance may not be important.

There are many types of irrationality that have been documented by psychologists that have not been considered by economists interested in OSH regulation. No consideration has been given to the wide variety of pathological self-destructive behavior which has been documented. However, it is not clear that it is the proper role for OSH regulation to protect people from themselves. There are also many other normal deviations from rationality that have been discovered in the process of research on decision making.[26] Some of these observations might be integrated fruitfully with more complete models of how markets will behave in the face of imperfect information about job risks.

The first thing that should be clear from the above presentation is that, despite the work that has been done, we know very little about the policy implications of the possible deviations from the pure competition model. The question is how we should proceed to investigate them.

The first assumption discussed was that markets were characterized by competition. A number of situations in which this is not the case were examined. Of these, the existence of noncompeting groups are not important to OSH regulation and too few workers are affected by minimum wages for this to be an important consideration. The discussion of monopsony labor markets suggests two questions which need to be answered. The first is the empirical question of the significance of monopsony and of the marginal worker arguments. Do more transient workers' tastes determine all workers' conditions and, if they do, are they substantially different from the tastes of other workers? The second is the theoretical question of the effect of different types of OSH policy. It would also be useful to consider the implications of disequilibrium for the effects of OSH policy. The role of government regulation in the presence of other distortions certainly needs to be considered. Finally, further work on the effects of unions would be useful. Current work which assumes surplus maximization models of union behavior should be extended to consider other types of union behavior and bargaining.

Despite the widespread belief that imperfect information is the best justification for OSH regulation, very little work has been done on the implications of different types of information problems for market performance and particularly for the impact of regulation. Although Viscusi's work provides some insight into how workers and firms will behave in certain situations, work in this area essentially must start from scratch. What is the nature of the information problems workers and firms face? Theoretical work which evaluates the implications for a variety of different possibilities can pinpoint important empirical questions and suggest methods for testing them.

Unlike the other assumptions, the implications for the existence of external economies is well understood. However, it seems unlikely that external economies are very important. If they are, that fact needs to be established by empirical work.

Finally, the violation of the rationality assumption poses two questions: the empirical question of the importance of the departures from rationality that have been identified and investigated, and the theoretical question of what the implications are of other departures that have been discovered by psychological decision-theory researchers but have not been considered by economists working on the problem of OSH regulation. Since all these departures can be characterized as problems with information processing, it seems that the best way to proceed may be to integrate the psychological observations into more general models of labor markets where workers are uncertain about the safety of jobs.

Of this list of needed work, what should have the highest priority? Since it is agreed widely that information problems are a major justification for regulation, and since so little is known about the implications of imperfect information, work in this area is an obvious priority. Beyond imperfect information, there seems to be a growing consensus in the profession that most labor markets are characterized by some degree of monopsony power. The classic case of the company town may not be very important for the labor market as a whole but transportation and workers' search costs may be. In addition, some of the worst cases of dangerous jobs are found in labor markets dominated by one employer.[27] Thus it would be useful to consider the effect of OSH regulation in such cases.

Only 23 percent of the labor force is covered by unions. However, nearly 40 percent of blue-collar workers are union workers,[28] and it is widely believed that many nonunion employers are affected by union contracts in their industry in setting wages and working conditions. Thus it would seem to be very important to know how unions will behave and what will be the effects of OSH regulation on bargaining.

Finally, even though there is no professional consensus on the existence of disequilibrium in labor markets, it would at least be interesting to know what the effects of different types of regulation would be under such conditions.

The next section of this paper begins the work of answering some of these questions. A framework for the analysis of information problems is suggested, and some important special cases are examined. An investigation of the effects of OSH regulation in the presence of monopsony, or a monopoly union, also is undertaken.

New Theory

Monopsony and Monopoly Unions

Let us consider the case where, in the absence of OSH regulation, the firm chooses the level of safety (s^*) and demands (L^*) labor to maximize profit and then pays the wage that is necessary to attract L^* labor. Spence (1975) has examined the behavior of a monopolist who sets price and quality. He found that the optimal policy necessarily involved regulating both quality and price. He also showed that if the regulator lacked the necessary information to pick optimal price-quality pairs, rate of return regulation could dominate a laissez-faire policy. These results would both be applicable in this case. What Spence does not show is the effect of regulating quality alone. To determine the effects of setting s* to a level other than the one that would be chosen by the monopsonist, we will assume a social welfare function of the form

$$W = R + E = R(\pi) + \int_0^{L^*} U(w,s) - a(i)\, di \qquad (5.1)$$

where R is the monopsonist's utility times an arbitrary weight.[29] R is monotonically increasing function of π, which is the monopsonist's profit. E is the employee's surplus, which is defined as the difference between the utility the workers receive from working for the monopsonist — U(w,s,i), which is a function of the wage (w), and the level of safety (s), and is identical for all workers — and the utility a worker would receive from his or her best alternative — a(i). Workers are ordered from 0 up according to their a(i)'s so that $a' > 0$. We are also assuming that there are enough workers that changes in labor supply and demand can be treated as being continuous.

Marginally increasing s above s* will improve welfare if $dW/ds > 0$. Since the firm has chosen s* and L^* to maximize profits $d\pi/ds = dR/ds = 0$. So

$$\frac{dW}{ds} = \frac{dE}{ds} = \frac{dL}{ds}\left[U(w,s) - a(L^*)\right] + \int_0^{L^*} \frac{dw}{ds} U_W + U_S\, di \qquad (5.2)$$

The wage w equals r(L,s) where r is defined implicitly by the equation

$$U(r(L,s),s) - a(L) = 0 \qquad (5.3)$$

Thus the first term in brackets in equation 5.2 is equal to zero, so the equation can be rewritten as

$$\frac{dW}{ds} = \int_0^{L^*} \left.\frac{a'}{U_W}\right|_{L^*} \frac{dL}{ds} U_W - \left.\frac{U_S}{U_W}\right|_{L^*} U_W + U_S\, di \qquad (5.4)$$

which will have the same sign as

$$\frac{\int_0^{L^*} U_S\, di}{\int_0^{L^*} U_W\, di} - \left.\frac{U_S}{U_W}\right|_{L^*} + \left.\frac{a'}{U_W}\right|_{L^*} \frac{dL}{ds} \qquad (5.5)$$

If the marginal rates of substitution of safety for money in utility (MRS) are approximately equal across all individuals, then the first two terms will cancel. Past authors have argued that the MRS of the marginal worker should be smaller than the MRS of other workers. If this is the case, then the difference between the first two terms should be positive. However, as was pointed out in the second section,[30] if there are large differences then there are incentives for both employers and workers to strike deals allowing workers to have different safety levels and different wage rates. This type of market segmentation should cause the MRSs of all workers receiving the same wage to equalize. The sign of dW/ds will therefore depend on the last term. Since a′ and U_w are both positive, the sign of the last term will depend on the sign of dL/ds. From the implicit function rule and the first order conditions for maximization

$$\frac{dL}{ds} = \frac{\partial^2 \pi}{\partial L \partial s} \Big/ \frac{-\partial^2 \pi}{\partial L \partial L} \tag{5.6}$$

Second-order conditions for profit maximization require that the denominator be positive so the sign of dL/ds will depend on the sign of the cross-partial of profits with respect to L and s. Taking a profit function of the general form

$$\pi = R(L,s) - wL \tag{5.7}$$

where R is revenue net of nonlabor input costs, we get

$$\frac{\partial^2 \pi}{\partial L \partial s} = \left[\frac{\partial^2 R}{\partial L \partial s} - \frac{\partial w}{\partial s} \right] - \frac{\partial^2 w}{\partial L \partial s} L \tag{5.8}$$

The term in brackets will be equal to zero if the marginal cost of safety per worker does not depend on scale and will be positive if it is decreasing with scale and negative if it is increasing. Applying the implicit function rule to equation 5.3 yields

$$U_W \frac{\partial w}{\partial s} + U_S = 0$$

or (5.9)

$$\frac{\partial w}{\partial s} + MRS = 0$$

Applying it again yields

$$\frac{\partial^2 w}{\partial s \partial L} = - \frac{\partial w}{\partial L} \frac{\partial MRS}{\partial w} \tag{5.10}$$

The first term, $\partial w/\partial L$, will be positive and $\partial MRS/\partial w$ will be negative; thus $\partial^2 w/\partial s \partial L$ will be positive. So if the MRS of the marginal worker is either equal to or less than that of other workers and the marginal cost of safety per worker is either decreasing or constant with respect to scale, then minimum safety standards may be welfare-improving even if monopsonists choose the optimal amount of safety for the level of employment they choose. If marginal costs are increasing with scale or if the marginal worker values safety more than other workers, the effect will be indeterminate.

The analysis basically is the same for a surplus maximizing union which faces a market of competitive employers. If we define S(s,i) as the producer surplus net of nonlabor costs created by the ith job — where jobs are ordered for each level of s from those producing the most surplus to those producing the least — and we assume that there is a sufficiently large number of jobs that they can be treated as being continuous, then

$$\pi = \int_0^{L^*} S(s,i) - w \, di \tag{5.11}$$

Since $w = S(s,L^*)$

$$\frac{d\pi}{ds} = \int_0^{L^*} S_s di - S_S(s,L^*)L^* - S_L(s,L^*) \frac{dL}{ds} L^* \tag{5.12}$$

S_s should be approximately equal for all jobs. If it is not, there are incentives for both the union and the employers to segment the market to allow wages and safety levels to be different on different jobs. If they are equal across jobs, the first two terms cancel and the sign of dW/ds will depend on the last term. S_L will be negative so the sign of dW/ds will be the same as dL/ds. Using the implicit function rule and the first- and second-order conditions for the maximization of E, it can be seen that the sign of dL/ds will be the same as $\partial^2 E/\partial L \partial s$. That will equal U_s which is positive, so in this case dW/ds unambiguously is positive.

Imperfect Information

Rea (1981) identifies three types of imperfect information which could complicate the analysis of OSH regulation:[31] (1) employees may be incorrect in their estimates of occupational risk and their influence on the level of risk; (2) it may be difficult for an employer to monitor the precautions taken by employees or to identify accident-prone workers; (3) insurance carriers may not be able to monitor precautions or correctly assess outcomes. In the second section, it was argued that the lack of "experience rating" of insurance does not contribute significantly to OSH problems. Thus the third type of imperfect information will not be considered. The source that figures most prominently in discussions of OSH is the first. The analysis which follows will be concerned primarily with the first problem.

As was noted earlier, it seems reasonable to believe that most workers at least recognize the possibility that some jobs may be more dangerous to their health than other jobs. In this case, the question is what information is available about job safety and how do people use that information to determine the safety of a particular job.

People trying to assess the safety of a job can go about it in two ways. One source of information available to them would be observations of the experience of people who have that job. The observations could be direct if the person trying to make the assessment knows people who work in that job or if he or she works in it. Alternatively, it could be indirect with the person hearing stories from others about the experience of people in that job. The individual may not use only information on the particular job in question but also on other similar jobs.

The second way people might try to assess the safety of a job would be to try to gain knowledge about the conditions of work, such as whether or not they would be exposed to certain chemicals, what sorts of safety equipment the employer had installed, etc. Once again this knowledge could be gained firsthand or indirectly. The information could be about the job the individual is considering or about similar jobs. People using this approach must also have knowledge about how working conditions relate to outcomes — how dangerous are different chemicals, how effective is a certain type of safety equipment. The two methods are obviously not mutually exclusive.

Ideally we would like a model of market behavior in which workers made use of both types of information. This must be left for future work. What follows is an analysis of static markets where workers make once-and-for-all decisions about where they are going to be employed. Each worker has a unique original endowment of information. Additional information is either unavailable or considered by the worker to be too expensive.

Two models will be presented. In the first, workers are certain about all aspects of job quality but uncertain about the danger associated with a particular hazardous substance or condition to which they know they are exposed. In the second, model workers have prior beliefs about the safety of employment at each of many employers but do not know job conditions exactly. The two models yield different results on some questions. The differences can be attributed to the assumptions about the structure of the informational imperfections.

Imperfect Information About a Known Hazard

Let us begin by examining a market for jobs which expose workers to a known level of some hazard. Workers maximize expected utility subject to available information, and will take a job if the expected utility of the best job available to them, given their information, is greater than zero (utility is being measured with respect to some best alternative). A worker's expected utility can be expressed as

$$EU_i = \int_{\Theta} (U_i(w_j,\theta)) P(\theta \mid e_j,\epsilon_i)\, d\theta \qquad (5.13)$$

where w_j is the wage people with job j are paid, U_i is the utility of that wage in state of health θ. P is the individual's subjective density function for states of health given the known exposure level of job j (e_j) and individual i's unique information (ϵ_i). Expected utility is obtained by integrating over the set of all possible states of health Θ. If a person knows the true probability of all states of health with certainty we will say that $\epsilon_i = 0$. We will also assume that $\partial EU_i/\partial\epsilon_i > 0$.

Demand for labor will come from firms facing an infinitely elastic demand for their product. The firms will act to minimize costs. We will assume completely free entry so that profits must equal zero. Nonlabor costs are the same for all firms and increase as the level of exposure is decreased. It is assumed that the amount of that increase will be independent of the exposure levels of other workers and the scale of production. Thus a worker's wage will be

$$w_j = W(e_j) = (p - c(e_j))F_L \quad W' > 0 > c' \qquad (5.14)$$

where p is the price of the good produced by the firm, $c(e_j)$ is the cost of nonlabor inputs per unit of output as a function of the worker's exposure level, and F_L is the marginal physical product of labor. If a firm were to pay a higher wage for a job with this exposure level it would be earning negative profits and would go out of business. If a firm paid a lower wage for a job with this exposure level, another firm could enter, hire the worker at a higher wage, and still earn positive profits. Finally, we will assume that there is no market for insurance and that workers can do nothing beyond choosing a safe job to limit exposure.[32]

Given these assumptions what will market equilibrium look like? First, all jobs with an exposure level e must pay a wage W(e). Given this constraint, workers will choose jobs which maximize their utility. If workers have different tastes or different endowments of information, they will most likely choose different jobs.

What are the welfare characteristics of such an equilibrium? First, someone who knows the true probability of all states of nature will choose an optimal level of safety and wages. For this person, the conditions of the purely competitive model will be met. However, someone who has an incorrect estimate of the probabilities of different states given different exposure levels will not necessarily choose the same job and such a person will be worse off than they would be if they knew the true probabilities. Note that this result does not depend on the distribution of information between people. Even if all workers were in some sense correct, on the average, workers with incorrect estimates of the dangers would still be worse off if they choose jobs which were different from the jobs they would have chosen if they had correct information. This state could persist as long as an individual continued to believe that his or her job was more or less safe than it was truly. Given that exposure to hazardous substances may have effects over very extended periods of time and the difficulty of attributing resulting illness to a specific cause, learning may be very difficult, if not impossible.

Is there any way that policy intervention can improve the lives of workers? Let us consider a number of possible actions a regulatory agency might take. We begin by considering exposure standards. It is possible that a policy-making body could have better information than some people in the market. It might also be too costly to communicate this information so that the government may consider safety standards to be a better way of dealing with such a problem.

What will be the effects of a standard? First, let us consider the case where all workers have identical tastes and alternative employments. We will also assume for now that the government's role in setting the standard will not affect people's assessment of the danger of the substance. In this case we can identify a unique optimal level of exposure.

What will happen if we require all jobs to have this level of exposure or less? Assuming that the true expected utility of such a job is at least as great as people's best alternative, those who remain employed will clearly be as well off or better off. However, some workers may decide to stop working in this market. These workers will be made worse off. Workers with $\epsilon > 0$ will not quit. They must see the subjective expected utility of the optimal job as being higher than it really is. Since it has been assumed that the true expected utility in this job is higher than the best alternative these workers will not quit. However, if there are any workers with $\epsilon < 0$ who are employed in jobs that are more dangerous than the standard, they may quit. If they do they will be worse off since they underestimate the true expected utility of their current job but still see it as being higher than their best alternative. Therefore, true expected utility of their current job must be higher than their alternative job so they are made worse off by quitting. Thus for a Pareto superior standard to exist, all workers with jobs which are more dangerous than the standard must be willing to take a job at the standard. This is not a very satisfying result. Even with these very strong assumptions about the homogeneity of worker preferences, we still cannot say for certain that a Pareto superior standard will exist. As with Rea's results reported in the second section, because the source of the market imperfection is worker misperception, worker behavior in response to standard setting may make them worse off.

If we allow the goverment's setting of a standard to influence people's estimates of the danger, the question becomes what sort of effect would it be likely to have. A good first guess would be that it would cause people's estimates to move closer to those of the government. In particular, those who think their job is more dangerous than it is actually may see the government's setting an exposure standard at a particular level as a signal that that level of exposure is relatively safe. If they did, they would be less likely to quit. However, it is also possible that they might suspect the government for setting the standard too low, in which case their behavior would be unchanged.

When workers' underlying preferences are different, the result only becomes more ambiguous. In this case, a Pareto superior standard will almost certainly not exist unless the distribution of workers over different types of jobs has very little to do with differences in tastes and almost entirely to do with differences in information. If all the workers in the most hazardous jobs are there because they believe the job to be safer than it is, then a standard will make them better off. If workers are aware that tastes vary, they will also be less likely to change their assessments of the danger of exposure when a standard is set, since they may attribute the government's choice to a difference in tastes and not in perceptions of the danger.

If we allow side payments so that those who benefit from the imposition of a standard can compensate the losers, then what are the conditions for Pareto dominance? This will obviously depend on the distribution of workers with different tastes and information and on the structure of costs in the market. In the case where all workers have the same tastes, it seems unlikely that there would be many workers who would overestimate the danger of a hazard but would choose a suboptimal amount of protection. These workers are saying, "This stuff is so dangerous that nothing practical provides me with any protection. I'm willing to work here under current conditions, but if they make me pay for nearly useless protection, I would rather work somewhere else." Such workers, if they exist at all, are probably considerably outnumbered by workers who underestimate the danger of the hazards with which they work. If this is the case, a standard with side payments which Pareto dominates the competitive outcome is very likely to exist. If workers' tastes differ, the important consideration would be whether the distribution of workers over jobs was due more to the differences in tastes or to differences in information. If it is the former, then a Pareto superior standard, even with side payments, is unlikely to exist.

If we now allow workers to purchase insurance, or if exposure depends on the protective actions of workers, then Rea's findings would be relevant. In addition to the ambiguities examined above, there would be the possibility that workers might change the amount of insurance they purchase or the safety precautions they take at work in response to standards. If they do, they could make themselves worse off. The first of these problems may not be of practical importance. If workers already see themselves as being safe in their current job, they would probably view the additional standards as making little or no difference in their safety and would not change their insurance pattern. The second problem may be of greater practical importance as workers may see exposure standards as mitigating the need for care on their part. Thus it would be important to design protection standards that are difficult for workers to circumvent.

The above analysis provides further evidence that the existence of imperfect information alone is not enough of a justification for standard setting. In addition, we must know that worker behavior will not undermine the effort and that less safe jobs exist primarily because of misinformation and not because of differences in workers' preferences and costs.

If the effect of standards is ambiguous, are there any other possible remedies which might be better? Three others will be considered: provision of information, an outcome or exposure tax, and liability.

If workers choose jobs which expose them to some dangerous substance because they believe that the substance is less dangerous than it really is, will giving them more information about the danger make them better off? Once again, the answer is frustratingly ambiguous. Consider the case where the government has commissioned a study of the health effects of a particular hazardous substance. The people doing the study are able to establish the shape of the dose-response function[33] with a great deal of accuracy and the government is going to disseminate the results. Clearly, if everyone believed the government study and changed their subjective assessments of the danger to conform to those found in the study then everyone would be at least as well off as they were before receiving the information. Anyone who changed jobs would be better off. However, we would not necessarily expect everyone to adjust their subjective assessments to conform exactly to the study. Depending on how the government disseminates the results of the study, not everyone will be directly exposed to the results. Many people may hear about it secondhand and discount the information accordingly. Even people who are directly exposed to the results may not know how to interpret them or may not understand the methodology. As such, they may not completely accept the findings. People with assessments of the danger that are very wrong may react to the information more by adjusting their assessment of the credibility of the source than by changing their assessment of the danger.[34] Finally, employers who use the dangerous substance or firms that manufacture it may attempt to confuse the issue by disseminating misleading information. Time and money could overcome these problems but the cost might be prohibitive. Thus it seems possible that, in many cases, the best the government would be able to do would be to obtain a partial improvement in people's information. Unfortunately, if the improvement is only partial, we cannot be certain that the effect will be to improve all individuals' welfare.

Consider a worker whose expected utility can be represented as

$$EU = \alpha w - P(e) \tag{5.15}$$

where w is the worker's wage, α is the marginal utility of income, and P(e) is the probability of contracting some disease given the exposure level e in the worker's job to some hazardous substance. The worker is self-employed and receives a payment of p for each unit produced and can produce one unit per period. Production necessarily involves some exposure to the hazardous substance. Exposure can be reduced to a level e_0 with no cost. To reduce exposure any more than that requires an expenditure of one dollar to lower exposure by one unit. The heavy line in the upper part of figure 5-1 shows the probability of not contracting the disease as a function of exposure. The dashed line is the utility cost from lost income of reducing exposure to a given level. The heavy line in the bottom part of the figure shows the worker's true expected utility for each exposure level — that is, the worker's expected utility evaluated using the true probabilities. The complication is that the worker does not know the true probabilities.

Let us assume that before the government publishes its report the worker believes the true probabilities to be those depicted by the curve labeled subjective probabilities before information (P_B^s). The worker's corresponding subjective expected utility is shown in the bottom of the figure (EU_B^s). If the worker is an expected utility maximizer, he will choose a job with an exposure level of e_1. Now the government releases its report, and the worker reacts by changing his or her assessment of the probabilities to those depicted by the curve labeled subjective probabilities after information (P_R^s). Even though the worker's assessments of the probabilities of contracting the disease are now closer to the true probabilities, the worker will choose a job with exposure level e_2 and will be worse off from the standpoint of true

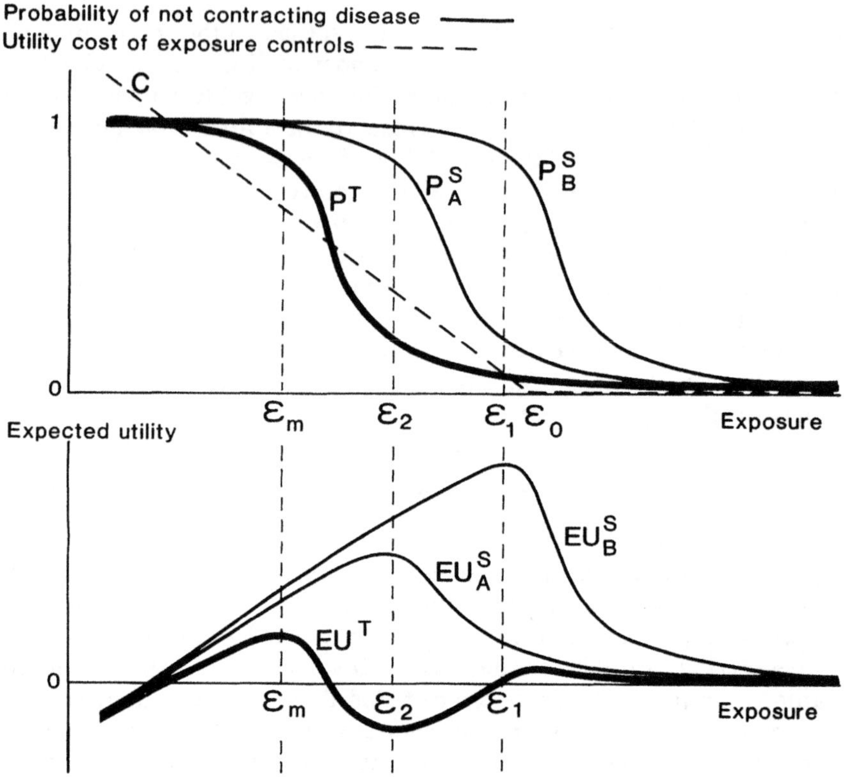

C : Utility cost of exposure control expenditures

P^T: True probability of not contracting disease

P^S_A: Subjective probability of not contracting disease after information

P^S_B: Subjective probability of not contracting disease before information

EU: Expected utility

Figure 5-1. Workers' Expected Utility with Varying Risks of Contracting a Disease after Exposure

expected utility. The worker would recognize this if his or her subjective assessment of the hazard of exposure conformed to the truth, but because it does not, the worker will be worse off. Thus, giving workers more information may make them worse off.

How likely is such an outcome? The result obtains because of the possibility of nonconvexities in expected utility as a function of exposure. Assuming that the utility function is well-behaved, nonconvexities could result from either the technology of exposure controls or, as in this case, from the dose-response relationship. Nonconvexities in the dose-response relationship are likely to exist for most carcinogens and toxic substances. Very high doses produce the undesirable outcome with near certainty. In some intermediate range, decreasing the dosage rapidly decreases the probability of the outcome. Such relationships are modeled by biologists and epidemiologists as logistic, cumulative normal, or piece-wise linear functions. The nonconvexities exist in a range where the probability of the undesirable outcome is very high. Any decreasing marginal costs of exposure control are also most likely at high levels of exposure. Since it is unlikely that misperception could persist for long with many people contracting the disease, information is unlikely to make people worse off unless the hazard is new and there is a long delay between the exposure to the substance and the onset of the symptoms of the disease.

Injury taxes, which have been proposed as an alternative to standard setting, allow firms flexibility in their determination of the level of job safety to provide while also creating additional incentive for the provision of safety. It has been pointed out that such an approach would not be practical for occupational health (Smith, 1976) where the cause of illness is hard to identify and when the time lag between exposure to a dangerous substance and the onset of symptoms may be as long as twenty years. However, the tax alternative is still available in this case if, instead of taxing outcomes, the government taxes exposure levels. Such an approach, if administrable, would probably be preferable if the market was like the one described above. At least this way some discrimination would be possible on behalf of those with very strong preferences for money income over safety. If employers have different costs of providing safety, then a tax system would allow flexibility for those with extremely high costs of controlling exposure.

Finally, let us consider the possibility of making employers liable for the full amount of the damage done to an individual by an occupational hazard. Under the current workmen's compensation laws, the liability for occupational injury or disease is limited to fixed amounts which do not compensate the individual for all losses. If the limits on liability were eliminated and workers were allowed to sue their employers when they suffered occupational injuries or diseases, what would be the consequence? If it were costless for workers to pursue such a remedy, if the legal system could determine with complete certainty whether or not an injury or disease was caused by the conditions of employment, and if all the individual's costs could be assessed, then even if all workers were totally unaware of the danger posed by workplace hazards, the entire cost of those dangers would be shifted to employers. If the employers had better information about the hazards than the employees, or if their insurance companies had or could obtain better information, then the results in such a market could approach those of a market with perfect information.

However, litigation is not costless, and courts are far from being perfect in their ability to determine cause and judge costs. Ordover (1978) has examined markets where consumers have recourse to costly litigation and Simon (1981) has examined the case where litigation is costly and the outcome is not known with certainty. The characteristics of such markets, if they can be predicted, are less desirable than those in which information is perfect. Both Ordover and Simon find that if litigation is costly the market will be inefficient. In addition, Simon finds that there may be market segmentation with undesirable distributional effects.

Thus none of these policies clearly dominates the others. To determine which would be most effective would require considerably more information, about the nature of the markets in which one intended to intervene than is currently available.

Imperfect Information about Outcomes

Let us now consider the second case of imperfect information. Here we will assume that workers know nothing about the actual working conditions of the firms they are considering for employment, but they do have a subjective assessment of the probability of undesirable outcomes for each workplace. As was noted earlier, these assessments may be formed using a wide range of information. However, if this information is not sufficient for the worker to identify the probability associated with each job precisely, and different workers are exposed to different information, then there will be a distribution of workers with different assessments of the danger of each job.

Take as an example the simplest case where workers form their expectations about each firm on the basis of the experience of people they know who have worked for the firm. If everyone knows a different set of people, and most people do not know more than a few others who work at each job, then each individual will have an assessment of the true probability for each job which is unbiased but will contain some sampling error. If we look at a large group of people and consider their assessments of the probabilities for all jobs, they will have a multivariate binomial distribution where the expected mean of the distribution will be the true probabilities and the variance will depend on the number of people each person knows.

To analyze this sort of market, let us assume that it is made up of N profit maximizing firms. Each firm faces a total revenue function $R_i(L)$, which is a function of the amount of labor it employs. The firm sets the wage and the level of safety in the jobs it provides. The cost per worker for firm i of providing safety level s is $c_i(s)$.[35]

Workers maximize subjective expected utility $EU(w_i, s_i, \epsilon_i)$, which is increasing in wages (w_i — wage for job i), safety (s_i — the true safety of job i), and the error of estimate in the person's assessment of the safety of the job (ϵ_i). If workers differ only in their assessments of job safety and choose the job which offers them the highest expected utility, given their assessments of each job's safety,[36] then the supply of labor to firm 1 can be described by the following equation

$$L_1^s = L \cdot P(EU_1 > EU_j \forall j, j \neq 1) = \int_{-\infty}^{\infty} \int_{-\infty}^{\epsilon_2^*} \cdots \int_{-\infty}^{\epsilon_N^*} \vec{f}(\vec{e}) d\vec{e} \quad (5.17)$$

where L is the total number of workers, N is the number of firms, $\vec{f}(e)$ is the density function of workers' errors, and ϵ_i^* is defined implicitly by the following equation

$$EU(w_1, s_1, \epsilon_1) = EU(w_i, s_i, \epsilon_i^*) \quad (5.18)$$

Note first of all that no matter how large the number of firms, the supply of labor to the firm will depend on the wage and safety conditions it offers.[37] This type of informational imperfection gives rise to monopsony power as has been noted by Perloff and Salop (1980). Thus market outcomes will be inefficient even if firms do provide the correct amount of safety.

The next thing to note is that the workers who do choose to work in a particular firm will be those who have the more favorable assessments of the firm's safety. If there are only a few workers at each firm, the expectations of each worker are unbiased, and the error in their assessments of all firms are not highly correlated, then we might expect that those who do take work with an employer will believe their jobs to be safer than they are in reality.

What level of safety will firms provide? Perloff and Salop prove the existence of a Nash equilibrium when employers all have the same costs. In a Nash equilibrium, every firm has maximized its profits subject to the decisions of the other firms.[38] If its profit function is

$$\pi = R(L^s) - L^s w - c(s)L^s \quad (5.19)$$

then the first-order conditions for profit maximization are

$$\frac{\partial \pi}{\partial w} = (R' - w - c)\frac{\partial L^s}{\partial w} - L^s = 0 \quad (5.20)$$

$$\frac{\partial \pi}{\partial s} = (R' - w - c)\frac{\partial L^s}{\partial s} - L^s c' = 0 \quad (5.21)$$

Thus companies will choose s so that

$$c' = \frac{\partial L^s}{\partial s} \Big/ \frac{\partial L^s}{\partial w} \tag{5.22}$$

For social welfare to be maximized companies should choose s so that

$$c' = \frac{\partial EU}{\partial s} \Big/ \frac{\partial EU}{\partial w} \tag{5.23}$$

Under what conditions will the R.H.S.'s of equations 5.22 and 5.23 be equal so that the optimal combination of safety and wages will be chosen by the firm? The only time we can count on it is when expected utility is a linear function of safety, when all workers have the same marginal utility of safety, and when expectations about safety are unbiased estimates of the true safety. If each worker's utility can be described as

$$U = f(w) + \alpha S \tag{5.24}$$

where S is perceived safety or $s + \epsilon$, then

$$\epsilon_i^* = [f(w_1) - f(w_i)]/\alpha + s_1 + \epsilon_1 - s_i \tag{5.25}$$

By substituting equation 5.25 into 5.17, differentiating with respect to s_1 and w_1 and then substituting the result into equation 5.22, we will find that the profit maximizing firm sets $c'(s) = \alpha/f'(w_1)$ which is exactly equal to $(\partial EU/\partial s)/(\partial EU/\partial w)$. Thus in this case, even though information imperfections give firms monopsony power and even though the workers in any given firm believe the firm to be safer than it actually is, firms will still provide the optimal level of safety.[39] This is possible because workers' assessments of the absolute safety of their job does not matter for the firm. What matters is that the market respond correctly to marginal changes in that level of safety. This will happen under these special conditions.

Is it realistic to expect that normally this will be the case? Probably not. There are a number of reasons to believe that the conditions described above will not hold. First, if workers' utility functions are not linear in safety, then safety may be either over- or underprovided. One such case which seems particularly likely is that increasing safety beyond a certain level will have diminishing effects on utility. In this case, if the marginal worker in a job overestimates its safety, then safety will be underprovided. Arguments made above suggest that marginal workers will overestimate job safety.

Second, if workers use more information than just their own and others' experience — for example, if they look at other firms in the same industry or area — then their assessment of any one firm's safety will be biased towards the mean of the group in which the firm is being considered. In particular, changes in the level of safety provided by any one firm will not be completely reflected in workers' assessments of the safety of that firm. Such a change will also improve workers' assessments of similar firms so its effect on demand will be further muted. In this case, firms will underprovide safety.

What would be the impact of safety standards in this sort of world? Consider the first case above where each firm chooses the level of safety that optimized welfare. Forcing some or all firms to increase the level of safety offered may cause a loss or gain in welfare if it has no effect on the monopsony power of the firm. This was shown in the first part of the third section. However, in this case the monopsony power arises because workers have different assessments of the actual safety of each job. If a uniform standard is set and is enforced well, and if workers knew this, they would expect all firms to have the same level of safety. If this happened, firms' monopsony power would be eliminated and welfare could be improved. If safety is being underprovided, then the standard would also improve welfare by increasing the amount provided. If cost-benefit analysis is used to determine the level of safety to be required by a standard, regulators should take into account both the individual gains from the increased safety and the gain in market efficiency from the reduction in monopsony power in computing the benefits. Currently, only the first is considered.

What about other policies? Outcome or exposure taxes could induce firms to provide more safety, and that could be beneficial if safety was being underprovided. However, the purpose of a tax as opposed to a standard is to allow flexibility so that all firms need not provide the same level of safety. Thus, a tax system would not provide the benefit of eliminating the monopsony power of firms.

A policy of providing workers with information could be effective in eliminating this problem entirely if a way could be found to gather and communicate the necessary information effectively. This would be a difficult task, to say the least. First, some way of correctly assessing the dangers in each workplace would have to be determined and then some way of conveying that information would have to be indentified. Such a task would probably be impossible. However, any information which decreased the dispersion of people's prior beliefs about the safety of firms also would lower the monopsony power of the firms and would, therefore, improve welfare. Publishing accident rates in local papers and/or requiring firms to inform workers of their health and safety records when they applied for jobs could improve this situation.

Finally, if firms could be held liable for occupational injuries and diseases beyond the current fixed limits and if the court system functioned perfectly and costlessly, then the firms would lose their monopsony power (as workers would no longer care about the safety of their jobs) and firms would have an incentive to provide the optimal level of safety. However, as we noted earlier, there are reasons to doubt that this remedy would be preferable when we consider that the court system is not perfectly capable of assessing causes and values and is far from costless.

Conclusion

The major point of this paper has been to show that in the absence of the assumptions of pure competition, we do not know much about how labor markets will behave with respect to OSH. A second purpose has been to evaluate the assumptions and to suggest directions for further research on this topic. Four significant assumptions were considered.

The first was that labor markets are competitive. Minimum wages and labor market segmentation were found to be unimportant considerations — minimum wages because so few workers are affected and labor market segmentation because it would affect the provision of OSH only through its effect on the distribution of income. That left monopsony, labor unions, regulation and disequilibrium to be considered. Several authors have examined the effect of monopsony on the provision of OSH. What has not been considered is the effect of different policies in the presence of monopsony. Viscusi's work on labor unions is important, but much more could be done here if different assumptions are made about union behavior. In general, little has been done on the effects of regulation when other imperfections are present. Finally, the effects of policy in the presence of sticky wages have not been considered.

With respect to the other assumptions, very little has been done on the effects of OSH regulation when workers have imperfect information about job safety besides Rea's work. More analysis is needed here and the literature on imperfect information and product quality should be surveyed for relevant work.

The articles examined here suggest only one potentially significant external economy. If insurance premiums are not adjusted to reflect the safety of each firm or the danger of each worker's job, then there will be less incentive for a firm to provide safe working conditions. The analysis of this problem in the second section calls into question whether this problem could be of any practical importance.

Finally, two different types of irrational behavior have been examined in the literature. Beyond these two departures from rationality, the psychological literature on decision making should be reviewed for descriptions of other relevant behavior.

The work in the third section analyzed the effects of policy in the presence of monopsony or monopoly labor unions, and presented a framework for examining questions of imperfect information. In addition, some preliminary results were presented. It was shown that safety standards may improve welfare, even if a monopsonist chooses the "optimal" level of safety, by increasing the number of workers that are hired. It was also shown that imperfect information — even biased estimates of safety — need not lead to serious market failure, that giving workers more information about job hazards can make them worse off, and that uniform standards may be preferable to the more flexible injury taxes if they improve the information environment and thus reduce the monopsony power which may result from imperfect information. Additional circumstances were identified in which standards or taxes which lead employers to offer more safety could make workers worse off, even if they are employed in overly dangerous jobs. Finally, it was suggested that in setting standards, regulators must consider the effect of the standards on the efficiency of the market as a whole as well as the employment conditions of the affected workers. The problem of the second best invariably lurks in the background of this entire discussion.

What remains to be done? More work is needed to integrate the different approaches to imperfect information. In addition, the observations from the decision-theory literature on irrationality of behavior might also be fruitfully incorporated into a more elaborate model. The topic of how unions will affect the provision of OSH with and without regulation could be investigated. Finally, the role of regulation in markets with socially determined wages might also be pursued.

The most important goal of empirical research should be to identify the importance of the different possible types of market failure. This work will not be an easy task, but even preliminary information on the importance of misinformation, monopsony power, and irrationality in the labor market are unavailable. Other questions relate to the nature and extent of the distortions caused by the imperfections and the possibility of ameliorating them through policy intervention.

The occupational safety and health issue is an important one. The current regulatory framework is expensive and the costs imposed on employers are not trivial. On the other hand, the benefits or potential benefits may also be quite large and well worth the expense. Such an important issue deserves far more attention from economists than it has thus far received.

Notes

1. One could take many different approaches to a review of this literature. I have chosen to look at it from the point of view of its usefulness to policy, since that has been the motivation for so many who have written on the topic. A review of this literature could also illuminate questions in the history of economic thought or the methodology of economic inquiry. I will not comment on these concerns since proper consideration of them would require another paper at least of this length.

2. For now we will not specify how we measure safety. It could be the probability of an accident per year, it could be the exposure level to some hazard, or it could be any combination of measures of things that matter to workers' well-being.

3. For example, lump-sum transfers might produce less distortion.

4. For example, see Chelius (1977), Oi (1973, 1974), Smith (1976), or Zeckhauser and Nichol (1978).

5. For example, see Olson (1981), Viscusi (1978a,b, 1979d, 1980a), Thaler and Rosen (1976), R.E.B. Lucas (1977). Smith (1979b) and Brown (1980) provide summaries of this literature.

6. Bergmann's (1971) crowding model of discrimination is particularly relevant.

7. Standard texts in this field are Doeringer and Piore (1971) and Edwards, Reich, and Gordon (1975).

8. For instance, transportation costs could differ between firms or workers might have to incur costs when changing jobs. It should be noted that mobility costs which arise because of specific training give rise to bilateral monopoly, not monopsony, and cannot be analyzed in this framework.

9. This would be the case if the level of safety was, of technological necessity, set to be the same for all workers in a firm. Viscusi (1980a) argues that workers have no incentive to reveal their tastes to the firm since the firm could then capture the whole surplus. This, he argues, will lead the firm to choose only one level of safety. However, workers could reveal their marginal preferences without revealing the size of their surplus, so Viscusi's argument does not hold. For instance, workers could take a firm's initial uniform wage and safety offer and bargain for mutually advantageous changes with the company. Indeed, we observe market segmentation within firms. In particular, segmentation by age is common. After some time with a firm, older workers will typically be promoted into jobs with different wages, skill requirements, and safety conditions.

10. Freeman discusses preferences for pension plans. Viscusi and Smith discuss job safety.

11. Viscusi (1980a) shows that if unions attempt to maximize total worker surplus and marginal workers prefer less safety than the average worker, unionized firms will pay higher compensating wage differentials.

12. Piore's dual market theory would predict such a result. It would also be consistent with an information model (such as the second one presented in the third section) if unionized firms held workers longer allowing them the chance to learn the true safety of the job.

13. Gramlich (1976) and Baldwin (1980) have argued that increases in minimum wages may have ripple effects. If they do, then more than 6.2 percent of the work force may be affected. However, this would require a sociological theory of wage determination. Such theories are considered below in the discussion of disequilibrium.

14. See Viscusi (1979d, p. 255).

15. Viscusi's argument against market segmentation in the monopsony case would be relevant here if it were true. He argues that workers will not reveal their preferences to employers because the firm could then take their entire surplus. However, workers may reveal their pref-

erences at the margin without revealing their total surplus (see note 9). Likewise, employers could bargain for marginal, mutually advantageous changes in wages and safety requirements with the union. If there were a sufficiently large number of employers who wanted a particular type of change, the union could simply break the market into two or more parts. Thus, it is unlikely that the marginal cost to the marginal firm and the average marginal cost would be very different.

16. Originally, John Dunlop (1944) proposed that unions be modeled as maximizing some function of wages and employment. The supposition was that the union would represent the collective preferences of its members. Arthur Ross (1948) objected to this view, arguing that the divergence of interests between the union leaders and the union's members had to be considered. Since then little innovative work has been done on the question of how to model union behavior. Analytical work involving unions has proceeded assuming some version of the Dunlop hypothesis. Three recent innovations are Atherton (1973), Farber (1978), and Blair and Crawford (1980).

17. This is basically Arthur Ross' (1948) view.

18. An exception is J.S. Mill (p. 388), who cited this as one of his two major objections to Adam Smith's compensating wages argument.

19. For example, see Solow (1980) and Akerlof (1980, 1982).

20. For example, see Smith (1976) or Zeckhauser and Nichol (1978). An exception is Chelius (1977, p. 63), who argues against regulation and in favor of a no-fault income maintenance system similar to the current workers' compensation program and a change in the rules governing employers' liability for industrial accidents and diseases. The change he advocates would allow employees to sue if gross negligence on the part of their employer results in injury or disease. Current workers' compensation laws limit employer liability in such cases. Chelius argues that such a framework would provide the proper incentives for both employers and workers to keep a safe work environment. However, analyses by Ordover (1978) and Simon (1980) of the effectiveness of torts for guaranteeing product quality suggest that such an approach might have undesirable distributional effects.

21. As of August 1983 ninety-two percent of all workers' compensation insurance is experience-rated according to conversations the author has had with researchers at the National Council on Compensation Insurance.

22. Of course, consideration has been given to formalizing such models in other fields such as finance and industrial organization. Some of this literature is considered in the third section.

23. As was noted above, this is likely to be the case in large labor markets.

24. See note 21.

25. Several authors (for a review, see Einhorn and Hogarth (1981)) have noted that rational behavior towards real world problems involving probabilistic outcomes may be hard to define. However, the behavior noted here is dysfunctional with any reasonable assumption about the appropriate normative model.

26. Slovic, Fischoff, and Lichtenstein (1977) review the literature on how people make probabilistic judgments and identify a large number of deviations from the Bayesian model of decision making. Nisbett and Ross (1980) provide a more recent review mixed with some interesting speculation on many of these issues.

27. For example, mining operations, which tend to offer very hazardous employment, often dominate their local labor markets. Many textile firms are located in small towns. Textile workers have a high incidence of lung disease from exposure to airborne cotton dust particles.

28. May 1980 Current Population Survey.

29. Since $dR/ds = 0$ the size of the weight does not matter. Any nonmarginal change will cause the monopsonist's welfare to deteriorate. If the change caused workers' welfare

to improve, the net effect would depend, in part, on the size of the weight.

30. In particular, see notes 9 and 15.

31. I have collapsed Rea's category five into his third category, and his fourth into his second.

32. Relaxing these assumptions would complicate the analysis but would not significantly affect the results.

33. A dose-response function describes the relationship between exposure to a substance and the probability of observing a certain outcome such as a symptom of an illness. Typically, dose-response curves are assumed to be logistic, normal, or piece-wise linear.

34. Psychological studies of persuasion suggest the likelihood of this outcome (Osgood and Tannenbaum, 1955).

35. We will assume workers do not insure themselves against injury or loss on the job and that they cannot directly affect the safety of their jobs. Relaxing these assumptions would complicate the analysis but would not significantly affect the results.

36. Depending on what one assumes about how much people know about the workings of the market, this may not be utility-maximizing behavior. In the case of product markets, if all firms face the same costs of providing quality, then in a Nash equilibrium Perloff and Salop have shown that all firms will offer the same quality product at the same price. If people realize this, they would be better off choosing between brands at random since this would eliminate the monopsony power created by the perceived differences. Of course, firms could then offer lower-quality products, at which point consumers might go back to choosing the product they thought was best. No pure strategy equilibrium would exist in this case. Thus, if people are assumed to be utility maximizers, it must also be assumed that they do not know that firms will produce homogeneous products.

If firms differ in costs or consumers differ in their access to information, firms will produce different quality products at different prices. If people understood the nature of the market equilibrium, these prices would carry information about the quality of the goods and, in some cases, they would carry all the information necessary to determine the quality. However, if other considerations are introduced into the model, such as allowing workers to have different tastes and productive characteristics in different jobs, the information required for someone to deduce quality from price becomes far too great to be realistic. Thus, it seems reasonable to assume that workers may limit their attention to the price and perceived quality of each job, as has been assumed here.

37. Perloff and Salop (1980) show that if the support for the density of the errors is bounded from above or if the density function is of a class such that

$$\lim_{e \to -\infty} \frac{\phi'(e)}{\phi(e)} \to \infty$$

(for instance, an normal density function), monopsony power will diminish as the number of firms becomes large. The result will not hold if one assumes an upper bound to job safety. In this case, the distribution of perceived safety will have a mass point at the maximum level of safety, and their proof will not go through.

38. This is probably a reasonable assumption if the number of firms is *not* very small.

39. However, if these workers purchase insurance against losses from job injuries, they may buy too little.

References

Akerlof, George A. "A Theory of Social Custom of Which Unemployment May Be One Consequence." *Quarterly Journal of Economics* (June 1980), 749–775.

Akerlof, George A. "Labor Contracts as Partial Gift Exchange." Mimeographed, Berkeley, 1982, (forthcoming in the *Quarterly Journal of Economics*).

Akerlof, George A., and Dickens, William T. "The Economic Consequences of Cognitive Dissonance." *American Economic Review* (June 1982), 307–319.

Atherton, W.N. *Theory of Union Bargaining Goals.* Princeton, N.J.: Princeton University Press, 1973.

Baldwin, Jean. *The Response of Wages to the Minimum Wage.* Unpublished doctoral dissertation, M.I.T., 1980.

Bergmann, Barbara R. "The Effect on White Incomes of Discrimination in Employment." *Journal of Political Economy* (March/April 1971), 294–313.

Blair, Douglas H., and Crawford, David L. "The Objective Function of a Democratic Union." CARESS Working Paper 80–24, 1980.

Brown, Charles. "Equalizing Differences in the Labor Market." *Quarterly Journal of Economics* (February 1980), 113–134.

Bureau of Labor Statistics, U.S. Department of Labor. "Earnings and Other Characteristics of Organized Workers." Bulletin No. 2105 (May 1980).

Chelius, James Robert. *Workplace Safety and Health: The Role of Workers' Compensation.* American Enterprise Institute, Washington, D.C., 1977.

Chelius, James R., and Smith, Robert S. "The Responsiveness of Injury Rates to Experience — Rating of Workers' Compensation Insurance." Paper presented at the seminar on incentive and disincentive issues in workers' compensation insurance, City College of New York, November 16, 1981.

Coase, Ronald H. "The Problem of Social Cost." *Journal of Law and Economics* (October 1960), 1–45.

Diamond, Peter. "Insurance Theoretic Aspects of Workers' Compensation." In Alan S. Blinder, and Philip Friedman (eds.) *Natural Resources, Uncertainty and General Equilibrium Systems.* New York: Academic Press, 1979.

Doeringer, Peter B., and Piore, Michael J. *Internal Labor Markets and Manpower Analysis.* Lexington, Mass.: Heath Lexington Books, 1971.

Dunlop, John. *Wage Determination Under Trade Unions.* New York: Austin Kelley, 1944.

Dunn, L.F. "Quantifying Nonpecuniary Returns." *Journal of Human Resources* (Summer 1977), 347–359.

Edwards, Richard C., Reich, Michael, and Gordon, David M. *Labor Market Segmentation.* Lexington, Mass.: D.C. Heath and Co., 1975.

Einhorn, Hillel J., and Hogarth, Robin M. "Behavioral Decision Theory: Processes of Judgment and Choice." *Annual Review of Psychology* (1981), 53–88.

Farber, Henry S. "Individual Preferences and Union Wage Determination: The Case of the United Mine Workers." *Journal of Political Economy* (October 1978).

Freeman, Richard B. "The Effect of Unionism on Fringe Benefits." *Industrial and Labor Relations Review* (July 1981), 489–509.

Gramlich, Edward M. "Impact of Minimum Wages on Other Wages, Employment and Family Incomes." *Brookings Papers on Economic Activity* (2:1976), 409–461.

Grether, David M., and Plott, Charles R. "Economic Theory of Choice and Preference Reversal Phenomena." *American Economic Review* (September 1979), 623–638.

Kahn, Shulamit. "Occupational Safety and Labor Market Immobility — Who Is the Marginal Worker?" Mimeographed, University of California at Irvine, November, 1980.

Kahn, Shulamit. Dissertation work in progress, M.I.T. (1982).

Kunreuther, Howard. "Limited Knowledge and Insurance Protection." *Public Policy* (Spring, 1976), 227–262.

Kunreuther, Howard, and Slovic, Paul. "Economics, Psychology and Protective Behavior." *American Economic Review* (May 1978), 64–69.

Lucas, R.E.B. "Hedonic Wage Equations and Psychic Wages in the Return to Schooling." *American Economic Review* (September 1977), 549–558.

Mill, John Stuart. *Principles of Political Economy.* London: Longmans, Green and Co., 1909.

Nisbett, Richard, and Ross, Lee. *Human Inference: Strategies and Shortcomings of Social Judgment.* Englewood Cliffs, N.J.: Prentice Hall, Inc., 1980.

Oi, Walter Y. "Workmen's Compensations and Industrial Safety." *Supplemental Studies for the National Commission on State Workmen's Compensation Laws,* Volume I. Washington, D.C.: U.S. G.P.O. (1973), 41–106.

Oi, Walter Y. "On the Economics of Industrial Safety." *Law and Contemporary Problems* (Summer 1974), 669–699.

Olson, Craig A. "An Analysis of Wage Differentials Received by Workers on Dangerous Jobs." *Journal of Human Resources* (Spring 1981), 167–185.

Ordover, J. "Costly Litigation in the Model of Single Activity Accidents." *Journal of Legal Studies* (June 1978), 261–343.

Osgood, Charles E., and Tannenbaum, Percy H. "The Principles of Congruity in the Prediction of Attitude Change." *Psychological Review* (January 1955), 42–55.

Perloff, Jeffrey, and Salop, Steven C. "Firm-Specific Information, Product Differentiation and Industry Equilibrium." Mimeographed, University of Pennsylvania and Federal Trade Commission, April 1980.

Rea, Samuel A., Jr. "Workmen's Compensation and Occupational Safety Under Imperfect Information." *American Economic Review* (March 1981), 80–93.

Root, Lawrence S. *Fringe Benefits, Social Insurance in the Steel Industry.* Beverly Hills, Calif.: Sage Publications, 1982.

Rosen, Sherwin. "Hedonic Prices and Implicit Markets: Product Differentiation in Pure Competition." *Journal of Political Economy* (January 1974), 34–55.

Ross, Arthur M. *Trade Union Wage Policy.* Berkeley, Calif.: University of California Press, 1948.

Russell, Louise. "Pricing Industrial Accidents." *Supplemental Studies for the National Commission on States Workmen's Compensation Laws,* Vol. III. (1973), 35.

Russell, Louise B. "Safety Incentives in Workmen's Compensation Insurance." *The Journal of Human Resources* (Summer 1974), 361–375.

Simon, Marilyn J. "Imperfect Information, Costly Litigation and Product Quality." *The Bell Journal of Economics* (Spring 1981), 171-184.

Slovic, Paul, Fischoff, Baruch, and Lichenstein, Sarah. "Behavioral Decision Theory." *Annual Review of Psychology* (1977), 1-39.

Smith, Adam. *An Inquiry into the Nature and Causes of the Wealth of Nations,* Volume 1. London: J.M. Dont & Sons, 1910, (1776).

Smith, Robert Stewart. *The Occupational Safety and Health Act, Its Goals and Its Achievements.* Washington, D.C.: American Enterprise Institute, 1976.

Smith, Robert Stewart. "The Impact of OSHA Inspections on Manufacturing Injury Rates." *Journal of Human Resources* (Spring 1979a), 145-170.

Smith, Robert S. "Compensating Wage Differentials and Public Policy: A Review." *Industrial Relations Review* (April 1979b), 339-352.

Solow, Robert M. "On Theories of Unemployment." *The American Economic Review* (March 1980), 1-11.

Spence, A. Michael. "Monopoly, Quality and Regulation." *Bell Journal of Economics* (Autumn 1975), 417-429.

Thaler, Richard, and Rosen, Sherwin. "The Value of Saving a Life: Evidence from the Labor Market." In Nestor Teolecky (ed). *Household Production and Consumption.* N.B.E.R. Studies in Income and Wealth. New York: Columbia University Press, No. 40, 1976, 265-298.

Tversky, A., and Kahneman, D. "Judgment Under Uncertainty: Heuristic Biases." *Science* (October 1974), 1124-1131.

United Sates Department of Labor, Bureau of Labor Statistics. "Earnings and Other Characteristics of Organized Workers, May 1980." Bulletin No. 2105 (September 1981).

United States Government Printing Office. *Report of the Minimum Wage Study Commission,* Volume 1. Washington, D.C., (May 1981).

Viscusi, W.K. "Labor Market Valuations of Life and Limb — Empirical Evidence and Policy Implications." *Public Policy* (Summer 1978a), 359-386.

Viscusi, W.K. "Wealth Effects and Earnings Premiums for Job Hazards." *Review of Economics and Statistics* (August 1978b), 408-416.

Viscusi, W.K. "Job Hazards and Worker Quit Rates; An Analysis of Adaptive Worker Behavior." *International Economic Review* (February 1979a), 29-58.

Viscusi, W.K. "The Impact of Occupational Safety and Health Regulation." *Bell Journal of Economics* (Spring 1979b), 117-140.

Viscusi, W.K. "Insurance and Individual Incentives in Adaptive Contexts." *Econometrica* (September 1979c), 1195-1207.

Viscusi, W.K. *Employment Hazards: An Investigation of Market Performance.* Cambridge: Harvard University Press, 1979d.

Viscusi, W.K. "Union, Labor Market Structure and the Welfare Implications of the Quality of Work." *Journal of Labor Research* (Spring 1980a), 175-192.

Viscusi, W.K. "A Theory of Job Shopping: A Bayesian Perspective." *Quarterly Journal of Economics* (May 1980b), 609-614.

Viscusi, W.K., and Zeckhauser, Richard J. "Optimal Standards with Incomplete Enforcement." *Public Policy* (Fall 1979), 437-456.

Zeckhauser, Richard and Nichol, Albert. *The Occupational Safety and Health Administration — An Overview.* United States Senate Committee on Governmental Affairs, Study on Federal Regulation, Washington, D.C., 1978.

6 STRUCTURE, PROCESS, AND THE LABOR MARKET

Samuel R. Friedman

Introduction

In the late 1960s, attention focused on the persistence of poverty and of income differentials on the basis of sex and (especially) race. Neoclassical economic theorists such as Becker (1957) held that such differentials were the results of tastes for discrimination that were uneconomic and, thus, that they would tend to be eroded by the forces of competition. Another branch of standard economic theory, once again led by Becker (1964), held that poverty and racial differentials in income stemmed heavily from differences in human capital. This implied that improved education and training programs should enable poverty and racial differentials to be reduced.

The first draft of this chapter was written while I was working at the Vera Institute of Justice on a study of youth-training strategies for the U.S. Department of Labor. The ideas expressed herein are mine and do not represent the views of Vera or the Department of Labor. Many people have helped me in developing these ideas, sometimes by disagreeing with them, including Janis Barry, Florence Dinerstein, Nancy DiTomaso, John Evansohn, Samuel Farber, Robert Fitch, Judith Friedman, David Gordon, Sally Hillsman, Mark Kotkin, Deanna London, Douglas MacDonald, Selma Marks, Jerome McElroy, Richard McGahey, Carol Nackinoff, Gary Nickerson, Ellen Riley, Susan Sadd, Randall Smith, Roberta Spalter-Roth, Mercer Sullivan, and June Swerdlin.

The activists of the 1960s and scholars who reflected their experiences did not accept this analysis. They saw that racial and sex discrimination were not eroded by competitive pressures and that graduates of raining programs and schools did not tend to escape from poverty. Thus, they tried to develop a politics that could end poverty and discrimination as well as a theory that could help explain why existing policies would not do the job.

The dominant theories critical of the neoclassical view were the dual economy and segmented labor market approaches. They stemmed from a common set of theoretical forebears — the institutionalists (Dunlop, 1958; Kerr, 1950, 1954; Reynolds 1951) and monopoly/oligopoly theorists (Baran and Sweezy, 1965; Galbraith, 1967). From these theorists they took ideas about how unionization improved pay and working conditions by setting up barriers to entry that reduce competition and by strengthening the impact of shop floor customs on the work process. They also incorporated ideas about the similar impact of professional organizations and about the importance of product markets in allowing large firms to grow, stabilize their product demand (and, thus, their work force), develop or buy new technology, and invest in capital-intensive production techniques.

The dual economy approach holds that there are two kinds of industries in America: (1) core industries characterized by large firms, little competition, high capital intensity and productivity, good labor conditions, and white male labor; and (2) periphery industries consisting of small companies with low capital intensity and productivity that compete with each other and offer low pay, unstable employment, and poor working conditions to their workers (who are disproportionately women and minorities).

Segmented labor market theorists focus less on industries and more on jobs as their unit of analysis. They see some jobs as part of well-defined career ladders with a firm, profession, or craft occupation. Primary jobs offer relative job security, advancement, and benefits, and tend to be held by white males. Other jobs, in the secondary segment, are not so blessed. Some of them are in marginal companies that offer low pay, little security, and no prospects for learning or advancement while some are with established employers who find it worthwhile to have part of their workforce situated in similarly unappealing jobs. Holders of secondary jobs are disproportionately minorities and women.

In this paper, I critically review each of these three approaches at some length in order to see what they can contribute to a new approach to labor market processes that potentially avoids these weaknesses. I review several other theories in less depth; they, nevertheless, contribute important insights to the model I develop. These theories deal with notions of class, of workers' developing shelters from the negative effects of competition for their jobs, and with the idea that the existence of workers without jobs weakens the bargaining positions of employed workers.

I then develop a new approach to the labor market — one that views economic and political processes as intertwined rather than separate and thus brings in history as part of economic reality. I see the characteristics of jobs and the social characteristics of job-holders (such as their sex and race) as the outcome of two interacting sets of conflict processes: (1) processes that define the nature of a job include struggles over pay levels, workplace safety, technology, and authority relations as well as characteristics of the industry, occupation, and firm; (2) processes that define the potential labor for the job (its reserve labor force) including struggles over who is allowed to be given the job as well as general social struggles over the conditions of the nonemployed and of those in less desirable jobs that affect the extent to which employers can replace workers. These two sets of processes interact in many ways. For example, employers often redesign their technologies in ways that de-skill jobs (Braverman, 1974), and this change in the job definition process affects who can be hired to do the work. In the other direction, the increase in the reserve labor force for most manufacturing jobs in the early 1980s has allowed many employers to increase workloads and to decrease both safety and pay; whereas the cooperation between the jobless and the employed from 1934 to 1940 enabled them to restrict the effective reserve labor force for most jobs and thus to unionize millions of jobs.

Finally, I discuss the implications of this analysis for policy and politics.

Human Capital Theory

Human capital theory is a branch of neoclassical economics. In one way, it represents a progressive development beyond the conservative orthodoxies of the Chicago approach — namely, it is a development within neoclassical theory that allows it to pay attention to, and develop policies to reduce, poverty and racism. Thus, proponents of the human capital approach could offer a response to the insurgency of the poor with proposals for training programs.

Like any neoclassical theory, human capital theory is based on a model of individual choice. An economy/society is viewed as composed of atomized individuals or families who make choices that shape their present consumption and future income. A critical set of such choices are decisions about how to use one's time and resources. The decision at the heart of human capital theory is whether to spend time and resources to obtain income in the present and thus maximize current consumption[1] or, instead, to use one's time and resources in obtaining skills and thus maximize future consumption.[2] Such decision making, then, is viewed as a matter of individual choice in which the individual is assumed to try maximize income — and in which only the question of whether the income to be maximized is present income or future income is a problem. Thus, as in all neoclassical models, social structure and culture are ignored in practice — although always with the proviso that they could be modeled in some future study as factors that condition individual utility functions or the options open to individual endeavor.

Why should investing in skills produce increased income? It is assumed that higher skills result in more productive labor and that the forces of competition lead employers to use workers in jobs which use these skills. These assumptions have been questioned by those who hold that skills are less important to a firm than personnel policies that separate workers by race or gender, that firms consider managerial control of the labor process more important than skill and thus organize production accordingly (Braverman, 1974; Edwards, 1979; Zimbalist, 1979), or that companies establish hierarchies of pay and status irrespective of skills in order to weaken workers' ability to resist management (Stone, 1973). The human capital approach further argues that workers' ability to change employers ("labor mobility") produces effective pressure on employers to pay each worker (or skill-category of worker) his or her marginal productivity.[3] Thus, increased skills for the worker get translated into employment at jobs in which marginal productivity and pay are higher. The extent to which increased skills increase wages depends on the technology of production (which determines both the increased productivity due to skills and the possibility of substituting lower-paid labor or new techniques that require fewer or less-skilled workers) and the supply and demand conditions of the market.

The implication of human capital theory is that training pays off for the trainees both by increasing their pay and by increasing the range of jobs open to them (since employers have lower training costs). Training programs should thus benefit the clients. If they do not, it is due to poor implementation (as in training clients in outmoded skills or failing to teach them well) or due to the faults of those enrolled in the program.

Another set of assumptions underlying human capital theory holds that differences in returns to investment in human capital among occupations, industries, races, and genders tend to be momentary deviations from a standard rate of return to such investment (with the proviso that mistakes can lead to wasted investment in human capital as readily as in other capital markets and that variations in individual ability create variations in increased skills per hour and dollar invested by the trainee). This assumption comes from the neoclassical model which holds that differences in rate of return get eliminated by the shift in investment from areas with low return to those with high return. This, in turn, reduces relative production in areas with low return, which leads to increased prices and thus to an increased marginal return to the company from its remaining labor force (after adjusting for employment decline due to decreased demand — with the departing workers presumably being absorbed by the expanding areas of production created by the new investment in areas with a high rate of return). Finally, this increased marginal revenue to the company due to increased prices leads to increased pay for its workers since the labor market equalizes marginal revenue with pay.

As a result of all these forces, the theory concludes that there is a unitary labor market in which human capital investment tends to pay off equally regardless of occupation, industry, sex, or race. Variations from this are analyzed in terms of market imperfections — with the underlying assumption that the forces of competition render such imperfections short-lived, unless they are the product of lasting state intervention that disrupts normal market mechanisms.

Further Critiques of Human Capital Theory

Three major kinds of criticisms have been directed at human capital theory: (1) policies based on it do not work; (2) its empirical descriptions are false; (3) it is theoretically incorrect. In this paper, we can only allude to major points rather than conducting a thorough review of the evidence and debate.

Policies

The claim that policies based on human capital theory do not work rests on the argument that a wide range of programs — from Manpower Development and Training and the War on Poverty through CETA — have attempted to train the poor so that they can get jobs and escape poverty. One criticism of human capital theory is that, in spite of all the money spent on such programs, the basic social problems they were meant to cure still remain. Thus, poverty still is widespread; unemployment has increased — particularly for youth and minorities; and a great many of the employed population still earn less than a poverty-level income. Human capital theorists can reply that the programs were poorly designed or too small to affect these ills — but the expenditure of $64 billion on such programs between 1963 and 1979 (Ginzberg, 1980, p. 3) without serious impact on unemployment or poverty raises doubts about such responses.

One also can consider programs based on human capital theory in terms of their impact on the individuals involved rather than in terms of their ability to affect aggregate labor force statistics. Borus (1980) reviews a number of experimental and comparison group studies of classroom training, on-the-job training (OJT), Job Corps, Youth Work-Experience, adult basic education, and adult work experience programs. He concludes (p. 35) that classroom, OJT, and work-experience programs "appear to yield benefits sufficient to justify the programs if the first year benefits continue relatively intact for five or more years. The evidence of the continuation of benefits, however, is not clear." Although recommending the continuation of such programs, he also finds that "training, at least as it currently exists, should not be viewed as the major weapon for fighting poverty. The gains in participants' earnings are measured in the hundreds of dollars and are unlikely to move many people out of poverty" (p. 40). It should be added that the Manpower Demonstration Research Corporation (MDRC) studies of supported work found that experimental/control differences in hours worked per month were short-lived for young school dropouts and for ex-offenders, although there is some evidence that gains might be more lasting for long-term AFDC recipients (Masters and Maynard, 1981; Maynard, 1980; Piliavin and Gartner, 1981).

In summary, then, the record of human capital policies provides little evidence to support human capital theory.

Empirical Descriptions

Human capital theory argues that people who invest in their own education or training should receive equal returns (net of differences in ability to learn) and that any differences that do develop in rates of return should be short-lived. It also argues that, ceteris paribus, people with more education or training should receive higher wages and be employed more steadily than people with less education or training.

These views were criticized by segmented labor market theorists because they contended that education would not affect returns in the secondary sector or, at least, that rates of return to education would be less in the secondary than in the primary sector. Dual economy theorists raised similar criticisms. Both segmentation and dual economy researchers have studied the returns to education (see Appendix I). Many, but not all, of these studies have found that regression equations measuring the contribution of human capital to earnings vary among segments and among industrial sectors. Some find education to be unrelated to income; others find that there are positive returns to education but that these vary among segments, sectors, races, or sexes; and others are consistent with human capital predictions. Thus, many of these studies find that labor market outcomes are not explained well by human capital theory, and most of them indicate that the labor market is not unitary but has different dynamics in different segments, sectors, races, and sexes. Since human capital theorists (and, more generally, neoclassical economists) hold that regression estimation is a valid test for their theory, these results indicate that their approach is inadequate.

Theoretical Critiques

Many of the theoretical critiques of human capital theory debate some of the assumptions discussed above. Those critiques will not be developed further here; instead, the focus will be on discussions of the nature of jobs, the job attainment process, and the labor market.

Osterman (1980, pp. 40–43) holds that human capital theorists' descriptions of individual decision making about job choice and human capital investment rest on the assumptions that "workers have careers, that the careers are in some nontrivial sense selected, and that once selected, the careers are followed." Alternatively, human capital theorists might assume that job choice by youths is a process of rational exploration to learn about the job market. However, Osterman's interviews of youths challenge these assumptions since he finds that:

1. The sequence of jobs held by youths do not follow career patterns. More often, the jobs are random with respect to skills and occupations.
2. Because most jobs are found through personal contacts, the range and role of careful search and rational choice seems limited.
3. Unemployed youths generally take the first job offered, and they do so even though they have applied for a wide range of jobs with varying characteristics. (p. 40)

The relevance of these findings for human capital theory might be challenged on the grounds that it requires only a small proportion of youth to act as rational maximizers for the marginalist dynamics of the market to hold true. As Osterman points out, however, this defense of the theory amounts to saying that it explains only a portion of economic behavior. Osterman's study suggests that the human capital approach is based on a faulty description of the process by which jobs and people are brought together and, thus, that the theory is unlikely to predict behavior well — at least for youth. Further research is needed on whether this critique is relevant for adult labor markets as well.

Neoclassical theory rests on the assumption that market processes are the outcome of a series of more or less uncoordinated individual decisions. These create an "invisible hand" that leads to an equilibrium in which each item produced is sold at a price set by its cost of production for the least efficient producer who is able to make any sales plus an average profit.

Marxists accept some of the underlying dynamic — namely, that competitive pressures force employers and workers to set their pices at lower levels and to buy their supplies at higher prices than they would prefer. However, Marx used a different approach to the price-setting mechanisms which he derived from the theories of Adam Smith and David Ricardo. This is the labor theory of value, which holds (as a first approximation) that commodities exchange at relative prices such that each side to the exchange transfers goods which have required equal amounts of labor. Marx would add several complications to this formula: (1) Since there is a standard price for most items, the value of a commodity is based on the socially necessary amount of labor put into each commodity (rather than the most efficient or, as the marginalists would have it, the least); (2) prices are derived from values such that the value is an underlying level, set by production dynamics, with prices fluctuating around the values as random short-term variations occur in supply and demand; and (3) as the most serious divergence between the formula and Marx's view, there is a systematic adjustment of prices from values to adjust to the most fundamental force that determines price-setting — namely, that investors compete with each other in such a way that there is a strong tendency for the rate of return on investments to be equalized among firms and industries. This means that relative prices tend to be raised above values for these industries in which competitive dynamics force the use of more than average capital per worker.[4]

As a further difference with neoclassical theory, Marx did not see these processes as simply individual decisions. He saw them as collective, influenced by class belief systems, politics, organization, and struggle. Thus, workers come to the market not as abstract individuals with abstract talents but as people with real ties to each other and with views about other workers, employers, and how to improve their lot. These ties and views may influence their ability to get jobs or their bargaining position for pay and benefits. Similarly, employers may come to treat workers of different races, sexes, or other traits differently in response to employing-class biases, divide-and-rule strategies, or a calculation that splitting pay levels or job assignments by such criteria allows a lower long-term total wage bill.

Furthermore, Marxist analysis maintains that capitalism generates an antidote to pressures by workers to increase their compensation — pressures that might tend to subvert the possibility of such long-term differential treatment of categories of workers by making it profitable to attract scarce labor by offering higher than normal pay to a member of a disadvantaged category. Marx argued that capitalism creates in many ways a reserve army of the unemployed that makes such efforts unnecessary (except in unusual circumstances such as major wars) by providing a supply of labor ready to fill vacancies at low wages, thus obviating the need to promote subordinated groups.

What does Marxist analysis imply for human capital theory and the analysis of low-income youth (or other categories such as sexes and races) in the labor market? First, Marxists would not expect workers of different categories to receive the same pay or even the same rate of return to education. Second, to the extent that higher educational attainment represents a greater input of labor in producing a worker, there should be a weak tendency for there to be a positive return to education. The empirical relationship is expected to be weak for two reasons. First, values are set by the socially necessary labor time that goes into a product. Much of the education received by low-income youth, for example, involves lower-than-normal productivities and capital inputs. Thus, less value is transferred per year of schooling. Second, given the existence of a large unemployment reserve, many people take jobs that do not use many of their skills — which means that they take jobs whose pay rates are set by what is needed to attract labor of lower value. Finally, Marxist critics of the human capital approach, such as Wright (1979), maintain that income determination is decisively affected by class. Workers, ceteris paribus, will earn less than members of the petty bourgeoisie, capitalists, or intermediate groups such as managers.

Dual Economy Theories and Economic Sectors

The late 1960s spawned radical analyses that synthesized previously existing theories with lessons learned from mass struggles. The basic intention (Mannheim, 1953) of dual economy theory (in the hands of Bluestone and O'Connor, at least) and of segmented labor market theory (according to Edwards, Gordon, and Reich, and, perhaps, Doeringer and Piore) was to point to economic structures that required elimination in order for New Left movement goals to be achieved. The development of these theories will be considered, in part, in terms of their efficacy in helping achieve the original intentions.

Dual economy theory, then, was a response to movement discoveries that blacks and women do not get a fair deal; that human capital-based training programs did not bring many blacks from "bad" to "good" jobs nor end their pervasive unemployment; that discrimination was not a short-term market imperfection, as Becker (1957) would imply, but a deeply rooted structure; that giant corporations have a stake in racism and have foreign interests, and that these same corporations have enormous power with which to defend their interests. These discoveries were made by mass movements of blacks and of students, who were radicalizing as they made the discoveries and who were looking for theories that would explain these discoveries while pointing to ways to change the structures.

However these movements were not rooted in the working class — and, indeed, saw the better-off, unionized sections of the working class as at best suspect and at worst as part of the system (and thus part of the enemy). Movement theoreticians found Baran and Sweezy's *Monopoly Capital* (1965) very congenial and found less radical work such as Galbraith's *The New Industrial State* (1967) at least as relevant. Thus, they developed a theory based around the dichotomy between giant corporations that dominate society and provide their male, white employees with a bourgeoisifying affluence, on the one hand, and the rest of the economy which they saw as containing disproportionate numbers of racial minorities and white women who were forced to eke out a bare existence, on the other. Such theories had several uses for the radical wing of the movement. They showed that problems like racism and sexism were not just superstructural but were rooted in the economic base. They pointed to the giant corporations as the enemy and therefore seemed anticapitalist at a time when the movements were becoming anticapitalist. Finally, they did all this while holding that unionized workers are beneficiaries of the system, rather than its victims. This view was congenial to movements composed of upper middle class whites and middle class blacks, plus some blacks from rural areas and the secondary labor market. It also meant the movements accepted their failure to link up with the worker insurgencies developing at the same time (Friedman, 1982; Georgakas and Surkin, 1975; Geschwender, 1977; Serrin, 1974; Weir, 1973).

The content of the early qualitative distinction between core and periphery sectors is reflected by the following quotation from Bluestone, Murphy, and Stevenson (1973, pp. 28–29).

> The core economy includes those industries that comprise the muscle of American economic and political power . . . the firms in the core economy are noted for high productivity, high profits, intensive utilization of capital, high incidence of monopoly elements, and a high degree of unionization. Workers who are able to secure employment in these industries are, in most cases, assured of relatively high wages and better than average working conditions and fringe benefits.

> Beyond the fringes of the core economy lies a set of industries that lack almost all of the advantages normally found in center firms . . . The peripheral industries are noted for their small firm size, labor intensity, low profit, low productivity, intensive product market competition, lack of unionization, and low wages. Unlike core sector industries, the periphery lacks the assets, size, and political power to take advantage of economies of scale or to spend large sums on research and development.

The implication of this theory is that human capital-style equalization of returns will not operate between the two sectors. Thus, those in the periphery (competitive) sector will receive lower incomes and lower returns to education, and do so in more dangerous, less pleasant, and more precarious jobs than those employed in the core (monopoly) sector. This sectoral structure is viewed as providing a structural basis underlying race and sex differences. This analysis provided the basis for proposals aimed at reducing discrimination and redirecting government expenditures to peripheral industries, at sharply increasing the minimum wage, and at having the government establish high-wage jobs open to periphery workers so that the oversupply of labor to the periphery can be brought down and periphery wages increased (Bluestone et al. 1973, ch. 10).

For reasons that will be presented more fully below, this two-sector qualitative categorization failed to describe the economic structure adequately. This led to two forms of quantitative development of the theory.[5] On the one hand, O'Connor (1973) introduced a state sector as a third sector and Hodson (1978) extended this to four sectors by considering construction and the state as separate sectors. On the other, Oster (1979) and Tolbert, Horan, and Beck (1980) used factor analysis to divide industries into two sectors in a quantitative manner. Finally, in the ultimate quantitative decomposition of the economy, Kaufman, Hodson, and Fligstein (1981) used a combination of factor and cluster analyses to define 16 sectors.

This quantitative multiplication did not just stem from attempts to reach greater levels of descriptive precision. Instead, it reflected a conceptual error underlying the original qualitative presentation of dualism: the assumption that there is an underlying core-periphery dimension that captures important elements of industrial structure. Friedman and Friedman (1979) pointed out that there is little empirical reason to believe that such an underlying dimension exists, and on theoretical grounds, one would not expect it. We held that market relationships, production relationships, and political relationships were all part of what dualists were claiming to be this one dimension and, therefore, the assumption of such an underlying dimension is a form of economic (indeed, market) determinism. Furthermore, analysis of the correlation matrices underlying dualists' factor analyses indicates that many of these variables are essentially uncorrelated, so there is no underlying duality dimension. To be blunt: the evidence that industries with high market concentration are not particularly likely to be capital intensive or unionized severely challenges dual economy theory. Kaufman, Hodson, and Fligstein (1981) essentially accept this logic in developing their 16-sector model.

In addition, it should be noted that the change from qualitative dualism to quantitative analysis involved changes in the policy relevance of the approach. The qualitative formulation included a severe critique of the current system as producing racism and other ills and proposed radically altering the role of the government in the economy (Bluestone et al. 1973). Even in Hodson's (1978) 4-sector model, a strain of generalized anticapitalism remains, although it is not tied to any specific proposals or strategies and the implications for racial struggles are downplayed. In Kaufman, Hodson, and Fligstein (1981), politics has disappeared.

In response to the multidimensionality of industrial structure, most dual economy theorists turned to the use of separate independent variables rather than categorizations.[6] This amounts to a change from quality and quantity to a new stage in which each variable is treated as a measure. This measure stage is best exemplified by Hodson (1981), Kalleberg, Wallace and Althauser (1981), and Bridges (1980).[7] Hodson divides his measures of industrial structure into (1) market factors such as profit rate, foreign involvement of the industry, corporate autonomy (the extent to which workers in an industry are employed by companies operating primarily in that industry), extent of government regulation, and growth (new capital expenditures per company); (2) technical workplace factors such as capital intensity; and (3) organizational workplace factors such as size and productivity. He also included measures derived from interviews with the individuals studied such as class (by dummy variables for occupational categories of managers, professionals, white collar workers, and manual workers) and unionization (of the individual and the industry). He treats sex, race, education, years of work experience, and weeks and hours worked as individual characteristics.

In explaining the logarithm of annual earnings, Hodson found that industrial structure was an important explanatory concept, but so were demographic and human capital characteristics, occupation, and unionization. Within his industrial structure variables, size, foreign involvement, concentration, and perhaps capital intensity have the greatest effect on earnings.[8]

Kalleberg et al. (1981) use a somewhat different set of measures: (1) economic segmentation variables are industry concentration, average firm size in the industry, the extent to which the industry's products are sold to governments, non labor-production costs per worker in the industry (which they call capital intensity), and the size of the establishment in which the individual whose income is measured works; (2) worker power measures are individual membership in a union or other employee association, individual length of service with current employer, skill of individual's occupation,[9] the degree of occupational licensing for people of a given industry and occupation (Freedman, 1976), and class (whether the individual exercises supervisory authority over others' labor); (3) individual characteristics are education, sex, and race; and (4) controls for region and age.

Kalleberg and his coauthors regressed log income on these variables separately for males and females and also in a pooled equation for both. In the separate equations for males and females, education had the largest (positive) standardized regression coefficient. In the pooled equation, education had the largest (positive) standardized coefficient except sex. Establishment size and occupational specific vocational training were also important and positive in all three equations,[10] as was concentration. Employee tenure with the given employer, which segmented labor market theory would predict to have a positive association with income in the primary market, also has a sizable positive association in all three equations. The standardized regression weight (beta) for unionization was positive for the pooled sample and for females.[11]

The Hodson and Kalleberg et al. studies agree in showing that industrial, firm, unionization, and occupational variables as well as education are important determinants of income. In this, they indicate that human capital explanations (or Marxist theories of labor value determination by the input costs of preparing labor power) have some support, in that education has a positive effect on income across the employed population as a whole and within each sex, but they show that structural factors, gender, and unionization (a political variable) are also important. The two studies disagree in a number of ways — most importantly over whether concentration increases or lowers income.

It was discussed above that the qualitative formulation of dual economy theory was associated with radical politics but that the quantitative formulation was apolitical. This was exemplified, in part, by Hodson's own works (Hodson, 1978; Kaufman, Hodson, and Fligstein, 1981). The formulation now before us looks at economic variation in terms of multidimensional continuous measures, which one would expect to be consonant with incremental policies in which the values of given variables are adjusted step-by-step to attain desired ends. Hodson (1981) indeed bears out this expectation. He calls for "a sectoral policy with different goals for different parts of the economy. Instead of raising the overall profit rate, this policy would focus on aiding workers in specific sectors in improving their situation.

Thus, closer government regulation of labor-intensive industries and greater support for employees in small businesses might be called for. In addition, the negative impact of concentration on employee earnings is but another reason to revitalize antitrust procedures against the great monopolies" (p. 23). Kalleberg et al., however, present no policy conclusions — although their analysis implies a similar approach.

At this point, we should consider the implications of the dual economy tendency for an improved understanding of poverty and of the actions that might be taken by the poor or others to improve their futures. We can see, first, that the improved theoretical and empirical grasp of the measure stage of this theory as compared with its qualitative formulation has been accompanied by a weakening of its policy proposals. Antitrust policies and unspecified government regulation of labor-intensive industries and small businesses do not provide as much of a handle as do proposals to reduce discrimination, increase the minimum wage, and increase and redirect government expenditures in ways that will help periphery workers. The qualitative stage analysis, on the other hand, was based on faulty theory. This implies that a new theoretical approach might help us to develop more useful policy.

Furthermore, the measure stage formulations are based on studies that examine general cross-sections of the employed. They do not focus on poor youth nor do they address the problem of explaining poverty per se or unemployment. This suggests, at the least, that any reformulation of dual economy theory should be integrated with the segmented labor market approach and critiques thereof.

As a final reason to try to go beyond the measurement formulation of dual economy theory, we should realize that the two studies we have considered explained only about half the variance in the natural logarithm of income. This is not a bad result for equations with 15 variables but it is far from a complete statistical explanation. Half the variance remains to be explained — and it is highly probable that the variables used would explain considerably less than half the variance for samples of youthful and/or low-income individuals.

How can we advance beyond the current formulations of dual theory? We can get some ideas by studying the contradictions in the current theory and its forebears.

Dual economy theory began as an explanation that rooted racism and sexism in the economic base while avoiding a Marxist analysis of class. It is suggestive that as the theory developed through its various stages it moved toward class formulations. In part, this was in response to Wright's analysis in which he shows the relevance of class variables (such as whether one is a taker of and/or giver of orders) to income determination (Wright, 1979), and in part it was due to critiques such as those of Friedman and Friedman (1979). By 1981, Kalleberg et al. were trying to develop explicit measures of workers' power as a major part of their explanatory scheme and Hodson (1981) included class measures such as union membership, union strength, and crude occupational proxies for class.

It thus seems logical that the next stage of theoretical development should include conspicuous use of individual class membership and of the institutionalized strength workers have in given industries and occupations. However, I propose that this is only a first step in reformulating the theory in class terms. The second step is to see that there are class and social conflict elements underlying most, if not all, of the other variables in the model and to develop variables that make this explicit and thus take account of the way power relationships actually affect income and other job characteristics.

In discussing his results, Hodson makes several remarks that suggest the value of this approach. In discussing his finding that concentration has a negative effect on earnings, he argues that "the market position of large oligopolistic corporations provides them with the ability to exploit their work forces to a greater extent than would otherwise be possible. That is, the discretionary resources provided by market power are utilized to undermine wages rather than to increase them" (1981, p. 15). He then goes on to argue that corporate size also provides resources but that "higher earnings associated with large size result from increased worker power in large corporations, not from the generosity of owners or from the use of wages as a mechanism of social control" (p. 25). Under other circumstances, as Friedman and Friedman (1979, pp. 7–8) pointed out, the resources available to large corporations can allow them to dominate their workers and thus to reverse the sign of the relationship between size and earnings. Indeed, recent givebacks in the automobile and steel industries suggest a future development of this sort (Nyden and Nyden, 1981). Hodson also argues that capital intensity can be interpreted as giving workers extra power that necessitates paying higher wages (1981, p. 16).[12]

This suggests, then, that a general reformulation of the variables of the model to make power relations more explicit would increase our statistical explanatory power. As an example of this, it would be useful to measure the extent of discretionary power afforded by size. This could be accomplished by creating variables for the extent to which the workers in an industry are actively involved in attempting to improve their collective rewards and conditions, and for the extent of management mobilization within and among firms. (See Kochan and Block 1977 for an interesting attempt to apply such measures.)

Similarly, we should go beyond thinking of sex and race as individual factors (Hodson, 1981, p. 13; Kalleberg, 1981, p. 663). The implication of sex and race for earnings and job security is clearly a politically determined variable. Effective mobilization by women or racial minorities in an industry, occupation, or community can affect the relative (and absolute) conditions of women and minorities in the labor force. On the other hand, successful racial division of workers has been an important factor underlying the lower wages of southern workers of all races. Thus, individual indicators of the race and sex of a respondent should be supplemented by measures of the relative mobilization, relative income, and segregation of women and subordinated races in given industries, occupations, and communities.

Other variables that affect the labor market power of workers versus employers, or of dominated groups versus superordinate groups also should be considered. These include occupational, industrial, and local unemployment rates; the stringency and benefit levels of local welfare and unemployment programs; and the general tenor of local politics.

Another critique of the measure stage of dual economy theory also is helpful in formulating some of the requirements for a new beginning. In Friedman and Friedman (1979), we pointed out that the qualitative stage of dual economy theory was economic determinist, and, perhaps, even market determinist. That is, the theory held that economic variables (and the market variables that affect the degree of competition/monopoly in particular) were decisive determinants of workers' fates, and thus questions of politics, organization, and ideology were treated as irrelevant. We also argued that dual theory was ahistorical and that this led to treating variables (the meaning and effects of which differ in different situations) in a timeless, reified manner. As an example of this, we showed that the characteristics normally pointed to as underlying the relatively good pay and conditions of workers at General Motors or U.S. Steel in the 1960s — company size, capital intensity, market concentration — had operated in the 1920s to strengthen management control over the worker and thus to worsen wages and conditions. By the measure stage, dual theory had moved beyond economic determinism[13] — but unfortunately it remained at a level of ahistorical institutional determinism.

Thus Kalleberg et al. (1981) measure workers' power only by institutional measures such as union membership, tenure with employer, skill-level of occupation, percentage of people in a given occupation and industry whose occupations are licensed in at least 30 states, and individual supervisory authority. Hodson (1981) relies on individual union membership and on percent of the industry that is unionized. Unfortunately, all of these measures (except possibly the management dummy variable) are simply ahistorical measures of institutional strength or attachments. They do not measure how this strength is used or whether the attachment strengthens employer control over the worker (e.g., workers being tied down by benefits that increase with tenure) or the reverse (e.g., workers in companies with longer average tenure having built up internal networks that help them to mobilize). As another example of this, percent union in an industry can, as Kalleberg et al. and Hodson assume, measure worker power, but it also can be the product of a highly bureaucratized union that serves employer interests rather than worker interests (Friedman, 1982; Serrin, 1974). To avoid this, we should attempt to avoid measures of institutional strength when it is possible to supplement or replace them with measures of behavior, mobilization, and side (whether the institutional strength is, in reality, used in behalf of or in opposition to its putative goals).[14]

In summary, we should incorporate the gains made in the measure stage (such as the multidimensional nature of industry structure), but we should go beyond this by introducing new qualitative aspects — class and social conflict. By making the power relationships explicit, this new beginning will also make visible (and accessible for analysis and action) the points at which policy intervention can have lasting positive results.

Segmented Labor Market Theories

In contrast to dual economy theory which looks at the capital structure of industries and firms, segmentation approaches look at job characteristics and labor markets. The two sets of theories share the same basic intentions (Mannheim, 1953), however: Both are attempts to provide an economic structural underpinning for the persistence of poverty, racism, and sexism; both see the growth of giant corporations as having restructured the labor market; and both advance critiques of the system and its theorists without developing a Marxist approach to questions of class or value.[15]

Doeringer and Piore (1971) presented an early segmentationist view. They identified two segments — primary labor market jobs with high wages, good working conditions, employment stability, chances of advancement, equity and due process in the administration of work rules; and secondary jobs with low wages and fringe benefits, poor working conditions, high labor turnover, little chance of advancement, and supervision that was often arbitrary and capricious. Workers in secondary jobs frequently display high rates of lateness, absenteeism, insubordination, petty theft, and pilferage. Disadvantaged workers, they argued, were confined to the secondary market by residence, inadequate skills, poor work histories, and discrimination. Relatively little mobility occurs between these two labor markets.

Structurally, Doeringer and Piore viewed the primary market as a series of internal labor markets in which there are stable employment opportunities and regularized lines of advancement. Some of these internal markets are specific to a given firm but others, in the crafts or professions, are specific to an occupation. The secondary labor market was seen as consisting of several different kinds of employment situations: work ouside of internal labor markets; work inside secondary internal labor markets in which the lines of advancement are short, the pay is low, and the work unpleasant; and secondary jobs that are attached to the bottom of internal labor markets in which the other jobs are primary.

Piore then moved to develop the theory underlying this question, an effort which still engages him. In Piore (1973), he focused on the relative stability of jobs and workers in three segments (secondary, lower tier primary, and upper tier primary) as the key, and on the presence of career ladders in the primary labor market and their absence in the secondary. An interaction between labor supply and demand factors determines the segment of a job.

On the supply side, secondary jobs tend to be filled from the lower-class subculture; lower tier jobs from the working class; and upper tier from the middle class. Thus, if a previously lower-tier set of jobs is opened to lower class workers, Piore saw this as creating an unstable situation in which the cultural characteristics of the lower class would cause the job to become secondary unless the stabilizing effects of the job (possibly helped by social programs) first resocialized the job-holders into a working-class approach to the employment situation.

On the demand side, the structure of technology shapes jobs. In some jobs, efficient operation requires considerable skill or knowledge, so employers set up mobility chains and other primary characteristics to train and retrain labor; whereas in other jobs, the technology can be operated by a low-pay, high turnover work force. Piore pointed out that the nature of the technology on a job is not exogenous — but is itself affected by the structure of product demand. Stable demand allows investment in technology and thus allows lower-tier primary jobs. Unstable demand is associated with a low degree of technological specialization and, thus, either with highly skilled upper-tier primary work or with secondary employment.

Thus, a job can move between segments, depending on whether demand for its products shifts and also depending on the social class that the labor market, in its current state, makes available to fill it.

Gordon (1971) generally agrees with Piore's formulations. He spells out some hypotheses that clarify the meaning of the term labor market segmentation. He hypothesizes, first, that "within the span of individual labor market careers, one will witness relatively little intermarket mobility (except occasionally among white males)'' and, second, that within different segments there exist ''*fundamentally different behavioral models* [emphasis in original] to explain the determination and distribution of income within each . . . for the interaction of job and worker characteristics in each market fosters different kinds of worker behavior and personality traits in those markets'' (Gordon 1971, p. 32).

Vietorisz and Harrison (1973) argued that segementation can occur because positive feedback allows divergent development (whereas equilibrium models are based on convergence due to negative feedback). They held that, in the primary segment, positive feedback between the development of technology and the attendant need for highly skilled workers produces a dynamic tendency towards improvement, whereas in the secondary segment, low technology and low skills feed back upon each other to produce a vicious circle downward. Thus, the segments diverge. This model explained why there is low mobility of workers between segments. On the other hand, the model is highly vulnerable to falsification if considerable mobility between segments is found to exist.[16]

Thus, by 1973, the theory of labor market segmentation was reasonably well developed. It was a theory that said that two or three separate markets exist for labor. These markets are distinct — meaning that the processes by which the buyers and sellers of labor-power arrive at deals in each market are separate from the processes in the other segments and, further, that there is a considerable degree of insulation among these markets. However, for labor markets to be insulated and distinct requires that the conditions in one market not affect those in another, and also that there not be much mobility of workers between markets (since such mobility means that the balance of supply and demand in one market affects the balance in the other).

Starting in 1973, a number of studies showed that there is considerable mobility between segments — a major challenge to segmentationist theory. Andrisani (1973, p. 56) found considerable intersegment mobility; over two-fifths of male youths (whether white or black) with first jobs in the secondary segment had current jobs in the primary segment.[17] Similar conclusions were reached by Lowell (1973), Rosenberg (1975),[18] and Buchele (1976). Rosenberg (1979, p. 8) summarizes: ''The results of virtually all the studies, using various measures of mobility, show upward mobility from the bottom of the occupational distribution.''

These findings undercut a key assumption of segmentationist theory: that there is little intersegment mobility and, hence, that the segments constitute different labor markets. However, this did not destroy the theory for three reasons. First, these and other studies indicated that the segments do differ in their dynamics (as indicated by equations that predict earnings and labor-market behavior in the segments). Second, these same studies found results incompatible with human capital theory — which meant that it was reasonable to try to modify segmentation theory in the absence of any clearly superior alternative theory.[19] Third, such a reformulation of the theory in terms of segmentation being a trait of jobs rather than labor markets was readily developed.

Osterman (1977) saw two separate (not logically linked) aspects to segmented labor market theory — an empirically suspect model based around the secondary labor market as a "mobility trap" and an "alternative intellectual framework" to neoclassical labor economics based around the idea that "there are different sectors of the labor market that operate according to different behavioral rules." He held that it "is perfectly possible that there is considerable intragenerational mobility between two labor market segments, each of which operates on a different set of internal economic rules."

As the theory has developed in later work (notably, Osterman, 1980; Berger and Piore, 1981; and Gordon, Edwards, and Reich, 1982), it has ignored the question of mobility among segments. Instead, it has worked out a theory of job segmentation and of the processes that cause jobs to become segmented. Piore (in Berger and Piore, 1981) has emphasized the interplay of two dynamics that create the distinction between primary and secondary jobs: First, that uncertain or unstable demand limits the ways in which employers develop and apply new technological equipment and processes, so that stability allows the development of stable semiskilled subordinate primary jobs whereas instability or uncertain demand pushes toward the use of cheap unskilled secondary labor. The second dynamic involves politics and groups' attempts to build shelters against instability. Thus, Piore sees the expansion (or development) of the distinction between primary and secondary segments as occurring in response to a sudden upsurge in labor militancy[20]; he views the actual institutional arrangements (like labor and social security laws in the U.S.) which define the segmentation as being preexisting legal frameworks or institutions; and he sees the labor force that gets relegated to the secondary jobs as deriving heavily from "preindustrial" groups and classes (often migrants or women). The relative importance of the demand/technological and the politics/shelter causes of segmentation can vary.

Gordon et al. (1982) study the history of the labor process and of the working class in the United States. They see segmentation as being a stage in this history. The earlier stages were initial proletarianization, in which workers were brought together into workplaces without serious modification of their pre-existing technology or work processes; and homogenization, in which large firms reorganized their labor processes (which required the breaking of the power of the crafts over technical knowledge and over production) and reduced most workers to a relatively undifferentiated mass of semi-skilled workers. The segmentation stage, as they see it, developed out of the homogenization stage in a process of social conflict. The labor upsurge of the 1930s put considerable power in the hands of workers in a number of industries and occupations. Employers responded to this in a complex process of segmentation. Gordon et al. unfortunately base their analysis of this process on a dual economy model.[21]

Thus, as they see it, core firms could afford to create stable, high-paying primary jobs on the basis of unions (or nonunion subordinate primary workers) trading off control over production for wages and conditions. Independent primary jobs developed to perform the creative, supervisory, skilled and/or initiatory tasks for core firms and the public sector, many of which had in past years been handled by craft institutions. The secondary segment, in their view, is composed of two groups of jobs. First, almost all jobs in periphery firms; second, jobs for large corporations which either prevent workers in entire enterprises from unionizing without establishing primary conditions (examples include electronics assembly and tobacco processing and manufacturing) or set up particular job sets as secondary (such as typing pools).

Summarizing, Gordon et al. (1982) and Piore (in Berger and Piore, 1981) both argue that labor market segmentation occurs through the interaction of economic factors (capital structure for Gordon et al. and the effects of unstable demand on the structuring of the work process for Piore) with the organization of workers into unions, primary work groups, and associations that provide them with shelters (Freedman, 1976) against negative pressures from the labor market. These arguments then require that the downward pressure on wages and conditions in the primary segment from job-seekers from the unemployed or from secondary segment jobs (i.e., the reserve labor force) are suppressed by the stabilizing forces described by the theories. Under these conditions, mobility of individuals among segments can be fairly high without a breakdown in segmentation.[22] One implication of these theories is that segmentation becomes unstable as a system in times of long-term economic crisis (such as the segmentationists characterize the 1960s). When formerly stable demand becomes unstable or nonexistent, when productivity under current labor control strategies deteriorates, and when profit rates fall, employers come under pressure to downgrade primary conditions and labor costs, even if this requires union-busting. As

Gordon et al. recognize (1982, ch. 5), this leads to a period of social conflict in which all aspects of labor control and labor markets become objects of contention. The policy implications of this for the poor and for those who work on behalf of the poor are not adequately spelled out by the Gordon group or by Piore. A crisis clearly holds out both horrendous possibilities (Reaganomics, poor laws) and real opportunities — such as the union organizing in the thirties provided for workers who became primary by their own power.

What is the empirical foundation for labor segmentation theory, given that considerable intersegment mobility occurs? Such a theory should be based on the following:

1. Evidence that job characteristics cluster into segments. This is the segmentation theory equivalent of the multidimensionality problem that undercut dual economy theory. What needs to be shown, then, is that jobs with some "secondary" characteristics are considerably more likely to have other "secondary" characteristics than are jobs that are "primary" on the first characteristic. Findings that these traits are statistically independent or only mildly associated tend to undercut the theory.
   Unfortunately, studies to test this have not been carried out — with one exception. My preliminary analyses of two data sets indicate that segmentation-relevant traits of jobs are, at best, mildly associated. For example, having a job with a written promotion policy has a correlation of only .13 with having learned new skills during the first month for a sample of improverished male and female youth. Job characteristics in a national Quality of Employment Survey of jobholders also have low intercorrelations. Thus, the study strongly suggests that there is no underlying "primariness" dimension and, therefore, segmentation models are ill-conceived on empirical grounds.
2. Evidence that earnings, hiring, firing, promotion, turnover, and other labor market outcomes occur differently in the various segments. Most segmentationists argue that human capital (and perhaps race and sex) affect incomes and other job characteristics in the primary segments but not in the secondary. This evidence is reviewed in Appendix II.[23]
3. In addition, the theory should use a wide range of historical and international comparative evidence to show that the predicted conditions lead to segmentaton. Piore (in Berger and Piore, 1981) presents a comparison of recent labor market histories for the United States, France, and Italy. Unfortunately, however, he does not develop the statistical

analyses needed to show convincingly that segmentation has actually occurred or that it has done so in the ways predicted by his theory.[24]

What are the policy implications of segmentationist thought? One is that training programs will do little good. This conclusion grows out of its critique of human capital theory and programs as well as Osterman's (1980) findings that primary jobs train workers in the needed skills. Thus, Osterman (1980, p. 158) proposes that black youths need help in placement and, in some cases, job-readiness training. More generally, if the main determinant of an individual's labor market fate is the segment of the job the individual gets, then programming should aid disadvantaged individuals in getting placed into primary jobs and/or help them establish networks among people in primary segments.

Another policy implication might be to put individuals through major educational programs like union apprenticeship or college. Segmentation theory implies that marginal differences in education matter little. However, major differences are accompanied by establishing primary networks and may, in addition, open up new hiring possibilities.

The third implication is that jobs should be changed from secondary to primary. Piore (1979) suggests that this can be done by reducing the variability and uncertainty of demand or the institutions by which this variability is handled. By the first, he means Keynesian-style management of aggregate demand but also more specific demand-management programs targeting particular industries or communities. Changing the institutions controlling job security, a second route he sees for making more jobs primary, raises questions of social power and conflict. This, of course, brings us back to our earlier discussion of Gordon et al. (1982) and the question of what policy initiatives might be useful for the poor in a period of general conflict over labor structures.

Selected Other Theories

The human capital, dual economy, and segmentationist analyses are perhaps the most salient, but are by no means the only, current approaches to explaining income determination and labor force dynamics. Several other views are worth mentioning.

Freedman (1976) developed a model in which income variation is studied by occupation and industry using Automatic Interaction Detection. She found 14 separate occupation/industry clusters, with major lines of division being the extent of part-time work, the extent of collective bargaining, and the extent of occupational licensing. Using personal rather than organizational factors as independent variables, she found that the extent to which the occupation/industry is composed of young workers and of women, and the educational level of the work force, are key in setting up eight occupation/industry clusters. She interpreted these results in an institutionalist framework, holding that competition tends to decrease workers' returns and that workers, in turn, try to set up shelter mechanisms to protect themselves. Thus, unionization and licensing are examples of shelters, and the low pay of youth and women is a consequence of their relative lack of power (which leads to their exclusion when others set up shelters and weakens their ability to establish shelters of their own).

Wright (1979) studied the importance of class in income determination. By class, he meant relations of production such as economic ownership, control over production equipment, control over the labor power of others, and being the buyer or seller of labor power. Workers, then, lack such ownership and control, and are sellers of labor power.

Wright's work is the first major Marxist analysis of earnings determination. As such, it presents one form of Marxist analysis of earnings. Of particular interest is Wright's demonstration that dividing the *labor force* or *employed/self-employed* population into segments (as do segmentationist and dual studies) is an incorrect procedure. Thus, we should view the question as one of how to study differences *within the working class* (and, of course, differences within other classes). Wright found that, for a cross-section of the working class, education has a substantial positive coefficient in an earnings regression and that neither race nor sex affects this income-return to education within the working class.

It should be noted that Wright's ideas do not lead directly to the questions that Friedman and Friedman (1979) pointed to, such as how earnings within the working class are affected by the political situation among workers and employers (e.g., unionization; rank-and-file democracy; militancy; employer organization; race/sex splits or movements among workers in an occupation, company, or industry) or by the market situation of the company or industry. The impact of production/technological characteristics (such as exploitation rates, organic composition of capital, de-skilling, etc.) might follow easily from his concern with relations of production as criteria among classes — but, then again, it might not.

Correspondingly, Wright did not develop an analysis where unemployed workers have a systematic relationship to the employed — whether in terms of a secondary labor market in which unemployment, work, welfare, and crime are simply different states within a long-term life pattern (as Bennett Harrison might argue) or in terms of either a reserve army of the unemployed or reserve labor force analysis.

Another approach looks explicitly at the reserve army of labor (Anthias, 1980; Beechey, 1977; Gardiner, 1975–76; Gordon et al. 1982, pp. 19–20, passim; Marx, 1967; Milkman, 1976; Rosenberg, 1977, 1981; Simeral, 1978; Sokoloff 1980). This analysis argues that capitalist production tends to create a pool of unemployed people and that this has several functions for capitalism. First, it means that new areas of production can form without being held back by labor shortages and that cyclical upswings are not cut short by an absence of workers.[25] Second, it provides employers with strong leverage in their relationships with workers and thus holds labor costs down, strengthening productivity and obedience. In the process, when reserve army workers get hired for relatively short times and then lose their jobs, they weaken workers' position in the labor market. The existence of such a reserve army and the maintenance of employers' ability to move them into and then out of jobs poses a threat of disorder (e.g., riots — as discussed in Piven and Cloward, 1979) with which management must deal. Conversely, restraints on management's freedom to lay workers off threatens profit rates. These problems are minimized to the extent that reserve army members are members of groups that are (or can become) looked down upon by the more stably employed workers. Hence, racial minorities, women, and immigrants tend to serve as the most effective sources of the reserve army.

Although controversial, the reserve army theory is compatible with the presence and effects of unemployment and with the social composition of the unemployed. However, it does not deal adequately with the existence of a wide range of different types of jobs.[26] Instead, it seems to assume that the unemployed form a potential employment source for most jobs and, hence, that they perform a function (allowing growth, holding down workers) for the whole economy.

Synthesis

The theories we have reviewed are attempts to explain income differences, the persistence of poverty, and the factors that shape workers' labor market experience. In this section, I will attempt to outline a new perspective on the labor market and job characteristics that encompasses what seems to be valuable in the above theories and that points out areas of ignorance that need to be studied in depth.

These phenomena can be seen as the outcome of a dialectic between two sets of processes. First, there are processes that *define the job*. These include struggles between workers and employers as well as characteristics of the industry, occupation, and firm. Second, processes that *define the potential labor for the job* centers around the nature of the reserve labor force for the job. But this, in turn, is shaped by the first process (the social and technical definition of the job), as well as by the social conflicts and economic dynamics that create and influence the potential employees.

Looking at labor processes in this way synthesizes some aspects of the analysis of supply and demand with two of Marx's key insights: First, the conditions of work create (and result from) constant conflict. Second, the existence and creation of potential job-holders disciplines and inhibits workers but also generalizes particular workplace struggles into a broader class conflict between the employing and working classes.

What are the processes and characteristics that affect the pay and conditions of a job? Wright (1979) showed that its class location is important. Our review of dual economy theory indicates that other production relationships are also important and may well be best conceived in terms that highlight class such as productivity, exploitation rates, and the organic composition of capital. In a similar vein, segmentationists point to another set of relationships that shape job returns: whether the job is part of an internal labor market and the kind of mobility chain (if any) of which it is a part.

Market relations also should be studied. These include concentration ratios and the political shaping of markets through regulations such as antitrust, occupational safety and health, and labor laws. Also, following the segmentationists, we would expect (among nonprofessional, noncraft occupations) jobs whose products face a stable demand to be more remunerative and to have more benefits and protections than those that are subject to wide demand fluctuations.

Political relationships also affect pay and job conditions. The nature and extent of worker and employer organizations are starting points, but the divisions that exist among workers in a firm, industry, or occupation (along lines of sex, age, or race, for example) and the relative success of workers and employers at building ties to local, national, and world community groups and power centers also are important. As a particular example, consider the ability of a group of workers to organize sufficient strategically located solidarity to stop production in a worldwide conglomerate.

Segmentationists argue that the outcome of the job-shaping process is a set of jobs divided into segments. As was discussed in the review of segmentation theory, the existence of such a unidimensional scale along which segmentation occurs has not been proven — nor, indeed, studied. This research is needed. In its absence, I will assume that no such segmentation dimension exists. Some jobs are better that some other jobs, but in many cases jobs that are better in one respect are worse in others.

The critical concept in understanding the dynamics of the creation of potential job-fillers and their relationships to jobs, as these affect the pay and conditions of the jobs and the social composition of the job-fillers, is that of the reserve labor force for a given set of jobs. This concept differs from that of the reserve army of the unemployed by being related to the job. Thus, the reserve labor forces for different jobs may differ; whereas there is only one reserve army of the unemployed.[27]

Of specific interest for the theory of segmentation, if segments exist, subordinate segments would be expected to serve as labor reserves for higher segments — which conforms with the finding that there is considerable mobility among jobs in different segments. The secondary labor force could thus be seen as a reserve labor force for the subordinate primary and, to a lesser extent, for the independent primary segment. When primary employment expands, secondary workers are there to fill the need. When primary employment contracts (particularly cyclically), the previously secondary workers tend to be the first let go (inasmuch as they were the last hired and are disproportionately composed of vulnerable groups — minorities, women, and/or those with criminal records).[28]

In time of major expansion of an industry or of the economy as a whole, employers need to hire from their reserves of labor. For this to occur, the potential employees need to have been kept from starvation while waiting. In modern America, there are several ways in which this is done. Some workers come from being home-bound housewives; others come from welfare; and some from living off the street. The relationship of these sections of the reserve army of the unemployed to that section of the reserve labor force[29] employed in less desirable jobs needs to be studied. Harrison (1977, 1979) has argued that social program participants, welfare recipients, street criminals, and workers in secondary jobs are really one group. Of particular relevance, we need to know whether employers prefer to hire those already employed in less desirable jobs to recruiting welfare recipients or people who have been living off the streets.

The entire reserve labor force keeps a large number of potential workers available for good jobs. This exerts a downward pull on the pay and conditions of the employed. However, as Piven and Cloward (1982) point out, the fact that welfare or low-income jobs give the labor reserve some income reduces its impact. Starving workers will take more risks and perform more unpleasant or disgraceful tasks than welfare recipients or holders of less desirable jobs.

The extent of the reserve for different kinds of jobs must be considered in any analysis of how pay and conditions are determined. The building up and exclusion of such reserves then becomes a subject of social conflict. This ties in with Freedman's (1976) analysis of shelters from the rigors of competition as workers try to shape job skills, licensing, apprenticeship programs, or union rules so as to reduce the number of reasonable replacements and as employers try to weaken these shelters by building up the relevant labor reserves. Examples of this process include the general weakening of university professors by the establishment of reserves of adjuncts and unemployed professionals; the ambushing of the seemingly strong air traffic controllers that was made possible by the training of a reserve in the military; and the general weakening of the construction trades by the building of reserves in home construction and their supplementation by manpower program trainees.

The conflict over the definition of the potential labor force for jobs is more complicated than simple employer-worker conflict, however. When workers set up a shelter by excluding other potential workers, the excluded workers can suffer. This introduces divisions into the working class. As was clear to the Wobblies early in the twentieth century, job trusting and exclusion by race, sex, or other criteria weaken the long-run solidarity of the working class. Thus, many sheltering mechanisms offer only short-run advantages to those sheltered, at a long-run cost to themselves and to other workers.

The excluded potential workers often try to end their exclusion and to buttress their social and economic position in the general society. Thus, such battles as the civil rights movement in the community, black caucuses on the job, and women's fight for public child care are parts of struggles over the definition of the potential labor for various jobs.[30]

Let us now take an overview of the reserve labor force process. The pattern is remarkably stable for an economy in constant flux, although the downward pressures exerted by the reserve labor force are more visible in hard times. In general, the pattern involves substantial mobility between better and worse jobs.

Relatively few members of subordinated categories of workers manage to retain primary quality jobs. When they do, this helps sustain images of the possibility of individual mobility and, therefore, helps to reinforce images among the reserve labor force of personal culpability in their own fates. This is true even though there is a large random contributing factor behind the success of a former reserve labor force member who gets and retains a good job. That is, behind such a success is the unexpected long-term maintenance of demand for the product of what was expected to be a short-term job. In addition, individual ability and/or reliability might well be required, but only exceptional personal traits or political circumstances would cause a reserve labor force member to be kept on a temporary job when slackening demand makes cutbacks advisable.

So far, we have considered the factors and conflicts that shape jobs and those that revolve around the reserve labor force. Now let us consider the dialectic between these two processes. It might be approached as a simple supply and demand equilibrium model, with the shaping of jobs defining the demand for labor of a given type, with the shaping of the reserve labor force defining the supply of labor, and with the price of labor varying so as to equalize supply and demand. Such a model would be a drastic oversimplification and, indeed, misrepresentation.

The job-shaping process is not simply a demand phenomenon but involves conflicts that incorporate supply issues as determinants of the outcomes. Similarly, the battle over shelters and the reserve labor force includes struggle over qualifications and other demand issues. Thus, supply and demand aspects in each process are part of the dynamic of the other process. Furthermore, the adjustment mechanism is not simply price fluctuation that leads to equilibrium. Instead, there is a broad conflict in which all aspects of the job and labor market both influence the outcomes and are themselves altered by the struggle. This can lead to seemingly illogical results if viewed from a neoclassical perspective. For example, even a huge oversupply of professionals and technology that allows much greater productivity probably would not be pushed to reduce the pay and conditions of college faculty so much that they abandoned their basic loyalty to the system; the possibility of saving huge sums has not led many employers to hire low-paid women to replace high-paid men; and, in construction, wages and unemployment increased together for years before seriously impairing the power of the unions.

Finally, in considering how to analyze jobs and labor markets, we should remember the question raised in the section on dual economy theory about the nature of ahistorical institutional variables. As an important example, the existence of a mass of unemployed seems to be prima facie evidence that employers' wishes will dominate. However, this is an institutional variable, and we need to go beyond it to look at the degree or potential of mobilization. These same unemployed can rapidly become a major threat to employer bargaining power. Indeed, the upsurge of the 1930s started among the unemployed and only then spread to the employed. In many struggles (such as the Toledo confrontation in 1934), the unemployed were a main force in changing power relations on the job. On the other hand, by 1938, the mobilization of the unemployed had decreased to such an extent that they again served as a labor reserve inhibiting the employed. A model that looked at unemployment simply as an institutional variable reflecting employer dominance would be unable to account for these events. More generally, research is needed on the circumstances and processes that lead to each relevant institutional variable changing from one meaning to another.

In conclusion, the model presented here is neither simple nor deterministic. In place of the elegant typologies of dual economy and segmentation theory and the magisterial calm fluctuations and equity that human capital theory posits, this model discusses the necessities of production and the dynamics of conflict. The other models are more elegant — but this review has shown that they are not adequate to deal with the clashing, inelegant forces that shape managerial needs, workers, jobs and the labor market. Nor is the model presented here complete. In part, this is because it is new and undeveloped. However, it also reflects the fact that it is a model developed to explain processes of conflict that involve dialectical leaps and reversals that are not neatly deterministic.

Policy and Political Implications

In spite of its lack of elegance, this model has a number of implications for policy to help the poor. It is convenient to present them in terms of policies for individual mobility and policies for collective mobility, although often a single policy involves both.

Policies for Individual Mobility

1. Individual-mobility programs cannot focus simply on getting participants into primary quality jobs. Getting such a job is not a break in the reserve labor force pattern since employers routinely hire reserve labor force members in good but temporary jobs. Programming needs to get participants placed and established in good jobs. This could be done by getting them placed artificially high on seniority lists (which has a potential for sparking major conflict); by placing them into good jobs at new plants or offices that are expected to expand; or by placing them in relatively secure sheltered jobs (like civil service *used* to be).
2. As an adjunct to such placement efforts, job-readiness training might be essential for some participants.
3. Further research is needed on the relationship of education to the ability to escape from the reserve labor force. Marginal differences in education do not seem to have large impacts on this. More ambitious programs that give participants support during major educational

experiences such as union apprenticeships or even multi-year programs that go up to and then through college are more likely to be effective.

4. The reserve labor force is composed heavily of those who are relatively easy to fire or lay off such as blacks, women, convicts, youth, and the working aged. Individuals will have a greater probability of escaping from the reserve labor force if employers find it harder to get rid of them. This can be helped along by antidiscrimination policies.

Policies for Collective Mobility

1. The qualitative formulation of dual economy theory pointed to making more of the economy resemble the core industries as one way to help poor workers. Analogously, we can use the findings of measure-stage analyses to find what characteristics of industries, occupations, or firms are associated with good jobs and then (if there are no likely side effects or complications) try to encourage development in the indicated directions. For example, since Hodson (1981) found a negative impact of concentration on employees' earnings, he suggests more antitrust action against large monopolies.
2. A main thrust of the argument of this paper is that jobs and labor market conditions are the outcome of conflict. Furthermore, the history of the last 50 years shows that major gains for groups of the poor were made in two periods: the thirties, when workers and unemployed waged massive struggles; and the sixties, under the impact of the black movement.[31] This raises questions about what programs can help the poor to empower themselves and what kinds of agencies can conduct such programs. Nonprofit agencies are obviously limited by their financing and requirements for political support. However, it would be useful to set up programs to train high-risk youth to turn their energies and aggressions away from *individual* conflict and toward *social* conflict by developing programs to train them in organizing skills. Similarly, it would be useful to train students in the tactics, strategies, and politics of organizing power for employed workers and for people unable to have jobs.

Politics

The proposals for collective mobility presented above are unlikely to be put into effect. They fly against the grain of current politics. The only times when similar proposals have been implemented (and, even then, only in ways that were self-limiting) were the community action programs of the 1960s and labor studies programs in a few schools — and these were responses to massive social movements that threatened existing economic and political arrangements. The reason for this is clear from the model of labor processes developed in this paper. Working conditions and the conditions of various sections of the reserve labor force are the result of social conflict. Programs of the kind described above would strengthen the position of workers and of the poor at the expense of the owners and controllers of capital. Since politics in normal times is dominated and defined by the corporate elite and their allies (Domhoff, 1967, 1970; Domhoff and Ballard, 1968; Mills, 1959; Parenti, 1974), policies that hurt their interests are not even widely discussed, much less implemented, except under conditions of mass upheaval.

If labor outcomes result from conflicts, this poses a series of choices for analysts and practitioners about which side to take in these conflicts. Do we support employers or workers? Those excluded from jobs or those building shelters by excluding them? Or do we try to stay neutral, perhaps trying only to influence the techniques of conflict (as in urging respect for the law or the use of mediation)? On this, let me say that attempts at neutrality or at influencing the techniques of conflict almost always support the status quo and, thus, the rich and powerful, since it is only through mobilizing for no-holds-barred conflict that workers and the poor develop their strength and understanding and thus become capable of winning gains (Friedman, 1982, chapters 1, 4, 11; Piven and Cloward, 1979).

More generally, the choice posed is a choice of sides between two classes. One can support the interests of employers and thus try to weaken workers' organizations, divide employed and unemployed workers from each other, make reserve labor forces more needy, and attack workplace health, safety, conditions, and pay. Or one can support the working class by strengthening workers' organizations, encouraging solidarity and cooperation between employed and unemployed, striving to end divisions among workers by combatting exclusions based on race, sex, and age, and supporting the struggles of the unemployed for social benefits and of the employed for better workplaces and pay.

Appendix I
Some Empirical Studies of Human Capital Predictions

In this Appendix, I summarize some of the studies of the returns to education that have been conducted by scholars interested in segmentation or industrial sector theories.

Segmentation theory research has found mixed results about the returns to education. Andrisani (1973) found a positive relationship between education and pay in a pooled sample of male youth, for white youth in the primary sector, for black youth in the primary sector, and for white youth in the secondary sector. However, he found no significant return to education for blacks in the secondary sectors. Osterman (1975) studied urban male heads of families. He found no significant return to education within the secondary segment but a significant return within the primary. Looking separately at blacks within the secondary, however, he did find a significant return to education. Buchele (1976, chapter 5) found, for out-of-school males aged 25–27, human capital variables such as education, IQ, training, and experience have no association with earnings in his bottom segment but that there is a positive return to education in the two segments just above the bottom. McGahey (1982) studied male arrestees. He found a positive relationship between education and gross hourly wages for his pooled sample. He found a positive return in both segments (but a higher rate of return in the primary) using ordinary least squares; a significant return in both segments using a two-stage least squares model (with total hours of work in the preceding two years as the other dependent variable); but a significant return only in the primary using a fully recursive procedure. McGahey also studied total hours of work, finding that education had a positive return (to hours) for his pooled sample under ordinary least squares and recursive models but not under two-stage least squares. He also found that within segments, total hours worked increased with education in both segments under ordinary least squares; education was similarly positively associated with total hours worked in the secondary segment but not in the primary under the recursive procedure; and there was no significant relationship in either segment under two-stage least squares. These studies are by no means conclusive, but they do indicate that human capital theory is not a consistent predictor of the returns to education.

Studies using the dual economy approach have also considered the return to education and how this differs among industrial sectors. Taylor et al. (1981) compared earnings functions computed separately (from Census Public Use Sample and Current Population Survey Data) for white males, white females, black males, and black females within core, periphery, and government sectors for each of the years 1960, 1970, and 1978. They found that returns to subcollege education in the periphery were nonexistent for women of both races but positive for men — although higher for white men than for black men. In the core and government sectors, there were significant positive returns for all four race/sex groups in all three years. These rates of return are not equal in the core since white males get higher returns to education. Returns to years of postsecondary education are significant and positive for all race/sex groups in each sector in 1978. In the periphery, such returns were higher for white males and lower for white females than for blacks of either sex. In the core, white males had the highest return to college education followed by black males, with females of both races getting the least benefit. In the government sector, returns to college years vary relatively little across race/sex groups.

Beck et al. (1980) found that dollar returns to human capital are greater for whites than nonwhites, men than women, and core sector workers than periphery workers. In each sector, nonwhite women, however, had a higher rate of return than white women. They found greater dissimilarity in dollar return to education among race/sex groups in the core than in the periphery.[1] Zucker and Rosenstein (1981) used four different taxonomies of industrial structure to determine whether sectoral differences were important determinants of earnings. They found years of education to be unimportant, but highest degree attained (the credential variable used in Beck et al., 1980) was generally both statistically significant and important. Furthermore, they found that differences between sectors in the values of educational coefficients were not significant.

Kalleberg et al. (1981) found that education has a positive effect on income with a number of industry, firm, and occupational variables controlled, and that the magnitude of the return to education does not vary between men and women.

Rumberger and Carnoy (1980) find that for males the returns to education vary across occupationally defined segments and by race but do not vary across industrially defined sectors.

Thus, in conclusion, both dual economy and segmented labor market studies raise serious questions about human capital theory. Some studies find education unrelated to income; others find that the returns to education vary among segments, sectors, races, or sexes; while the results of still others are consistent with human capital predictions.

Note

1. In an earlier work (Beck et al., 1978), these same authors found years of schooling to be a significant determinant of annual earnings only in the periphery; and dummy variables for the highest degree (high school or junior college; bachelors, postgraduate) significant only in the core. Their findings were challenged by Hauser (1980), however, who argued that sampling errors had produced the evidence of heterogeneity in the earnings equations between sectors.

Appendix II
Some Empirical Evidence on Segmentation and Labor Outcomes

This Appendix summarizes some of the studies on how segments differ in their labor outcomes.

Andrisani (1973) found that male youths' human capital is positively associated for both races with earnings in the primary sector and for whites (but not for blacks) in the secondary sector. This is, at best, weak support for segmentation theory.

Osterman (1975, p. 518) is more supportive of the theory. He found for males in the secondary segment, annual earnings depend only on the amount of time worked (hours worked previous week and weeks unemployed) and not on age, sex, or race; that in both the upper and lower primary tiers, age, age squared, education, and hours worked previous week were significant; and that race and weeks unemployed were significant in the lower tier but not in the upper (perhaps because the number of cases was far larger for the lower tier).

Rumberger and Carnoy (1980) found a significant positive return to a high school diploma (but not to college education) for white males but not for black males in the secondary segment. In the primary subordinate and primary independent segments, both white and black males received significant returns to education.

McGahey (1982) estimated equations for a sample of male arrestees. His ordinary least squares equations indicated substantial similarity of primary and secondary segment equations in estimating the total hours worked in the preceding two years. The major difference beween the segments was that race (being black or Hispanic) has a greater negative impact on hours worked in the secondary segment. Similarly, ordinary least squares showed similarity between primary and secondary earnings equations. However, McGahey then estimated recursive equations to take account of the two-way interaction between earnings and hours worked. He found different determinants of hours and earnings between the two segments. Interestingly, human capital variables seemed more important in predicting hours worked in the secondary segment than in the primary — which is not what would be predicted — and the above finding that minority racial status had a greater negative impact on hours worked in the secondary segment remains in the recursive equations. The recursive equations on earnings are also supportive of segmentation theory. Most importantly, much more of the variance in earnings is explained for the primary than for the secondary segment (R^2 of .357 versus .123), which supports the segmentationist view that these variables are important only in the primary segment. In the secondary segment, only experience and race are significant; whereas in the primary, age, education, and race are significant.

Turnover has been studied by Rosenberg (1975) and Buchele (1976). Segmentationist theory had originally argued very strongly that turnover would be much higher and job tenure much lower in the secondary segment as compared to the primary. However, these studies show relatively small (but nevertheless statistically significant) differences. Thus, Buchele found, for middle-aged white males, that secondary workers have mean tenure of 11.3 years — which is hardly evidence of instability — whereas subordinate primary workers have 13.8 years and independent primary supervisory workers have 15.2.

Notes

1. Current income might also be maximized to earn capital which can then be invested in income-producing property. This, however, is not an option for most of the poor.

2. A particularly conservative similar theory was presented in Banfield (1970), *The Unheavenly City*, in which he postulated that differences in ability and desire to defer gratification underlie income differences and, in fact, are the constitutive factor in class formation.

3. The formulations and weaknesses of marginal productivity theory are explored in more depth in Thurow (1975), Appendix A.

4. More precisely, relative prices are raised in industries in which the ratio of expenditures for nonwage items to expenditures on wages is above average.

5. Indeed, the pattern of development of dual economy theory is an interesting example of the Hegelian dialetic of quality-quantity-measure-new beginning. See Findlay (1958), James (1948, pp. 67–73), Hegel (1931, 1951).

6. This is not true of all dualists. Gordon, Edwards, and Reich (1982) retain a dual model. Their presentation does not deal directly with the criticisms and evidence that have undercut the core-periphery distinction — perhaps because they are unaware of it. However, their position is, to an extent, defensible. They emphasize that their unit of analysis is the firm. Since most of the evidence against the core-periphery dichotomy is on an industry level, it is hard to attack a firm-level theory with it. However, it should be noted that one of the key concepts in their analysis — that of market power (and thus the concept of monopoly and monopoly profits) — is usually thought of as industry trait rather than a characteristic of the firm. Also, although their theoretical discussion is on the level of the firm, the evidence they present (pp. 192-200) on behalf of the claim that the core and periphery differ is on an industry level. They also focus mainly on differences among manufacturing industries; when they extend this, they exclude mining, construction, and transportation (p. 200). Furthermore, their presentation deals first with a subset of the economy in which the component variables are more likely to be correlated; and then in extending their analysis they exclude those major sections of the economy in which the reversed sign of the correlation, or the lack of correlation among these variables — and thus the underlying multidimensionality — are most noticeable.

On the positive side, they do attempt an historical analysis. However, its completeness and accuracy is limited by their using a monopoly-competitive distinction that fails to deal with the large degree of independence of market relations, production relations, and politics with one another and, indeed, with variation within these three categories.

7. Bridges is not reviewed in detail because he devoted little effort to categorizing the independent variables which he used as measures of industry characteristics. It is of interest that he found that larger firms tend to employ more women, contrary to dualist predictions, although dual economy theory would have correctly predicted that capital intensive industries employ relatively few women.

8. Contrary to qualitative dual economy predictions, Hodson finds a negative association between concentration and earnings. He interprets this as meaning that "the market position of large oligopolistic corporations provides them with the ability to exploit their work forces to a greater extent than would otherwise be possible."

9. This is the Specific Vocational Preparation score from the *Dictionary of Occupational Titles*.

10. Neither variable occurs in Hodson's model.

11. Being a manager, or working in an industry that sells to governments, helps male incomes and being in an industry with large scale helps women.

12. Hodson and Kaufman (1982, p. 736) trace this power to the fact that workers' negligence or sabotage can cause serious costs. In addition, strikes or even absenteeism can cause expensive equipment to stand idle.

13. And, even more, beyond market determinism. Hodson's (1981) treatment of technical and organizational relations within the firm is a total break with market determinism.

14. Underlying this critique of institutional variables is a more general critique of the use of variables in much social science research. Many variables are the result of complex conflict processes. Measuring them at a given point in time simply inflates the importance of a momentary response pattern into that of a characteristic trait. In Friedman (1982, ch. 12), I show how analyses that rely on apathy as a trait can go astray and miss the important dynamic elements in a situation. Similarly, in economics, it has proven fruitful to look at price-quantity outcomes by analyzing both supply and demand functions and their interaction.

15. As Gordon (1971, p. 40) puts it, "The dual labor market theory offers a specific analysis of the labor market which can be interpreted in class terms, but the dual market theory itself does not rely on the concept, does not link the distinction between primary and secondary markets to other potential class divisions, and does not consistently base its hypotheses on evaluations of the group interests of employers or employees in either market."

16. In addition, it suffers from a theoretical error in assuming that technological development corresponds with the production of highly skilled jobs. Braverman (1974) discredits this critical argument.

17. Such upward escape from the secondary segment was not associated with human capital.

18. Rosenberg suggests, without much elaboration, that a reserve labor force model might therefore be appropriate.

19. See Kuhn (1962) for further discussion of the dynamics of competition among theories.

20. He has in mind France in 1968, Italy in 1969, and the United States in 1936-37.

21. They do not take account of the critiques discussed in the previous section. They would probably argue that: (1) The studies that show multidimensionality were based on industry data whereas their theory is on the firm level (which is weakened by their using industry-level data themselves — with major industrial categories omitted from consideration in such a way as artificially to reduce multidimensionality); (2) they are only studying those sections of the economy

for which such a core-periphery model is appropriate — and consider other sections not relevant to an emergent dual system. This argument, of course, covers all contrary evidence (at the expense of rendering one's domain of study insignificant).

22. However, neither set of theorists has taken adequate account of the meaning of the mobility findings for theory or policy concerning poverty and the poor. Rather than discussing this here, it will be discussed along with the theoretical proposals from other sections in the section on synthesis.

23. Almost all research on secondary labor markets has been on males. I am currently analyzing data for impoverished youths of both sexes that indicates that the ways in which segments have been defined operationally are inappropriate for studying women. Preliminary analysis indicated that these definitions have a higher percentage of women than of men in this sample getting primary jobs. It also indicates that neither segment nor human capital explains much of the variance in earnings.

24. Gordon et al. present historical data which they claim is based on segmentationist ideas. However, their data uses Oster's (1979) dual economy factor to show that the core and periphery diverged between 1947 and 1977. Their evidence is thus dualist rather than segmentationist.

25. Indeed, it is often argued that periods of upswing encourage increased productivity (which contributes to unemployment) and also leads to latent sources of labor such as underemployed traditional agriculturalists or home-bound women entering the labor market — which replenishes the reserve army.

26. The reserve labor force model proposed in the section on synthesis is a partial attempt to extend the theory to take account of this problem.

27. Some scholars such as Simeral (1978) would see the stagnant section of the reserve army as including many holders of secondary jobs. I see this as implicitly a formulation about a reserve labor force for the primary segment.

28. Rosenberg (1975) and Buchele (1976) both find considerable downward mobility, although they find even more upward mobility. A reserve labor force model requires considerable circulation. Since both Rosenberg and Buchele deal with males in a relatively tight labor market (1966 to 1970), their findings seem consistent with reserve labor force ideas.

29. I conceive of the reserve army as one part of the reserve labor force.

30. Some organizations among discriminated-against groups struggle over job definitions as well as potential labor definitions. The Dodge Revolutionary Union Movement (Geschwender, 1977; Georgakas and Surkin, 1975) and many women's caucuses (Tepperman, 1976) have fought both to open jobs to blacks or women and to improve the nature of the jobs they have.

31. In addition, the postwar economic boom helped by raising many incomes and moderating unemployment. Obviously, policies to restore the health of the economy would be of interest to us — but nobody knows how to do it, or even if it can be done.

References

Andrisani, Paul James. *An Empirical Analysis of the Dual Labor Market Theory.* Unpublished doctoral dissertation, Ohio State University, 1973.

Anthias, Floya. "Women and the Reserve Army of Labour: A Critique of Veronica Beechey." *Capital and Class* (Spring, 1980) 50–63.

Averitt, Robert T. *The Dual Economy: The Dynamics of American Industry Structure.* New York: Horton, 1968.

Banfield, Edward C. *The Unheavenly City.* Boston: Little, Brown, 1970.

Baran, Paul, and Sweezy, Paul. *Monopoly Capital.* New York: Monthly Review Press, 1965.

Beck, E.M., Horan, Patrick M., and Tolbert, Charles M., II. "Stratification in a Dual Economy: A Sectoral Model of Earnings Determination." *American Sociological Review* (October 1978), 704–720.

______ . "Industrial Segmentation and Labor Market Discrimination." *Social Problems* (December 1980), 113–130.

Becker, Gary S. *The Economics of Discrimination.* Chicago: University of Chicago Press, 1957.

______ . *Human Capital.* New York: Columbia University Press, 1964.

Beechey, Veronica. "Some Notes on Female Wage Labour." *Capital and Class* (1977).

Berger, Suzanne, and Piore, Michael J. *Dualism and Discontinuity in Industrial Societies.* New York: Cambridge University Press, 1981.

Birnbaum, Howard. "The Economic Effect of Career Origins." In Richard C. Edwards, Michael Reich, and David M. Gordon (eds.) *Labor Market Segmentation.* Lexington, Mass.: Lexington Books, 1975, 151–171.

Blaug, Mark. "The Empirical Status of Human Capital Theory: A Slightly Jaundiced Survey." *The Journal of Economic Literature* (September 1976), 827–855.

Bluestone, Barry. "The Tripartite Economy: Labor Markets and the Working Poor." *Poverty and Human Resources* (July/August 1970), 15–35.

______ . "The Characteristics of Marginal Industries." In David M. Gordon (ed.) *Problems in Political Economy: An Urban Perspective.* 2d edition. Lexington, Mass.: D.C. Heath, 1977, 97–102.

Bluestone, Barry, Murphy, William M., and Stevenson, Mary. *Low Wages and the Working Poor.* Ann Arbor: Institute of Labor and Industrial Relations, 1973.

Borus, Michael E. "Assesing the Impact of Training Programs." In Eli Ginzberg (ed.) *Employing the Unemployed.* New York: Basic Books, 1980, 25–40.

Bowles, Samuel, and Gintis, Herbert. "The Problem with Human Capital Theory — A Marxian Critique." *American Economic Review* (May 1975), 74–82.

______ . "The Marxian Theory of Value and Heterogeneous Labor: A Critique and Reformulation." *Cambridge Journal of Economics* (June 1977), 173–192.

Braverman, Harry. *Labor and Monopoly Capital.* New York: Monthly Review Press, 1974.

Brenner, Robert. "Agrarian Class Structure and Economic Development in Pre-Industrial Europe." *Past and Present* (February 1976), 30–75.

Bridges, William P. "Industry Marginality and Female Employment: A New Appraisal." *American Sociological Review* (February 1980), 58–75.

Buchele, Robert Kent. *Jobs and Workers: A Labor Market Segmentation Perspective on the Work Experience of Young Men.* Unpublished doctoral dissertation, Harvard University, 1976.

Cain, Glen G. "The Challenge of Segmented Labor Market Theories to Orthodox Theory: A Survey." *The Journal of Economic Literature* (December 1976), 1215–1257.

Doeringer, Peter B., and Piore, Michael J. *Internal Labor Markets and Manpower Analysis*. Lexington, Mass: Lexington Books, 1971.

______. "Unemployment and the 'Dual Labor Market.' " *The Public Interest* (Winter 1974), 67–79.

Domhoff, G. William. *Who Rules America?* Englewood Cliffs, N.J.: Prentice-Hall, 1967.

______. *The Higher Circles*. New York: Random House, 1970.

Domhoff, G. William, and Ballard, Hoyt B. (eds.) *C. Wright Mills and The Power Elite*. Boston: Beacon Press, 1968.

Dunlop, John T. *Industrial Relations Systems*. New York: Holt, 1958.

Edwards, Richard. *Contested Terrain*. New York: Basic Books, 1979.

Edwards, Richard C., Reich, Michael, and Gordon, David M. (eds.) *Labor Market Segmentation*. Lexington, Mass: Lexington Books, 1975.

Findlay, J.N. *Hegel: A Re-Examination*. New York: Oxford University Press, 1958.

Freedman, Marcia. *Labor Markets: Segments and Shelters*. Montclair, N.J.: Allanheld, Osmun & Co., 1976.

Friedman, Samuel R. *Teamster Rank and File: Power, Bureaucracy, and Rebellion at Work and in a Union*. New York: Columbia University Press, 1982.

Friedman, Samuel R., and Friedman, Judith J. "Class Conflict in a Dual Economy: A Critique of Some Current Theories." Presented at Annual Meeting of the American Sociological Association, 1979.

Gagliani, Giorgio. "How Many Working Classes?" *American Journal of Sociology* (September 1981), 259-285.

Galbraith, John Kenneth. *The New Industrial State*. Boston: Houghton Mifflin, 1967.

Gardiner, Jean. "Women and Unemployment." *Red Rag* (1975-76) as cited in Beechey (1977).

Georgakas, Dan, and Surkin, Marvin. *Detroit: I Do Mind Dying*. New York: St. Martin's Press, 1975.

Geschwender, James A. *Class, Race, and Worker Insurgency*. New York: Cambridge University Press, 1977.

Ginzberg, Eli (ed.) *Employing the Unemployed*. New York: Basic Books, 1980.

Gordon, David M. *Class, Productivity, and the Ghetto: A Study of Labor Market Stratification*. Unpublished doctoral dissertation, Harvard University, 1971.

______. (ed.) *Problems in Political Economy: An Urban Perspective*. 2d edition. Lexington, Mass.: D.C. Heath, 1977.

Gordon, David M., Edwards, Richard, and Reich, Michael. *Segmented Work, Divided Workers: The Historical Transformation of Labor in the United States*. New York: Cambridge University Press, 1982.

Harrison, Bennett. "Institutions on the Periphery." In David M. Gordon, (ed.) *Problems in Political Economy: An Urban Perspective*. 2d edition. Lexington, Mass.: D.C. Heath, 1977, 102–107.

______. "Welfare Payments and the Reproduction of Low-Wage Workers and Secondary Jobs." *Review of Radical Political Economy* (Summer 1979), 1–16.

Hauser, Robert M. "On 'Stratification in a Dual Economy.' " *American Sociological Review* (August 1980), 702–12.

Hegel, G.W.F. *The Logic of Hegel.* Oxford: Clarendon Press, 1931.
______. *The Science of Logic.* London: Allen and Unwin/Macmillian, 1951.
Hodson, Randy. "Industrial Structure as a Worker Resource under Corporate Capitalism." Presented at annual meeting of The Society for the Study of Social Problems, 1981.
______. "Labor in the Monopoly, Competitive, and State Sectors of Production." *Politics and Society* (1978), 429–480.
Hodson, Randy, and Kaufman, Robert L. "Economic Dualism: A Critical Review." *American Sociological Review* (December 1982), 727–739.
James, C.L.R. *Notes on Dialectics: Hegel, Marx, Lenin.* Westport, CT: Lawrence Hill & Co., 1948.
Kalleberg, Arne, Wallace, Michael, and Althauser, Robert P. "Economic Segmentation, Worker Power, and Income Inequality." *American Journal of Sociology* (November 1981), 651–83.
Kaufman, Robert L., Hodson, Randy, and Fligstein, Neil D. "Defrocking Dualism: A New Approach to Defining Industrial Sectors." *Social Science Research* (March 1981), 1–31.
Kerr, Clark. "Labor Markets: Their Character and Consequences." *American Economic Review* (May 1950), 278–91.
______. "The Balkanization of Labor Markets." In E. Wight Bakke et al. (eds.) *Labor Mobility and Economic Opportunity.* Cambridge, Mass.: M.I.T. Press, 1954, 92–110.
Kochan, Thomas A., and Block, Richard N. "An Interindustry Analysis of Bargaining Outcomes: Preliminary Evidence from Two-Digit Industries." *Quarterly Journal of Economics* (August 1977), 431–52.
Kruse, William J. "An Empirical Study of Labor Market Segmentation: Comment." *Industrial and Labor Relations Review* (January 1977), 219–220.
Kuhn, Thomas. *The Structure of Scientific Revolutions.* Chicago: The University of Chicago Press, 1962.
Lowell, Ruth Fabricant. "The Dual Labor Market in New York City." Paper presented at Human Resources Administration's Welfare Research Conference, New York City, December 1, 1973.
McGahey, Richard M. *Labor Market Segmentation, Human Capital, and the Economics of Crime.* Unpublished doctoral dissertation, New School for Social Research, New York, 1982.
Mannheim, Karl. "Conservative Thought." In Paul Kecskemeti (ed.) *Essays on Sociology and Social Psychology.* New York: Oxford University Press, 1953, 76–164.
Marx, Karl. *Capital,* Volume 1. New York: International Publishers, 1967.
Masters, Stanley H., and Maynard, Rebecca. *The Impact of Supported Work on Long-Term Recipients of AFDC Benefits.* New York: Manpower Demonstration Research Corporation, 1981.
Maynard, Rebecca. *The Impact of Supported Work on Young School Dropouts.* New York: Manpower Demonstration Research Corporation, 1980.
Milkman, Ruth. "Women's Work and Economic Crisis: Some Lessons of the Great Depression." *Review of Radical Political Economics* (Spring, 1976) as cited in Beechey (1977).

Mills, C. Wright. *The Power Elite.* New York: Oxford University Press, 1959.

Nichols, Albert L., and Zeckhauser, R. "Government Comes to the Workplace: An Assessment of OSHA." *The Public Interest* (Fall 1977), 39–69.

Nyden, Philip W., and Nyden, Gwendolyn Evans. "The Illusion of Stable Jobs: The View from Workers in Steel, Auto and Other Core Industries in Recession." Presented at annual meetings of the Society for the Study of Social Problems, 1981, 4–20.

O'Connor, James. *The Fiscal Crisis of the State.* New York: St. Martin's Press, 1973.

Oster, Gerry. "A Factor Analytic Test of the Theory of the Dual Economy." *Review of Economics and Statistics* (Febarury 1979), 33–39.

Osterman, Paul. "An Empirical Study of Labor Market Segmentation." *Industrial and Labor Relations Review* (July 1975), 508–23.

______. "Reply." *Industrial and Labor Relations Review* (January 1977), 221–24.

______. *Getting Started: The Youth Labor Market.* Cambridge: The M.I.T. Press, 1980.

Parenti, Michael. *Democracy for the Few.* New York: St. Martin's Press, 1974.

Piliavin, Irving, and Gartner, Rosemary. *The Impact of Supported Work on Ex-offenders.* New York: Manpower Demonstration Research Corporation, 1981.

Piore, Michael J. "Fragments of a 'Sociological' Theory of Wages." *American Economic Review* (May 1973), 377–384.

______. "Notes for a Theory of Labor Market Stratification." In Richard C. Edwards, Michael Reich, and David M. Gordon (eds.) *Labor Market Segmentation.* Lexington, Mass.: Lexington Books, 1975, 125–150.

______. *Birds of Passage: Migrant Labor and Industrial Societies.* New York: Cambridge University Press, 1979.

Piven, Frances Fox, and Cloward, Richard. *Poor People's Movements.* New York: Vintage Books, 1979.

______. *The New Class War: Reagan's Attack on the Welfare State and Its Consequences.* New York: Pantheon Books, 1982.

Reich, Michael, Gordon, David M., and Edwards, Richard C. "A Theory of Labor Market Segmentation." *American Economic Review* (May 1973), 359–365.

Reynolds, Lloyd G. *The Structure of Labor Markets.* New York: Harper and Brothers, 1951.

Rosenberg, Sam. *The Dual Labor Market: Its Existence and Consequences.* Unpublished doctoral dissertation, Brandeis University, 1975.

______. "The Marxian Reserve Army of Labor and the Dual Labor Market." *Politics and Society* (1977), 221–28.

______. "A Survey of Empirical Work on Labor Market Segmentation." Working Paper No. 138, Institute of Industrial Relations, University of California, Berkeley, Calif., 1979.

______. "Male Occupational Standing and the Dual Labor Market," *Industrial Relations* (Winter 1980), 34–49.

______. "Occupational Mobility and Short Cycles." In Frank Wilkinson. *The Dynamics of Labor Market Segmentation.* New York: Academic Press, 1981, 229–240.

Rumberger, Russell W., and Carnoy, Martin. "Segmentation in the U.S. Labour Market: Its Effects on Mobility and Earnings of Whites and Blacks." *Cambridge Journal of Economics* (June 1980), 117-132.

Serrin, William. *The Company and the Union.* New York: Vintage Books, 1974.

Simeral, Margaret. "Women and the Reserve Army of Labor." *Insurgent Sociologist* (Fall 1978), 164–179.

Sokoloff, Natalie J. *Between Money and Love: The Dialectics of Women's Home and Market Work.* New York: Praeger, 1980.

Stone, Kathy. "The Origins of Job Structures in the Steel Industry." *Radical America* (November/December 1973), 19–64.

Taylor, Patricia A., Gwartney-Gibbs, Patricia A., and Farley, Reynolds. "The Changing Structure of Earnings Inequality, 1960–1978." Paper presented at meetings of the American Sociological Association, 1981.

Tepperman, Jean. *Not Servants, Not Machines: Office Workers Speak Out.* Boston: Beacon Press, 1976.

Thurow, Lester G. *Generating Inequality.* New York: Basic Books, 1975.

Tolbert, Charles, Horan, Patrick M., and Beck, E.M. "The Structure of Economic Segmentation: A Dual Economy Approach." *American Journal of Sociology* (March 1980), 1095-1116.

Vallas, Steven P. "Marxism and The Labor Process." *Socialist Review* (November/December 1980), 151-158.

Vietorisz, Thomas, and Harrison, Bennett. "Labor Market Segmentation: Positive Feedback and Divergent Development." *American Economic Review* (May 1973), 366–376.

Wachter, Michael L. "Primary and Secondary Labor Markets: A Critique of the Dual Approach." *Brookings Papers on Economic Activity.* (3: 1974), 637–693.

Weir, Stanley Lewis. "Rank-and-File Labor Rebellions Break into the Open: The End of an Era." In Staughton Lynd (ed.) *American Labor Radicalism: Testimonies and Interpretations.* New York: John Wiley and Sons, 1973, 148–83.

Wilkinson, Frank. *The Dynamics of Labor Market Segmentation.* New York: Academic Press, 1981.

Wright, Erik Olin. *Class Structure and Income Determination.* New York: Academic Press, 1979.

Wright, Erik Olin, Costello, Cynthia, Hachen, David, and Sprague, Joey. "The American Class Structure." *American Sociological Review* (December 1982), 709–726.

Zimbalist, Andrew (ed.) *Case Studies on the Labor Process.* New York: Monthly Review Press, 1979.

Zucker, Lynne G., and Rosenstein, Carolyn. "Taxonomies of Institutional Structure: Dual Economy Reconsidered." *American Sociological Review* (December 1981), 869–884.

7 THE PHILLIPS CURVE CONTROVERSY AND ORTHODOX VISIONS OF THE LABOR MARKET

Kathryn E. Allen

> (T)he fact is that *economic* theories, whether current or in the past, were not born of pure intellectual curiosity but in response to problems that were encountered historically by the community. Involved inextricably with the problems, there were always conflicting interests at stake which favored the resolution of these problems in favor of one or the other of the contending economic interests. Theoretical or more general arguments were adduced in their support to prove that the solution offered was "justifiable" on a more general ground. (Bharadwaj, 1976, p. 12)

In this passage, Bharadwaj submits that the materialist mode of analysis is the most logical approach to the study of policy prescriptions arising from, and in response to, specific sets of circumstances. The divergent responses of economic theorists to the breakdown of the Phillips curve relation (which is reflected in the coexistence of rising unemployment and rising inflation) present an appropriate subject for a materialist study of the development of economic theory. Widespread frustration with macroeconomic stabilization policies has rekindled interest in the microeconomics of unemployment; the debate centers largely upon the proper interpretation of the workings of the labor market.

Following a brief introduction to the literature in the first section, the second part of this paper examines three distinct interpretations of the labor market, each of which spawns a different policy approach. Despite the divergence of these perspectives, all are rooted in the broader ideological framework of the class from which they arise: the managerial class. While a thorough analysis of the class is not pursued in this paper, a brief discussion of its major characteristics is appropriate.[1]

Managers are those who "already for the most part in contemporary society are actually managing, on the technical side, the actual process of production, no matter what the legal and financial form — individual, corporate, governmental — of the process [of production]. (Burnham, 1941, p. 80). Their special ideology maintains that "knowledge and knowledge systems are important in shaping outcomes" (Gouldner, 1979, p. 5). In short, managers are "cashing in on [their] education" (Gouldner, p. 7).

Two broad attributes identify what I shall call the managerial mentality. First, managers see themselves as instruments of human progress. Burnham writes that managers "tend to identify the welfare of mankind as a whole with their own interests and the salvation of mankind with their assuming control of society" (1941, p. 193). The motivation of the class, then, is the pursuit of the power that its members consider essential to the betterment of society. Second, managers see workers as generally incompetent. This view facilitates the emergence of a vanguard or "brain" — a role in which some managers cast themselves. This fosters conflict within the class over the preservation of the capitalist relations of production.

While they seek control of the forces of production, managers are not capitalists. As Burnham points out, the "position, role, and function of the managers are in no way dependent on the maintenance of capitalist property and economic relations; they depend upon the technical nature of the process of modern production. Consequently, the preservation of the capitalist relations is not an absolutely decisive question for the managers" (1941, p. 91). Managers, then, are not constrained by the profit motive. Gouldner argues that "elimination of the old [capitalist] class is an historical option open to the New Class" (1979, p. 7). Whether, and to what extent, this option should be exercised is a major question facing the managerial class.

The managers' command of the economy hinges on the extent to which they are able to mobilize the forces of production in their own interest.[2] The art of persuasion provides the managers' most powerful weapon in their quest to constrain and influence policy on economic matters. Clearly, however, the resolution of the questions that face class members is the subject of much intraclass dispute. The competition of ideas among the intellectuals over the ongoing necessity of capitalism and the role of the state in the marketplace constitutes the debate. Defining the best solution is the goal of all their arguments.

The third section presents a Marxist critique of the orthodox approach to the labor market. While Marx never analyzed the managerial class in depth, he remains the analyst of unemployment under capitalism *par excellence.*[3] In his view, issues of the voluntariness of unemployment, the rationality of workers' expectations, and the response of economic agents to tax cuts would contribute virtually nothing to a scientific study of unemployment. Rather, the inquiry must focus on the relationship between the workers and those who effectively control the means of production.

Theoretical Background

The classicals[4] perceived unemployment to be a strictly voluntary phenomenon. The central feature of classical theory (which Friedman and others have revived) is the notion of the long-run neutrality of money. Unemployment, then, is perceived as a function of real forces. According to Keynes, two fundamental assumptions underlie what he termed classical labor market theory: (1) the wage is equal to the marginal product of the labor; and (2) the utility of the wage when a given volume of labor is employed is equal to the marginal disutility of that amount of employment.[5] Up to the point at which marginal cost exceeded marginal product of each additional worker, there was always an incentive to employ all workers available. Unemployment resulted only when labor (through trade unions, etc.) managed to push money wages above the money value of the marginal product of labor. Since the marginal disutility of labor, as well as the real wage, was perceived to be determined by labor itself, then labor could be held responsible for its own unemployment.

Keynes rejected the classical presumption that persistent unemployment is voluntary. In particular, he criticized the notion that workers can control the level of real wages through the wage bargain. He wrote: "(t)here may be no expedient by which labour as a whole can reduce its *real* wages to a given figure by making revised *money* bargains with the entrepreneurs" (1964, p. 13). Moreover, he expressed serious doubts as to the efficacy of a cut in money wages as a tool for expanding employment (1964, ch. 19).

Keynes argued that involuntary unemployment exists whenever

> *(i)n the event of a small rise in the price of wage-goods relatively to the money-wage, both the aggregate supply of labour willing to work for the current money wage and the aggregate demand for it at that wage would be greater than the existing volume of employment.* (1964, p. 15 emphasis in original)

The point at which involuntary unemployment disappears corresponds to the fulfillment of the second classical assumption discussed above; this is Keynesian full employment.[6] That point is not, however, determined by labor itself. Edgar O. Edwards explains Keynes' position:

> The labor supply is simply *not effective* in determining employment at a real wage above that consistent with full employment. The spending decisions of income recipients and the output decisions of entrepreneurs are the dominant forces . . . labor supply decisions are subordinate to the others. (1959, p. 424 emphasis in original)

To the extent that Keynes demonstrated that workers could be (and were) unemployed through no fault of their own, he revolutionized the function of government. The state became the employer of last resort. As policy-makers accepted the theory that government could manage aggregate demand — through monetary and fiscal tools — to expand employment opportunities, macroeconomists increasingly influenced governmental strategies. It has become apparent, however, that conventional stabilization measures alone are inadequate to deal with the problem of the coexistence of inflation and unemployment. In response, a new body of literature has emerged purporting to describe the fundamental dynamics underlying the aggregates and, more importantly, to devise formulae for effective policymaking.

Case Studies

Liberal Neoclassical Economics

Liberal neoclassical economics enthusiastically embraces government intervention in the economy. Comprising an important fraction of the managerial class, and unlike conservative neoclassicals, liberals recognize the unstable nature of extreme laissez faire. As E.K. Hunt observes, "(g)overnment for the liberals is a benevolent, neutral, objective, and fair political power that can generally be relied on to intervene in the economy whenever the actual economic and social conditions differ markedly from those depicted in the model of perfect competition" (1979, p. 422).[7] The writings of Robert Solow and James Tobin are representative of the liberal view of the labor market.

Both of these authors perceive unemployment as the outcome of a failure of the labor market to clear. Solow attributes this phenomenon largely to nominal wage inertia, which makes employment vulnerable to unexpected fluctuations in aggregate demand (1980, p. 8). He attributes several general institutional characteristics to the labor market.

First, the labor market is segmented, which contributes to wage stickiness by limiting competition. Moreover, both workers and entrepreneurs develop a "stake, a rent, in the durability of the relationship" (1980, p. 9). Both may be induced to break those ties but not easily. This impedes the mobility of labor and contributes to wage rigidity. This point, Solow claims, distinguishes his customer market model from the auction market model adopted by the conservative neoclassicals.

Second, some "nontrivial source of nonemployment income" is available, so that "it becomes easier to maintain a labor pool in the presence of fluctuating employment" (1980, p. 9). He observes that unemployment insurance may prolong search activity, but that this outcome is not necessarily bad. "(T)he optimal search strategy for the individual might provide less than the socially optimal amount of search, and unemployment compensation could be regarded as a corrective subsidy" (1980, p. 5).[8] Solow argues that whether its effects are positive or negative, however, "the unemployment compensation system is an important determinant of behavior on both sides of the labor market" (1980, p. 5).

Third, the labor pool is stable so that social conventions assume some importance. While this notion relates to the first general characteristic, it purports to transcend the importance of job security and to expose the broader objectives of labor market participants. Solow, like Tobin, argues that workers are bound by a set of constraints different from those of other economic agents. He explains that workers seem bound by a "code of good behavior enforced by social pressure" (1980, p. 5). As a general rule, this code impedes wage cutting even in periods of excess supply because workers do not undercut each other by offering to work for less.

Fourth (and Solow's only unqualified empirical claim), the real wage elasticity of the demand for labor is approximately one-half, lower than the classicals believed. Workers, facing relatively inelastic demand, understandably resist wage cutting. Solow also criticizes the modern classical school for substituting a high elasticity of supply for Pigou's high elasticity of demand. While this provides them with another rationale for voluntary unemployment, the assumption is a poor reflection of reality and is of little help in explaining why labor markets fail to clear. In Solow's view, "what looks like involuntary unemployment is involuntary unemployment" (1980, p. 3).

Solow's analysis leads him to advocate an active stabilization role for government. He concludes that "if the labor market is often not in equilibrium, if wages are often sticky, if they respond to nontraditional signals, then there is a role for macro policy and a good chance that it will be effective" (1980, p. 10).

Tobin, like Solow, sees unemployment as a nonmarket clearing phenomenon. Labor markets fail to clear because money wages fail to adjust rapidly enough (1972, p. 9). In particular, money wages are sticky downward; Tobin presents several reasons why there even may be upward pressure on wages in the modern labor market.

Part of this pressure is attributable to employees' expectations. "The employee expects that his wages and terms of employment will steadily improve, certainly never retrogress" (1972, p. 12). Tobin's analysis is based on his notion of the labor market as a system of relatively stable relationships, "more like a rental housing market" (p. 12). Workers' wages, therefore, are less responsive to the existence of an excess labor supply.

In addition, Tobin argues that "(e)ven when a market is in equilibrium, it may outdo the recent wage increases in related markets" (1972, p. 13). This results in what he terms "true cost-push inflation. Since the economy is in a constant state of sectoral flux, there is no way to control average wages so as to reconcile them with productivity growth."

Finally, Tobin discusses the "secular increase in the prevalence of administered wages and prices" (1972, p. 14). He recognizes the power of large unions to push wages above competitive rates but notes that wages and prices are administered even in competitive sectors of the economy. The pervasiveness of this phenomenon results in slower money-wage adjustments to excess supply and demand.

Within this framework the dynamics of Tobin's labor market model are straightforward. At any given moment, labor markets vary widely with respect to excess demand or supply. Using a weighted average of these markets, one can determine their status in the overall performance of the economy. If overall demand is deficient, then unemployment is increased. Nevertheless, the upward pressure on money wages prevents them from adjusting in response to the deficiency in demand. The result is stagflation.

Based on his analysis, Tobin concludes that the economy has an inflationary bias (1972, p. 9). This means that price stability is compatible only with a situation of excess vacancies. Since he describes full employment in terms of the equality of vacancies and unemployment, full employment is not compatible with zero inflation within the framework of his model.

Conservative Neoclassical Economics

The conservatives (or monetarists) are ardent supporters of qualified laissez faire.[9] As open advocates of the interests of the capitalist class, their objective is to facilitate the maximization of surplus value. They resist policies aimed at altering the wage-profit ratio to the detriment of capital. They believe that, in the absence of governmental meddling, labor markets tend to clear; thus, the economy tends, in the ordinary sense, toward full employment. Their policy prescription, then, favors minimal government intervention.

Natural Rate Hypothesis (NRH). Through a variety of labor market models, proponents of the Natural Rate Hypothesis (NRH) argue that the long-run Phillips curve is vertical and that the family of short-run (negatively sloped) Phillips curves result from misinformation and suboptimal adjustment to economic realities. Milton Friedman, an ardent proponent of the NRH, states, "The natural rate of unemployment is the level that would be ground out by the Walrasian system of general equilibrium equations." At that level, real wages tend to rise at a normal secular rate, i.e., a rate that can be maintained indefinitely. Further, the economy is generating no more inflation than people expect. This also implies continuous or near-continuous labor market clearing.

Friedman, unlike Solow and Tobin, sees the labor market as a "textbook-variety commodity market" (1977, p. 19). The quantity of labor that a worker is willing to supply depends on his perceived real wage. In other words, the money wage bargain is made based on the worker's prediction of future inflation. Friedman assumes that workers will discover changes in their money wages immediately, but, due to information costs, they adjust more slowly to changes in the general price level.

The short-run Phillips curve results, then, from errors in prediction. If the actual rate of inflation exceeds the expected rate, the individual worker temporarily perceives an increase in his real wage. He supplies more labor and unemployment falls. Once his expectations about the rate of inflation catch up with actual inflation, he realizes that his real wage has not changed (or may have decreased), and he contracts his labor supply. Unemployment returns to its original level but at a higher plateau of inflation. If the government tries to keep unemployment below this "natural rate," it must pump up the money supply to keep pace with (or outrace) the workers' expectations of higher money wage scales. The gap between expected or desired wages and actual wages can never be closed, and accelerating inflation results. A temporary decrease in unemployment is traded for a permanent increase in the rate of inflation.

This model implies that, although money-wage increases are spurred by excess demand for labor, it is misguided government meddling, rather than labor's actions, which brings about inflation. In addition, it implies that in an equilibrium world all unemployment is voluntary. Friedman's policy prescriptions, therefore, are aimed at a qualified return to the invisible hand of the free market, or at least to a fixed money supply growth rule to provide an optimal rate of inflation that is perfectly predictable. Since all unemployment below the natural rate is voluntary, there is no real need for the government to use monetary and fiscal policy to expand the economy. At any rate, to do so would require accelerating inflation. Moreover, as Duboff points out, "just about any rate of joblessness might represent full employment," thus eliminating the need to peg full employment at some quantifiable level. The NRH becomes a rationale for maintaining chronic unemployment and for preserving a wage-profit ratio that is favorable to capital.

Edmund Phelps views labor market dynamics in a somewhat different way. He argues that labor markets are characterized by "seriously incomplete information concerning wage rates in the economy" (1968, p. 131), so that a certain amount of search employment is normal. Workers determine their "acceptance wage" by equating the "marginal costs and gains from search" (Santomero and Seater, 1978, p. 519). An increase in aggregate demand may cause workers to abandon their search prematurely (that is, before they have reached the socially optimal level) because they see higher money wage offers in other markets and fail to realize that prices are also rising.

This phenomenon is best illustrated with Phelps' island model, in which information flows are costly; workers must forego a day of work and travel to other islands in order to sample wages. He envisions an auction each morning on each island which determines the market-clearing money-wage and employment level.

Initially, he assumes a decrease in demand. If workers on every island see this as at least partially island-specific, they may assume that wages on other islands have not fallen as much. Some workers will travel to other islands to sample wages, and "the acceptance wage on each island will fall less than proportionally to product prices" (Phelps, 1969, p. 150). As a result, the labor supply is contracted voluntarily.

Charles Holt (1980, p. 387) takes issue with this notion of unemployment. He adds the concept of job availability, defined as the ratio of vacancies to unemployment, to the labor market equation. This causes him to reject the notion of a unique market-clearing wage. He writes

> Turnover in the labour market continually generates new vacancies and unemployed workers. These stocks grow until enough mutually satisfactory job-worker matches occur that new hires offset the inflow of vacancies and unemployment, and a stock-flow equilibrium is reached. However, many equilibria can occur — with vacancies high and unemployment low, or vice versa . . . The concept of market clearing ceases to be sufficient to determine an equilibrium because both residual variables, vacancies and unemployment, always exist applying opposite pressures on market transactions. (p. 389)

The notion that equilibrium can occur when unemployment exceeds vacancies implies the existence of involuntary unemployment even when the labor market clears.[10] This provides a more open-ended view of labor market dynamics for policy-makers because one need not view all search unemployment as voluntary. Moreover, policy-makers need not be faced with accelerating inflation in order to increase employment. They are forced neither to hold the line on the wage-profit ratio (to the advantage of the capitalist class), nor to maintain a pool of unemployed labor.

Rational Expectations (REH) as a Critique of the Adaptive Model. John Muth postulated that economic agents endeavor to form expectations of relevant future variables by making the most efficient use of all information provided by past experiences. This is the basis of the REH. Muth wrote: "It is sometimes argued that the assumption of rationality in economics leads to theories inconsistent with, or inadequate to explain, observed phenomena, especially changes over time . . . Our hypothesis is based on exactly the opposite point of view: the dynamic economic models do not assume enough rationality" (1961, p. 316). Colander and Guthrie summarize Muth's position as follows: "(O)n average, economic units' predictions are as correct as those of the relevant economic model" (1980–1, p. 221).

Within this framework, the adaptive expectations model is irrational because it allows for only gradual convergence of expected and actual rates of inflation. By definition, rational expectations cannot permit such systematic errors. REH models imply that even Friedman's conservative prescriptions are unwarranted and would be ineffective in the short run.

Policy-makers do not even have the choice of strong or weak deflationary policy because attempts to stabilize the economy through stated monetary or fiscal policies will be undermined if perfectly anticipated. "Government policy can be effective only to the extent that it deceives people" (Santomero and Seater, 1978, p. 530).

On its face, the REH model falls short of a viable alternative to active stabilization policies. It is unlikely that individuals are able to interpret economic signals, much less incorporate them into a sophisticated model. Nevertheless, economic agents clearly do react to policy changes. As Neil Berkman points out, the contribution which the REH school makes to economic theory is the realization "that stabilization policy is not a 'game' against nature whose reactions do not alter in response to policy stimuli but a game against intelligent agents whose reactions depend on policy moves" (p. 29).[11]

Supply-Side Economics. The supply-siders consider themselves classical growth theorists — their objective is to raise the nation's overall capacity to produce. In their view, the unemployment which this country is presently experiencing is an undesirable and unnecessary waste of resources (Feldstein, 1973, p. 18).

Like the monetarists, supply-siders blame economic instability on government intervention in the marketplace. While the monetarists stop short of unwavering monetary restraint, however, the supply-siders advocate a return to the gold standard.[12] They argue that the control of the quantity of money is an inappropriate goal of policy (*Business Week,* 1981a, p. 80). Rather, the government should guarantee a quality product — the money supply (Laffer, 1981a, p. 80). Returning to the gold standard would, they argue, effectuate supply-side employment strategies.

The supply-siders, represented here by Martin Feldstein and Arthur Laffer, target unemployment compensation programs and the tax rate as major disincentives for productive employment. They argue that policy changes in these two areas will yield benefits to both labor and capital which, in turn, will stimulate economic growth.

Feldstein argues that "(t)here is little room for doubt about the qualitative conclusion that our current system of unemployment compensation increases the rate and duration of unemployment" (1973, p. 38). He discusses three principle sources of unemployment, all of which are exacerbated by unemployment compensation: seasonal and cyclical variations in the demand for labor, weak labor force attachment, and unnecessarily long durations of unemployment (1973, p. 30).

Cyclical unemployment reflects the sensitivity of employment to changes in aggregate demand; Feldstein considers the bulk of this type of unemployment to be involuntary. While government commands a variety of tools with which it could reduce this sensitivity (e.g., substantial tax penalties for volatile employment or a guaranteed annual wage), Feldstein believes that "(c)ollective bargaining agreements can achieve any desired degree of employment security through the same techniques" (1973, p. 20). Leaving decisions of this nature to collective bargaining more accurately reflects workers' preferences and provides for a more efficient allocation of resources. According to Feldstein, unemployment compensation distorts this outcome because the price of unstable labor has been artificially subsidized, so that employers organize production in a way that makes too much use of unstable employment (1973, p. 34). He reasons that, in the absence of transfer payments, workers would demand a higher wage to compensate them for the lack of job security which accompanies cyclically sensitive types of employment. Unemployment compensation becomes a subsidy which masks this externality and produces an excessive amount of unstable unemployment.

This analysis also applies to seasonal unemployment, but Feldstein advances one step beyond it by asserting that this type of unemployment is clearly not involuntary. This assertion raises the true question of work incentives. To the extent that unemployment compensation reduces or eliminates the cost of temporary unemployment (as Feldstein argues that it does), seasonal workers have no incentive to find interim employment quickly, if they find it at all. This is clearly one type of unemployment which, if it exists to any great degree, a growth theorist cannot tolerate. Feldstein argues that the proper policy is nonintervention. This would prevent distortion of the economic signals by which the labor market yields an efficient allocation of resources.

The problem of weak labor force attachment involves workers with low skill and little education (1973, p. 21). It is a problem with the quality, rather than the quantity, of available jobs. In Feldstein's view, "(l)owering the rate of unemployment requires steps to bring the characteristics of the actual jobs and the standards of the acceptable jobs closer together" (1973, p. 22). Manpower training programs, one possible means to this end, seem to have positive but small effects (1973, p. 24). Another means, which Feldstein endorses, is to reduce the attractiveness of not working through changes in the rules governing transfer payments. This is his major policy prescription; training programs are merely a potential supplement in his analysis.

Feldstein believes that unemployment compensation prolongs joblessness far beyond the socially optimal length of time. As noted above, transfer payments reduce or eliminate the costs of being unemployed. This encourages workers to engage in more extensive search activity. Since search involves such a low marginal cost, even after a long search period the worker can afford to accept a job which is not substantially superior to his previous job. While this behavior may be rational from the individual's point of view, it is not efficient for the economy as a whole. Note that this is precisely one of the points where Solow has taken up the cudgel.

To be sure, Feldstein is not suggesting that all employable resources should be employed; he realizes that a certain amount of unemployment is both necessary and desirable. He seeks to maximize economic growth, which requires resources to be employed up to their most efficient point. His main premise is that macroeconomic demand management policies fail to (and, in fact are unable to) reach that point.

Arthur Laffer advocates the use of another specific policy tool in the quest to maximize growth — tax cuts. He points to the Kennedy-era tax cut as evidence that supply-side policies work to stimulate the economy and contain inflation.[13] In his view, Keynesian policies promote a low rate of growth and a high rate of unemployment.

Laffer's analysis regards tax-rate changes as equivalent to relative price changes (*Business Week,* 1980, p. 77). His basic premise, then, becomes a restatement of the obvious: "All else equal, the greater the cost to the firm of employing each worker, the less workers the firm will employ" (1981, p. 33a). The worker, on the other hand, is concerned exclusively with the amount of his take-home pay. Laffer asserts that "(t)he greater net wages received, the more willing the worker is to work . . . if net wages received fall, workers will find work effort less attractive and they will do less of it" (1981, p. 33).

Laffer's target is the tax wedge, which he defines as the difference between what it costs a firm to employ worker or acquire a unit of capital and what the worker or saver receives net (1981, p. 33). Figure 7–1 illustrates this concept. He argues that an increase in the wedge increases the price paid for, and reduces the price received by, a factor of production, reducing both the demand for and supply of that factor (1981, p. 36). In Laffer's analysis, the converse is also true.

Viewed in this way, his model is neither novel nor complex. In fact, its simplicity may prove to be its downfall. He suggests that the tax cut would both increase the take-home pay of the worker and decrease the cost to the employer. It would, therefore, stimulate employment by increasing both the demand for and supply of labor. There are several problems with this analysis on its own terms.

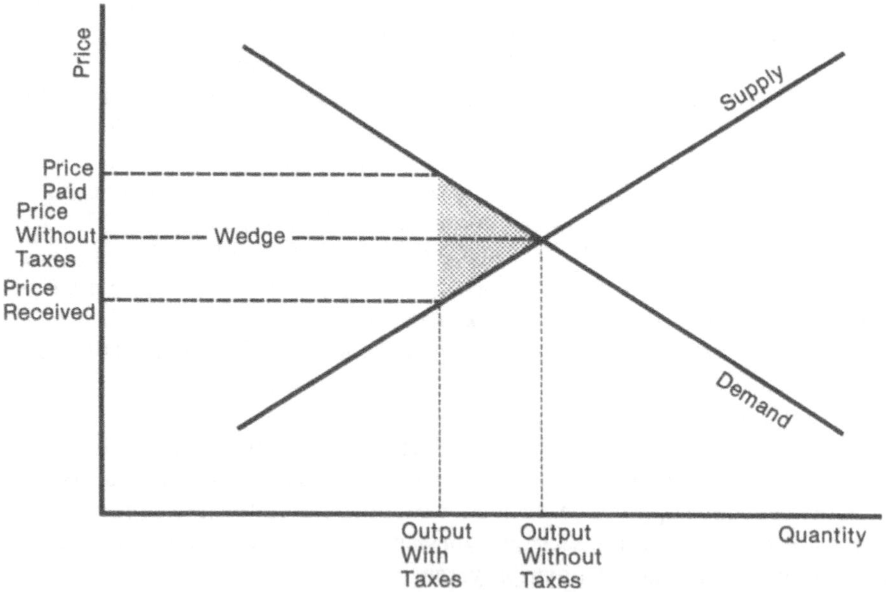

Figure 7–1. The Laffer Tax Wedge

First, it is not clear that both the worker and the employer will share in the benefits of the tax cut. In the event of a decrease in the amount required to be withheld from his paycheck, the worker is unlikely to accept an offsetting decrease in his gross salary. Unless he does, however, the cost of his employment to the employer will not be reduced, and the boost to the demand for labor upon which Laffer depends will not be forthcoming. Rather, if Laffer's assumptions concerning the supply of labor hold true, there may be more unemployment after the tax cut than before since the supply curve will have shifted outward.

Second, if both the demand for and supply of labor are relatively inelastic (see Solow, 1980, p. 7), then the tax cut may produce little or nothing in terms of increased employment even if it works as Laffer assumes. He makes no observations, empirical or otherwise, concerning the relative elasticities of demand and supply.

Third, as Alice Rivlin points out, "(t)he economic theory of household behavior leaves it unclear whether lowering tax rates will increase or reduce work effort" (Laffer, 1981, p. 41). Laffer's only response is that "for the economy as a whole . . . the effect of a tax rate cut can be presumed to lead to more work" (1981, p. 41). Again he musters little evidence to support this position.

Laffer tells us that labor and capital are not hostile entities and that increases in wages and profits are not mutually exclusive. It is difficult to see how he can make such statements without at least addressing the Marxist position that growth can occur only, in an essential sense, at the expense of the worker.[14]

The Marxist Alternative

Marxists would find the theories discussed above perhaps ingenious but largely meaningless contributions to a materialist study of the development of society's productive forces. In this view, one can only explain the existence and nature of unemployment in terms of the prevailing mode of production. The mode of production is determined by the social relations of production which govern the appropriation of surplus labor time. The inquiry must focus, then, on the substantive relation between the worker and the means of production or, more pragmatically, between the worker and those who effectively control the means of production.

The capitalist mode of production is characterized by the relations of production between labor and capital. The laborer is separated from the means of production. Thus he can realize his productive capacity only by engaging in relations of production with the capitalist. Marx wrote: "[I]nstead of being able to sell the commodities in which his labour has been objectified, [he] must rather be compelled to offer for sale as a commodity that very labour-power which exists only in his living body" (1977, p. 272).

The capitalist is the buyer of labor-power. Marx described the capitalist:

> . . . as the conscious bearer of this movement [of transforming money into capital], the possessor of money . . . His person, or rather his pocket, is the point from which the money starts and to which it returns. The objective content of the circulation we have been discussing — the valorization of value — is his subjective purpose, and it is only in so far as the appropriation of ever more wealth in the abstract is the sole driving force behind his operations that he functions as a capitalist, i.e., as capital personified and endowed with a consciousness and a will . . . His aim is . . . the unceasing movement of profit-making. (1977, p. 254)

At the highest level of abstraction in Marx's analysis, the real value of a commodity is measured by the labor time required for its production; labor-power is the only commodity whose value is less than the value it produces. The capitalist seeks to maximize this difference and, thus, to maximize the "portion of value which costs him nothing and is nevertheless realized through the sale of those commodities [which labor produces and which are owned by the capitalist]" (1977, p. 769). This is the essence of valorization.

Ceteris paribus, he may accomplish this by stimulating the productivity of labor; "[t]he objective of the development of the productivity of labour within the context of capitalist production is the shortening of that part of the working day in which the worker must work for himself, and the lengthening, thereby, of the other part of the day, in which he is free to work for nothing for the capitalist" (1977, p. 438). Herein lies the key to the creation of capitalism's surplus population: "in proportion as the productivity of labour increases, capital increases its supply of labour more quickly than its demand for workers" (1977, p. 789). In this way, capital is able to set free a part of the working class. Marx pointed out the irony of this situation: "The working population therefore produces both the accumulation of capital and the means by which it is itself made relatively superfluous; and it does this to an extent which is always increasing" (1977, p. 783).

Of course, the size of this reserve army fluctuates with the uneven movement of the process of accumulation. As Marx explained, "[w]hen this periodicity has once become consolidated, . . . the production of a relative surplus population — i.e., a population surplus in relation to capital's average requirements for valorization — is a necessary condition for modern industry" (1977, p. 786). It behooves the capitalist to have at his disposal a supply of idle hands, so that he can take advantage of economic upswings quickly and efficiently. During downswings, he can release workers to reach the point at which his purchases of labor correspond to his current requirements for valorization.

As the foregoing discussion indicates, the size of the industrial reserve army is not directly dependent on the size of the population. The process of valorization has separated the laborer from his labor-power. As productivity is increased, the over-work of the employed part of the working class swells the ranks of its reserve, while, conversely, the greater pressure that the reserve by its competition exerts on the employed workers forces them to submit to over-work and subjects them to the dictates of capital" (1977, p. 789). Thus, the dynamics of capitalist mode of production, rather than absolute population growth, spur the creation and maintenance of the reserve. As Marx explained

> The appropriate law for modern industry, with its decennial cycles and periodic phases which, as accumulation advances, are complicated by irregular oscillations following each other more and more quickly, is the law of the regulation of the demand and supply of labour by the alternate expansion and contraction of capital, i.e., by the level of capital's valorization requirements at the relevant movement, the labour-market sometimes appearing relatively under-supplied because capital is expanding, and sometimes relatively over-supplied because it is contracting. It would be utterly absurd, in place of this, to lay down a law according to which the movement of capital depended simply on the movement of the population.

Viewed from the perspective of the capitalist, then, one might say that full employment is the purchase of that amount of labor-power corresponding to capital's average requirements for valorization.[15]

As noted above, the production of relative surplus population is a reflection of the laws of motion of the capitalist mode of production. "The fact that the means of production and the productivity of labor increase more rapidly than the productive population itself expresses itself, therefore, under capitalism, in the inverse form that the working population always increases more rapidly than the valorization requirements of capital" (1977, p. 798). It follows, then, that issues of the voluntariness of unemployment, the rationality of workers' expectations, and the response of economic agents to tax cuts contribute nothing to a scientific study of unemployment. The scientific analysis of unemployment, however, can be found in the pages of *Capital.*

Notes

1. For a more in depth analysis of the managerial class, see James Burnham's *The Managerial Revolution* (1941) and Alvin Gouldner's *The Future of Intellectuals and the Rise of the New Class (1979).*

2. Gouldner (1979, p. 17) observes that the managerial class may at times ally itself with the working class to improve its own position against the old class.

3. Darity (1981–82, p. 177).

4. I define the classicals as Keynes did in the *General Theory,* p. 3, note 1.

5. Again, I rely upon Keynes' interpretation of the classical postulates. This facilitates understanding of Keynes' critique but does little violence to classical theory.

6. While there is some disagreement on this point, I find support for it in the *General Theory,* pp. 15–16. Keynes states: "It follows from this [his] definition [of involuntary unemployment] that the equality of the real wage to the marginal disutility of employment presupposed by the second postulate, realistically interpreted, corresponds to the absence of 'involuntary' unemployment. This state of affairs we shall describe as 'full employment'. "

7. It can be argued that this difference is a reflection of an ideological dispute among members of the managerial class over the proper role of the private sector and the treatment of the victims of capitalism — the unemployed.

8. Solow's premise rests upon a study by Peter Diamond and Eric Maskin. Diamond and Maskin construct their study using all the conventionally accepted techniques of discourse, thus reducing the issues to empirical disputes rather than matters of theoretical conceptualization.

9. One major unanswered question concerning the monetarists is: Why do they stop short of dismantling the Federal Reserve? It seems that the logical conclusion of their argument would point to that result, yet they advocate a fixed money growth rate scheme instead. Their willingness to preserve the Federal Reserve may result from an ultimate willingness to turn to monetary tools in pursuit of their policy goals or a fear of the absence of an agency of the last resort that controls the quantity of money.

10. Again, see Darity (1981–82).

11. Berkman's view is similar to the notion of reasonable expectations presented by Collander and Guthrie. They anticipate at least some role for stabilization policies.

12. This list of ramifications associated with a return to the gold standard are beyond the scope of this paper. I mention it here only to contrast the basic philosophies of the supply-siders and the monetarists.

13. Laffer points frequently to this tax cut in support of his position, even though it was developed and implemented by those who called themselves Keynesians.

14. Laffer couches his analysis in terms of labor, capital, and surplus value (1981, p. 33), without ever addressing the source of these terms. He ignores Marx's position that "within the capitalist system all methods for raising the social productivity of labour are put into effect at the cost of the individual worker . . ." (1977, p. 799). He encourages labor to adapt itself to the needs of capital, an adjustment which capital will make automatically, according to Marx.

15. I do not attempt to attribute this conclusion to Marx. This is my own interpretation, made for the purpose of juxtaposing, in traditional language, the Marxist conception of unemployment with the conceptions presented in the second section.

References

Bharadwaj, Krishna. *Classical Political Economy and the Rise to Dominance of Supply and Demand Theories.* Calcutta: Longman Orient, 1976.

Blatt, John M. "Classical Economics of Involuntary Unemployment." *Journal of Post Keynesian Economics* (Summer 1981), 552–9.

Brunner, Karl and Meltzer, Allan. *The Phillips Curve and Labor Markets.* Amsterdam: North-Holland, 1976.

Burnham, James. *The Managerial Revolution.* New York: John Day Co., 1941.

Business Week:

"A Guide to Understanding the Supply-siders." December 22, 1980, 79–78.

"Supply-siders vs. Monetarists." August 24, 1981a, 78–82½

"Building a Base for a Savings Economy." September 7, 1981b, 86–87.

"Reagan's Interest Rate Dilemma." September 14, 1981c, 28–29.

"A Return to the Gold Standard." September 21, 1981d, 114–120.

Cagan, Phillip. "The Monetary Dynamics of Hyperinflation." In Milton Friedman (ed.) *Studies in the Quantity Theory of Money.* (1956).

Cherry, Robert. "What is Natural About the Natural Rate of Employment?" *Journal of Economic Issues* (September 1981), 729–43.

Colander, David C., and Guthrie, Robert S. "Great Expectations: What the Dickens Do Rational Expectations Mean?" *Journal of Post Keynesian Economics* (Winter 1980–1), 219–34.

Darity, William Jr. "Beveridge and the New Search Unemployment. *Journal of Post Keynesian Economics* (Winter 1981–2), 171–180.

Duboff, R.B. "Full Employment — History of a Receding Target" *Politics and Society* (7:1977), 1–25.

Edwards, Edgar O. "Classical and Keynesian Employment Theories: A Reconciliation." *Quarterly Journal of Economics* (August 1959), 407–428.

Feldstein, Martin. "The Economics of the New Unemployment." *The Public Interest* (Fall 1973) 3–42.

Fellner, William. "Phillips-Type Approach or Acceleration?" *Brookings Papers on Economic Activity* (2: 1971), 469–83.

Friedman, Milton. *Studies in the Quantity Theory of Money.* 1956.

______ . "The Role of Monetary Policy." *American Economic Review* (March 1968), 1–18.

______ . "Nobel Lecture: Inflation and Unemployment." *Journal of the Political Economy* (June 1977), 451–472.

Gittings, Thomas. "The Inflation-Unemployment Tradeoff." *Economic Perspective* (September/October 1979), 3–9.

Gordon, D.F. "A Neo-Classical Theory of Keynesian Unemployment." In Brunner and Meltzer (ed.) *The Phillips Curve and Labor Markets.* Amsterdam: North-Holland, 1976, 65–97.

Gouldner, Alvin W. *The Future of Intellectuals and the Rise of The New Class.* New York: Seabury Press, 1979.

Holt, Charles C. "Labor Market Structure: Implications for Micro Policy." *American Economic Association* (May 1978), 342–7.

______ . "Wages and Job Availability in Segmented Labor Markets." In Edmund Malinvaud, and Jean-Paul Fitoussi (eds.) *Unemployment in Western Countries.* London: Macmillan Press, Ltd., 1980, 385–419.

Hunt, E.K. *History of Economic Thought: A Critical Perspective.* Belmont, Calif.: Wadsworth Publishing Co., 1979.

Hymans, Saul. "Comments and Discussion." *Brookings Papers on Economic Activity* (2: 1971), 514–515.

Keynes, J.M. *The General Theory of Employment, Interest, and Money.* First Harbinger Edition, New York: Harcourt, Brace, and World, Inc., 1964.

Laffer, Arthur B. "Supply-side Economics." *Financial Analysts Journal* (September/October 1981), 29–43.

Lipsey, R.G. "The Relation Between Unemployment and the Rate of Change of Money Wage Rates in the U.K., 1861–1957, A Further Analysis." *Economica* (February 1960), 1–31.

______. "The Micro-Theory of the Phillips Curve Reconsidered." *Economica* (February 1974), 62–70.

Lucas, R.E., and Rapping, L.A. "Price Expectations and the Phillips Curve." *American Economic Review* (June 1969), 342–50.

Lucas, R.E., and Rapping, L.A. "Some International Evidence on Output-Inflation Tradeoffs." *American Economic Review* (June 1973), 326–34.

Lucas, R.E., and Prescott, E.C. "Equilibrium Search and Unemployment." *Journal of Economic Theory* (February 1974), 188–209.

Lutz, Mark A. "Stagflation as an Institutional Problem." *Journal of Economic Issues* (September 1981), 745–68.

Marx, Karl. *Capital,* Vol. 1. Translated by Ben Fowkes, New York: Vintage Books, 1977.

Modigliani, Franco. "The Monetarist Controversy, or Should We Forsake Stabilization Policies?" *American Economic Review* (March 1977), 1–19.

Muth, John. "Rational Expectations and the Theory of Price Movements." *Econometrica* (July 1961), 315–335.

Okun, Arthur. "The Mirage of Steady Inflation." *Brookings Papers on Economic Activity* (2: 1971), 485–498.

Parsons, Donald O. "Unemployment, the Allocation of Labor and Optimal Government Intervention." *The American Economic Review* (September 1980), 626–35.

Patinkin, Don. "Price Flexibility and Full Employment." In Max G. Mueller (ed.) *Readings in Macroeconomics,* New York: Holt, Rinehart and Winston, 1966.

Phelps, E.S. "Phillips Curves, Expectations of Inflation, and Optimal Unemployment over Time." *Economica* (August 1967), 254–81.

______. "Money-Wage Dynamics and Labor-Market Equilibrium." *Journal of the Political Economy* (July/August 1968), 678–711.

______. "Short-Run Employment and Real Wage in Competitive Markets." *International Economic Review* (June 1969), 220–32.

______. "The Emerging Microeconomics in Employment and Inflation Theory." *American Economic Review* (May 1969), 147–60.

______. "The Natural Rate Controversy and Economic Theory." in N. Swan and D. Wilton (eds.) *Inflation and the Canadian Experience,* Kingston, Ontario: The Industrial Relations Center, Queens University, 1971.

______, and Taylor, J.B. "Stabilization Powers of Monetary Policy under Rational Expectations." *Journal of the Political Economy,* (February 1977), 173.

Phillips, A.W. "The Relation Between Unemployment and the Rate of Change of Money Wage Rates in the U.K., 1861–1957." *Economica* (November 1958), 283–299.

Piore, Michael J. "Unemployment and Inflation: An Alternative View." In Piore (ed.) *Unemployment and Inflation.* New York: M.E. Sharpe, Inc., 1979.

Rima, Ingrid H. *Labor Markets, Wages, and Employment.* New York: W.W. Norton and Co., Inc., 1981.

Ross S., and Wachter, M. "Wage Determination, Inflation, and the Industrial Structure." *American Economic Review* (September 1973), 675–92.

Samuelson, Paul A., and Solow, Robert. "Analytical Aspects of Anti-Inflation Policy." *American Economic Review* (May 1960).

Santomero, Anthony, and Seater, John. "On the Phillips Curve." *Journal of Economic Literature* (June 1978), 499–545.

Sargent, Thomas, and Wallace, Neil. "Rational Expectations, the Optimal Monetary Instrument, and the Optimal Money Supply Role." *Journal of Political Economy* (April 1975), 241–254.

Smyth, David J., and Holmes, James N. "The Employment Ratio and Potential Labor Surplus in Phillips-type Relationships: A Note." *Journal of Post Keynesian Economics* (Fall 1981), 75–80.

Solow, Robert M. "On Theories of Unemployment." *The American Economic Review* (March 1980), 1-11.

Tobin, James. "Inflation and Unemployment." *American Economic Review* (March 1972), 1–18.

Tuchscherer, Thomas. "The Unnatural 'Natural' Rate of Unemployment." *Journal of Post Keynesian Economics* (Fall 1981), 25–31.

Wheeler, David. "Is There a Phillips Curve?" In Michael J. Piore (ed.) *Unemployment and Inflation.* New York: M.E. Sharpe, Inc., 1979.

III COMMENTS

COMMENT ON CHAPTERS by Blau and Datcher

Saul D. Hoffman

In the past two decades or so, labor economics has been one of the major growth areas in the field of economics. Developments in theory, econometrics, and in the quality of available data have all been important, but the major impetus, I think, has been increased public interest in many of the issues analyzed by labor economics. Some of this interest and research has been in the evaluation of specific government policies — minimum wage legislation and the Negative Income Tax experiments, for example. But some of the broader issues of labor economics, especially those which concern the personal distribution of income, have recieved the most attention. The research output on income inequality, labor market discrimination, and equality of opportunity has been enormous.

Two of the chapters in this book — the ones by Blau and Datcher —undertake to summarize part of this literature. Blau's paper is a very thorough treatment of the research on sex-based earnings differences. It includes not only a careful summary of the relevant empirical literature but also an overview of the relevant economic theory and research methodology. Datcher's subject is narrower and less closely tied to major currents in labor economics. Her chapter focuses on the literature — much of it noneconomic — on race differences in the acquisition of education.

Despite the differences in focus — sex rather than race, earnings differences versus educational differences — the two chapters have much in common. They ultimately draw on much of the same theory and use the same methodology. Moreover, the research summarized by Datcher logically underlies the research presented by Blau in that the differences in workers' skills (e.g., education) which are treated as exogenous from the standpoint of labor market discrimination studies become the subject of analysis. Taken together, the chapters are interesting, not only for their own contributions, but also because the body of literature they discuss illustrates many of the strengths and weaknesses in the current state of theory, practice, and application in labor economics.

Because Blau's work is broader, I will begin by discussing some of the issues raised by her work and the body of research it summarizes. Much of these comments are, I think, also applicable to Datcher's writings. I will, however, also offer some more specific comments about Datcher's chapter.

The Analysis of Earnings Differences

I want to begin by noting how thorough and even-handed is Blau's discussion of the sex-discrimination literature. It is an excellent guide to a very large and diverse set of issues. Rather than comment directly on the details of her paper — and I would have little to disagree with — I want to address some related issues that she does not treat as fully. Most of my comments pertain equally to the analysis of earnings differences by race, since the theory and methodology is quite similar.

In reading Blau's chapter, I was struck by a number of things which, taken together, suggest something about this body of literature. First, the literature of earnings differences by sex (not to mention race) is truly voluminous. I counted 127 entries in the bibliography and these include only the major studies. This is all the more noteworthy since most researchers are drawing on a relatively small number of common data sources and the literature covers a relatively short time period. Second, the researchers have, on the whole, been extremely ingenious, both in the construction of hypotheses from imperfect data and especially in the interpretation of empirical results. There seems to be no result so secure that a clever skeptic cannot construct a plausible, alternative explanation. Third, it is striking how weakly related the empirical work is even to the relevant economic theory and, correspondingly, how little guidance that theory gives the empirical work. Indeed, my conjecture is that it is precisely the vagueness of the theory which has yielded the multitude of studies and unleashed the creativity of researchers.

In this case, where theory does not restrict or guide empirical practice to any significant degree, the range of hypotheses and interpretations is bound to be large. More critically, there is no obvious way to measure progress in the refutation of hypotheses. That leads to my last observation: after a great many empirical studies of individual earnings, we still have no clear evidence of which of several competing explanations of earnings differences is the most appropriate. I will try to show below that this reflects both inherent weaknesses in some of the relevant theory and an enormous (and not fully appreciated) gap between the theoretically relevant concepts and the data that is available.

What Theory?

The first thing to note is how little economic theory is actually used in the empirical work on earnings.[1] The theory of wage determination that constitutes the core of labor economics is hardly considered. There is, for example, virtually no mention of labor demand or labor supply, short-run versus long-run equilibria, nonpecuniary job characteristics and compensating wage differentials, the effects of monopsony and labor immobility, the returns to unique skills, and so on. Even the theoretical literature on labor market discrimination is used only indirectly. The works of Becker and Arrow are used primarily as a reminder that the concept of discrimination applies only to the situation of perfect substitutes and also, as Blau notes, to introduce skepticism about the compatibility of discrimination and profit-maximizing behavior.

In practice, as Blau emphasizes, empirical research on earnings differences has been couched primarily within the framework of the human capital market. Curiously, this has been true both for those researchers who count themselves as supporters of that model and those who would place themselves among its critics. It is common to include references to alternative views of wage determinations, such as the dual/segmented labor market, radical/Marxist approaches, or institutional wage setting, but these are rarely, if ever, tested directly. The battleground on which the alternative explanations are tested is the explanatory power of the factors designated as measures of human capital. Indeed, much empirical work takes an unorthodox form in which some researchers use the human capital model to show its importance while others use it to demonstrate its impotence.

The human capital model plays such a central role in the analysis of earnings difference that it is worth considering it more closely than does Blau. The model has attained a rather anomalous position. On the one hand, it is widely accepted, as evidenced both by its inclusion in the main body of economic theory (it even appears in textbooks about economic principles) and its central role in all empirical work. On the other hand, it is widely criticized, and the depth of feeling frequently is quite strong. There are not many areas of economics where researchers are as polarized.

Like most of microeconomic theory, the human capital model operates at two distinct levels of analysis. At an aggregate level, the model provides a theory of long-run equilibrium wage rates. Interestingly, it is essentially a cost-based theory, just like the competitive model of long-run price. The wage premium attached to any human capital investment must offer a rate of return comparable to other investments; otherwise it would not be profitable for individuals to undertake the investment. There is, by this reasoning, no need to inquire independently into the effects of human capital acquisition on worker productivity. All investments made in an equilibrium setting must be productivity-enhancing, otherwise profit-seeking firms would not offer the wage premiums necessary to induce individuals to bear the costs necessary to acquire the skills. None of this figures explicitly in empirical work, but it is an essential part of the story. There is, I think, very little guidance from the human capital model about short-run wage determination. In that time frame, separate supply and demand analysis for each occupation — the older theory of occupational wage differences — is the appropriate analysis.

More theoretical and empirical attention is focused on the human capital model's description of individual behavior regarding the accumulation of human capital. Decisions about education and on-the-job training have received special emphasis. Given some objective function expressed in terms of utility or income and a set of parameters describing the expected costs and benefits of acquiring human capital, the model can be used to characterize optimizing behavior. This is yet another application of a constrained maximization procedure and thus it fits comfortably within the general neoclassical approach.

At this level, the theory is used to suggest several things. First, an individual's level of acquired skills is viewed as a matter of choice — the result of a conventional maximization process. An individual's skill level — and thus earnings in a competitive labor market — therefore becomes endogenous and, moreover, it can be considered as optimal, at least in terms of the objective function and the relevant parameters. Second, optimal human capital accumulation will differ among individuals if the relevant investment parameters differ accordingly. This idea ultimately provides the central theoretical prediction and empirical guidance of the model: average earnings will differ among groups of individuals, defined by race, sex, ability, age, etc., if systematic differences exist in the parameters for these groups.

This last idea has been used in at least two different ways in the analysis of earnings difference by sex and race. For example, in the Mincer-Polachek approach to male-female earnings differences, parameter differences exist because of the traditional division of labor by sex in households. But since that labor allocation is viewed as both efficient and voluntary, the resulting differences in human capital and in earnings are regarded as voluntary as well. But other economists have recognized that parameter differences could just as well be due to discrimination and that, in this way, discrimination may have a lasting impact on average skill differences and wage differences between groups. Blau rightly gives strong emphasis to this feedback effect and the related "perceptual equilibrium" problem discussed by Arrow.

As a purely theoretical proposition, the human capital model seems to me to play the same role in the theory of personal income distribution that the perfectly competitive model plays in the theory of market price. It describes both the maximizing behavior of individuals under various constraints and the resolution of the market in long-run equilibrium. Especially as a description of individual behavior, it includes ideas with which I think most economists would agree: that skills are endogenous; that the acquisition of skills is costly; and that an individual's decisions regarding the acquisition of human capital are related to some purposeful objective and hence can be modeled as a constrained maximization problem. One need not, I think, believe that all markets are perfectly competitive and in long-run equilibrium nor that individuals are omniscient planners to find value in this approach. Since the parameter constraints in the problem can be varied, a wide range of situations potentially can be approached in this way. The important point is that adopting a human capital maximization view does not compel a researcher to ignore discrimination or institutional restraints where these can be suitably modeled in terms of the constraints facing an individual.

I have tried to argue that the main propositions of the human capital model are not objectionable and the approach itself is not inherently restrictive. Why is there, then, so much objection to the use of the human capital model, especially in applied work? The dislike, I think, reflects several things which essentially are unrelated to the ideas I have outlined above. There is, first of all, the very conservative labor market policy implications of the model, especially as argued by some of its more zealous advocates.[2] Second, and more fundamentally, there are serious problems with the empirical formulation of the human capital model. Empirical work with the human capital model is weakened by data problems which have made ascertaining its validity or importance highly problematic. The problems arise because neither an individual's stock of human capital nor the current level of investments is observable. Researchers thus must resort to proxies; the result is the widely used human capital earnings function in which earnings are regressed on years of education and years of work experience, which are assumed to measure human capital accumulation at school and on the job, respectively. But education could be just a credential or a correlate of skill or a screening device, and work experience could be simply seniority status, independent of any continued skill acquisition. The possibilities are as large as economists and other social scientists are clever. The result is a body of empirical work which goes by the human capital designation but actually is weakly related to that theory.

The weak fit between the theory and the empirical work frequently is overlooked both by advocates and critics of the human capital model. On the one hand, advocates will cite results as support for the model without acknowledging that alternative explanations for those findings exist. In extreme cases, the model can no longer be even potentially refuted by the data. A vivid case in point is Johnson and Stafford's finding that female academics earned less per additional year of work experience than male professors, a result which they then attributed to differential investments in human capital rather than discrimination. But what, then, would have been evidence of discrimination? On the other hand, critics occasionally treat anomalous results or lack of explanatory power as evidence that the theoretical propositions of the model are refuted.

My own position here is more agnostic. The potential problem of the human capital model seems to me to be not so much that it is wrong as that available data will not allow us to either reject or support it with confidence. Support for the model ultimately rests as much on one's belief in the strength of profit-maximizing behavior and on how close to competitive markets are than on any direct empirical evidence.

Alternative Approaches

However unsatisfactory the human capital approach may be as the basis for empirical investigation, the alternative earnings determination models which are frequently invoked seem demonstrably inferior. The continued support for dualist models seems especially notable in this respect. I say that as one who not so many years ago wrote a labor economics dissertation embracing much of the dual labor market literature. Not only was the model originally formulated almost without any reference to traditional economic behavior (i.e., profit-maximization, utility-maximization), but it yielded few testable hypotheses — not even as to the composition of the primary and secondary sectors themselves! I think it is fair to say that in the decade or more since the first publication of these ideas, there have been neither major theoretical developments nor any credible empirical confirmation of any of its predictions.[3] As evidence of this, it is interesting that most of the regularly cited dual labor market articles date from the early 1970s.

I think that the continued popularity of the dualist approach stems much more from lack of enthusiasm for the human capital model than from any direct evidence in its own favor. Indeed, many of the claims on behalf of the dual labor market model seem to be of the form "if not model A (the human capital model) then, therefore, explanation B (the dual labor market model or any other preferred explanation)."[4] I think we should be able to agree that that is not an acceptable methodology. In this case, reversing the process (i.e., considering the dualist approach directly) and using the same logic would lead to strong support for the human capital model.

I think labor economists should be willing to give serious attention to profit-maximization and/or utility-maximization and should, as a result, be skeptical of explanations which cannot be posed in those terms. As I indicated in my discussion above of the human capital model, I think that suitably modified maximizing models have more potential for explaining earnings and other labor market phenomena than vaguely drawn dualist or institutionalist approaches. As examples of broader approaches which seem promising, I would cite the social capital work of Loury and some of the recent work by Akerlof which examine some of the sociological elements of employment and earnings.

Empirical Practice

As Blau notes, virtually all empirical studies of earnings differences by sex or race utilize a statistical decomposition procedure credited to Oaxaca and Blinder, which separates mean earnings differences into one portion due to differences in estimated coefficients and a second part due to differences in the average levels of the independent variables. In practice, it is common to regard the latter portion as representing the effect of human capital differences and, hence, deserved, while the former category shows the effects of discrimination. Using this procedure, it is possible to conclude, using what I think are representative numbers, that about 40 percent of the female-male earnings gap and about one-half of the black-white earnings gap are deserved.[5]

There are at least two ways in which we might interpret the discrimination versus human capital differences issue. There is a narrow view, by which I mean an effort to determine the importance of labor market discrimination in explaining earnings differences. In this view, we need only inquire into the equality of treatment of individuals by race or sex, taking as given their productivity-related traits. More broadly, however, we might ask about the role of discrimination in any form in accounting for average wage differences, in which case we want not necessarily to regard human capital differences as given. These differences would properly be treated as endogenous, as in the literature discussed by Datcher. Few analyses of earnings differences by sex or race attempt to quantify discrimination from the broad view,[6] while the narrower approach is seriously impaired by the poor fit between theory and data.

Consider the narrow approach first. Because of the inability to measure human capital, it is not clear that the decomposition procedure does, in fact, accurately measure the portion of earnings difference due to discrimination and human capital differences. For example, does a finding of lower returns to job experience for women or blacks reflect discrimination or is it due to differences in on-the-job training which are inaccurately measured by the simple counting of years of experience? Standard procedure would place this in the discrimination category, but in the Mincer-Polachek view it belongs (at least in this narrower view) among the human capital differences. There is no obvious way to resolve this with the quality of data likely to be available.[7] The same is true of possible unmeasured differences in the quality of education. Typically, researchers know only the amount of education, so there is ample room for conjecture about differences in college or high school quality, course of study, class rank, the socioeconomic status of one's classmates, and so on. The inability to measure the relevant concepts sharply undercuts the confidence we can place in the decomposition results. It also, I think, accounts for many of the very ingenious explanations of why some coefficient differences may have one interpretation or may mean something altogether different.

There are some other problems as well with this narrow approach. As commonly used, no distinction is made between differences in coefficients or means which are statistically significant and those which are not. Numerically large subportions of the discrimination and human capital components frequently arise from differences which are not themselves statistically significant, even though there is not sufficient reason to believe that the means or coefficients are different. In addition, the results are highly sensitive to the exact specification of the model, and not just in the sense of whether certain variables (for instance, occupation in male-female analyses) should or should not be included. Rather, our knowledge of the correct specification of an earnings function is sufficiently inexact, that coefficient differences which could be attributed to discrimination are likely to be found in the analysis of earnings differences between any two groups. For instance, I found that 40 percent of earnings differences between white males in the South and white males in other regions was due to discrimination, even though I am unable to suggest a reasonable explanation of why that should be true.

If, however, we are interested in considering the causes of earnings differences from a broader standpoint, then the typical decomposition results are likely to be misleading. Consider the procedure as it would be applied to the analysis of earnings differences between black and white men and between white men and white women. The results in the latter case are discussed by Blau. There is, I think, little reason to believe that any more than a trivial portion of the difference in earnings by race should be due to differences in human capital, which are not themselves due to discrimination. To believe otherwise, one would have to cite genetic differences which affect skills or perhaps time preference differences which affect human capital accumulation. Certainly education differences due to segregation or to parental income differences should not be construed as being unrelated to discrimination. In the case of earnings differences by sex, it is at least arguable, via the Mincer-Polachek argument, that some human capital differences are not the result of discrimination. I have tried to put that carefully: I do not mean to accept the Mincer-Polachek argument, but only note that it could be valid.

In practice, however, most empirical studies using the decomposition procedure conclude that human capital variables are less successful in explaining earnings differences by sex than by race, exactly the opposite of the argument just presented. This result is almost inevitable, given the methodology and the measurement problems. Because most studies treat workers's skills as exogenous (i.e., they attempt to measure discrimination in the narrow view), earnings differences due to differences in average levels of measure traits are attributed to the human capital category. Blau does discuss this in the case of the treatment of years of work experience for women. Second, easily measured human capital variables, in particular, educational attainment, differ substantially by race and trivially by sex. The inability to measure human capital acquired on the job greatly reduces the likelihood of finding similarly large human capital differences between men and women.

Conclusion on Blau

Many of my comments thus far have been critical of theoretical and empirical practices in the literature on earnings differentials. Now I want to try to place that criticism in proper perspective. I think much of the early theoretical and empirical research in earnings differences was extremely valuable in defining issues, suggesting possibilities, and providing empirical magnitudes. We learned quickly and clearly that no simple explanation existed for the observed earnings differences in the sense that even discrimination defined narrowly could not be eliminated as a cause of the difference. But, having made those points and absorbed those insights, I think researchers have hit a dead end.

Consider, for example, the concluding paragraph in the second section of Blau's review of the empirical studies of male-female earnings differences: "We have seen that on a priori grounds the human capital model provides a viable alternative to labor market discrimination as an explanation for sex differences in market outcomes. However, on the basis of our review of the empirical evidence, we conclude that it cannot provide the full explanation and that discrimination most probably plays a role. As our review also makes clear, precisely quantifying the importance of discrimination relative to other factors is not an easy matter. Moreover, the effort to determine which model of discrimination is most consistent with the data and to determine the mechanisms by which these discriminatory outcomes are produced is still in its early stages." This is, I would agree, a perfectly accurate description of the findings thus far. The problem is that the same statement could have been written five years ago.

Much of the recent research in this area seems to be a replication of a previous study, varying only by the year of observation, data set, age group, etc., or adding some small wrinkle to the dependent variable or the independent variables. There are no fresh theoretical approaches to report, and the ability to draw new information from inadequate data seems to be exhausted. It has not been possible to resolve the issues or even to refine the empirical magnitudes much further. I am convinced of two things about the future course of research in this area: first, that measurable human capital differences will never account for a sufficiently large portion of earnings differences by race or sex as to end all argument; and second, that reasonable people will be able to identify ways in which the available measures are inadequate and suggest that, with better data, the results could be quite different.

Family Background and Educational Attainment

Datcher's chapter concentrates on reviewing a series of studies which have examined the extent to which race differences in educational attainment are due to the poorer family backgrounds of blacks. The studies are all quite similar: some measure of educational attainment is regressed on some set of family background measures and the race differences in means and estimated coefficients are examined. Although it is not made explicit, most of the studies use a Oaxaca-Blinder decomposition procedure. The studies differ in terms of the age groups examined, data set studied, year of analysis, and extensiveness of family background measures. Because Datcher is primarily interested in whether these family background effects have been diminishing over time, she focuses on whether differences by race in these effects are smaller for younger cohorts than for older ones.

Let me begin on a positive note. I think attention to the process that I would call skill acquisition is critical. Treating workers' skills as endogenous is important in extending our understanding not only of average earnings differences by race or sex but also of the personal distribution of income. As Datcher carefully emphasizes in the beginning of the chapter, equality of opportunity depends on eliminating those differences in education which are the result not of differences in ability but of differences in family background.

Although the primary thrust of the paper is empirical, the paper begins by describing what Datcher terms weak and strong versions of equality of educational attainment. I actually found these definitions a bit distracting. The weak version, according to Datcher, is satisfied when, if there were no racial differences in average background characteristics and ability, blacks would obtain as much schooling as whites. This seems to correspond to a situation in which the effects (regression coefficients) of background and ability are equal for blacks and whites. Actual educational attainment by race would nevertheless be unequal, since substantial differences in background variables do exist. The strong version, however, is not satisfied until the social origins of blacks do not handicap their educational achievement. To me, this suggests a situation in which neither coefficients nor means of background variables differ. The only legitimate cause of differences in educational attainment would be ability differences and, since there is no evidence that there are such differences, equality of education by race is the expected result.

Although this weak versus strong distinction is useful for understanding the causes of differences in educational attainment, I am not sure that it adds much to the paper or to the more general concerns of researchers in understanding the process of educational attainment. For example, most of the research that Datcher summarizes tells us about neither the strong nor the weak criteria but instead, about something in between. As summarized by Datcher, most of the studies (see table 4–1) tell us how much higher the educational attainment of blacks would be if they had the family background characteristics of whites but if these characteristics still affected their own educational attainment exactly as before. Thus the equality of background characteristics, required by the strong criterion, is met, but the quality of family background effects (coefficients) required by both criteria, is not.[8]

The application of the two criteria to the theoretical framework also is not completely successful. The three theories which are discussed — a restricted human capital version, a social capital extension of this, and a radical view — are presented not so much for how they provide insight into the educational attainment decision, but for how they fit into the weak versus strong criteria. I agree that it is important to note the different ways in which background differences affect educational outcomes — directly through financial ability via the external effects of neighborhood differences, or through differences in the nature of schooling in different communities. It seems to me much less important whether or not they fit into weak or strong equality criteria.

In any event, the discussion of empirical studies on educational attainment is largely independent on these preliminaries. The research is very pragmatic in the sense that it is answer-oriented and offers little in theoretical or empirical work for the nonspecialist. On the whole, it appears that educational differences have narrowed sharply for younger cohorts versus older ones and, moreover, that a very large share of the remaining difference is due to differences in family background. The important point here, it seems to me, has been made by Freeman,[9] but is not stressed by Datcher: the mechanism (i.e., coefficients) by which the status of one generation affects the educational attainment of the next is now quite similar for blacks and whites.

Consider, for example, Datcher's summary of Freeman's work. She notes that he found that "75 percent of the 1.6 difference in years of schooling between young black and white men can be accounted for by poorer mean black backgrounds compared to only 49 percent of the 3.7 difference between older black and white men." But, turned around, this means that over half of the education difference by older men was due to differences in the status-transfer mechanism, while for the younger men only a quarter is due to the status-transfer mechanism. In other words, older blacks were doubly disadvantaged; not only were their backgrounds less favorable, but even those with more favorable backgrounds were not helped as much as whites with similar backgrounds. For younger blacks, this latter effect has been substantially reduced; the major impediment to equality of educational attainment is their less favorable backgrounds. In terms of Datcher's framework, this suggests that the weak criterion has nearly been met.

The latter part of the paper is a detailed discussion of studies using more elaborate background measures. Measurement error problems are also discussed in terms of their likely impact on the research findings. I have little to add here other than the observation that the two economics papers discussed (by Morgenstern and Akin and Garfinkel) might not merit such a full presentation. They are not very timely and the data, especially in Morgenstern's paper, leave much to be desired. I think that Datcher's own work in this area is a significant improvement over previous research. Specialists will want to consult directly that work.

Conclusion on Datcher

As it stands, I am not sure that this body of literature suggests a significant direction for future research in labor economics. Much of it seems to straddle both the economic and sociological approaches to educational attainment without doing justice to either. Recent developments in both fields are not covered in the paper, presumably because they focus on educational attainment by individuals rather than on race differences in average attainment. I think future research will emphasize the individual level of analysis.

In the economics literature, I would note the recent research on the determinants of postsecondary education (see Fuller, Manski, and Wise, 1982, and the sources noted there). These studies are characterized by the use of much better data,[10] greater attention to modeling economic decision making, and the use of more sophisticated econometric techniques. One interesting feature of this work is that the empirical specification is more closely tied to economic theory; independent variables include foregone earnings, tuition costs, scholarship aid, student ability, and so on. The sociological literature on status attainment has considered explanatory variables more like those in the studies reviewed by Datcher but have taken greater care to specify the causal mechanisms. In contrast, the research discussed by Datcher is essentially a reduced-form approach. A good sampling of the state of the art in the sociological literature is presented in a recent volume of *Sociology of Education* (January, 1983). The interested reader will want to examine directly the papers there.

Notes

1. It is only fair to note that all of the criticisms which follow apply fully to my own research. On occasion, I will use some of that work to illustrate a point.

2. If voluntary human capital investment differences are the cause of wage differences between men and women, then interventionist labor market policies cannot be easily justified. This kind of argument was made in the *1974 Economic Report of the President* which drew heavily on the research of Mincer and Polachek.

3. See Cain for an early critique of the evidence and Duncan, chapter 4, for an analysis of the model using longitudinal data from the Panel Study of Income Dynamics. In general, Duncan finds much more relative income mobility and job mobility across sectors of the economy than is consistent with the dual labor market model.

4. A good example of this logic appears in *Women, Work, and Wages: Equal Pay for Jobs of Equal Value* by Treiman and Hartmann. They write (p. 45) that "the institutional view offers a more fruitful perspective from which to understand . . . wage differentials between men and women, especially since . . . attempts to explain earnings differences by productivity differences have not been very successful."

5. These figures are from Corcoran and Duncan, which is based on data which is more extensive than that used in most studies.

6. Interestingly, Blinder's original article considered this broader view as well as a narrower, reduced-form approach.

7. The Panel Study of Income Dynamics data for 1976 include a measure of on-the-job training derived by asking individuals about the length of time it would take "the average new person to become fully trained and qualified." Although this measure is superior to (estimated) years of work experience, it is far from perfect and is, in any event, unlikely to be regularly available. See Duncan and Hoffman for details.

8. The effect of inequality in returns to various characteristics can be determined from the information provided by Datcher as that fraction of the total difference not due to differences in means. That figure is not presented by Datcher in her discussion of any studies.

9. See Freeman, pp. 24–29.

10. The new data is from the National Longitudinal Survey of the High School Class of 1972.

References

Akerlof, G. "A Theory of Social Custom of Which Unemployment May Be One Consequence." *Quarterly Journal of Economics* (June 1980), 749–75.

______ . "Labor Contracts as Partial Gift Exchange." *Quarterly Journal of Economics* (November 1982), 543–70.

Arrow, K. "Models of Job Discrimination," and "Some Mathematical Models of Race in the Labor Market." In A.H. Pascal, (ed.) *Racial Discrimination in Economic Life.* Lexington, Mass.: D.C. Heath and Co., 1972a, 83–102.

Becker, G. *The Economics of Discrimination.* Chicago: University of Chicago Press, 1957.

Blinder, A.S. "Wage Discrimination: Reduced Form and Structural Estimates." *Journal of Human Resources* (Fall 1973), 436–55.

Cain, G. "The Challenge of Segmented Labor Market Theories to Orthodox Theory: A Survey." *Journal of Economic Literature* (December 1976), 1215–57.

Corcoran, M., and Duncan, G.J. "Work History, Labor Force Attachment, and Earnings Differences Between the Races and Sexes." *Journal of Human Resources* (Winter 1979), 3–20.

Duncan, G.J. *Years of Poverty, Years of Plenty: The Changing Economic Fortunes of American Workers and Families.* Ann Arbor, Michigan: Institute for Social Research, 1983.

_____, and Hoffman, S. "On-the-Job Training and Earnings Differences by Race and Sex." *Review of Economic Statistics* (November 1979), 594–603.

Economic Report of the President. Washington, D.C.: U.S. Government Printing Office, February, 1974.

Freeman, R. "Black Economic Progress After 1964: Who Has Gained and Why?" In Sherwin Rosen (ed.) *Studies in the Labor Market.* Chicago: The University of Chicago Press, 1981.

Fuller, W., Manski, C., and Wise, D. "New Evidence on the Economic Determinants of Post-secondary Schooling Choices." *Journal of Human Resources* (Fall 1982), 477–98.

Johnson, G., and Stafford, F. "The Earnings and Promotion of Women Faculty." *American Economic Review* (December 1974), 888–903.

Loury, G. "A Dynamic Theory of Racial Income Differences." In P.A. Wallace and A. LaMond (eds.) *Women, Minorities, and Employment Discrimination.* Lexington, Mass.: D.C. Heath, 1977.

Mincer, J., and Polachek, S. "Family Investments in Human Capital: Earnings of Women." *Journal of Political Economy* (March/April 1974), (Part 2), S76-S108.

Oaxaca, R. "Male-Female Wage Differentials in Urban Labor Markets." *International Economic Review* (October 1973), 693–709.

Sociology of Education (January 1983), 56.

Treiman, D., and Hartmann, H. (eds.) *Women, Work, and Wages: Equal Pay for Jobs of Equal Value.* Washington, D.C.: National Academy Press, 1981.

LABOR ECONOMICS, PREFERENCES, AND THE RATIONALITY ASSUMPTION: A COMMENT ON BLAU, DICKENS, AND MALVEAUX

Samuel L. Myers, Jr.

The Blau, Dickens, and Malveaux chapters share an alarming and perhaps heretofore insufficiently appreciated theme. The unambiguous message in these three chapters is one that concerns a failure of microeconomic labor market models. The standard models, it seems, fail to explain sex differentials in wages, racial differences in unemployment, and the provision of such workplace amenities as safety. An unusually consistent tale is told by Professors Blau, Dickens, and Malveaux.

The tale is alarming because each of the topics with which the respective authors deal is of profound public policy importance. What we are being told, essentially, is that although policy is being — and has been — developed and implemented upon the presumed truths of received conventional economic wisdom emanating from micro models of the labor market, the models themselves appear quite suspect. The tale is appreciated woefully because by now the intricate gymnastics upon them frequently are performed in a public policy vacuum.

That there is indeed an explanatory failure is easy enough to believe. Blau relates convincing evidence of significant wage disparities between men and women. But neither the standard models of discrimination nor of human capital provide satisfactory explanations as to why these disparities should persist in competitive markets in long-run equilibrium. Malveaux presents equally convincing evidence that reveals a continued racial disparity in unemployment rates. The same models that fail to explain sex discrimination also fail to provide illuminating insights about why black unemployment rates are so high. Still other models, really a few new modeling twists — specifically, theories of search and imperfect information — that Malveaux fears are inadequate to the task of unraveling the mystery of racial differences in unemployment are found by Dickens to be virtually the only — if not the most frequently employed — tools for understanding safety hazards in the workplace. Then, even these models, or variations thereof, flounder along with all the competitive market deviants (unions, minimum wages, regulations, and so on) when they are called upon to guide public policy.

What is striking about these three chapters is the total adherence to a key postulate of neoclassical microeconomic theory: rationality of firms and consumers. Actually, there is an *almost* total adherence to the postulate of *consumer* rationality. Except for Dickens' flirtation with a few variants of deviant consumer behavior, the possibility of nonutility or nonprofit maximizing behavior and the attendant implications are not seriously entertained by any of the authors. It seems that an important potential weakness in the standard model of labor markets goes virtually unchallenged.

This is especially disturbing because organizational theorists — who, incidentally, are often at odds with economists on a variety of issues — claim that if there is any market where the textbook economic man, the rational self-interested materialistic maximizer, is unlikely to emerge in full-dress, ceremonious regalia, it is in the organized, structured workplace.[1] Each of the labor market theories that are found lacking by Blau, Dickens, and Malveaux is based on the rationality assumption. It is somewhat incongruous, then, that these three papers that deal with virtually identical theoretical issues applied to equally important foci for public policy all fail to pick up on the possibility that the theories' failure rests with one basic, flawed postulate.

The reason why a challenge to the rationality assumption is so crucial in debunking labor markets models rests with the role preferences play in human capital, discrimination, job search, and even segmented labor market theories. A lesson from the economics of crime literature is instructive. The Becker (1968) model of crime predicts that increased certainty and severity of punishment reduces participation in illegitimate activities. This is so because rational, self-interested potential criminals acting on the margin and appropriately weighing their costs and benefits find that punishment reduces the expected utility from illegitimate pursuits.

Why, then, are blacks, who experience more certain and more severe punishment than whites, more likely to engage in crime? There are two possible answers. The first and immediately obvious one is that the legitimate opportunities faced by blacks and whites diverge, perhaps due to labor market discrimination. Blacks with their lower wages and higher unemployment rates have higher expected returns to crime than whites do, so they engage in more crime. Even I (Myers, 1980) have grabbed this idea and milked it for what it is worth, fully realizing that reliance upon notions of discrimination requires admission of market inefficiency, which in the Becker world cannot be sustained in the long run.

The second answer, the one the Malveaux generally ignores in her discussion of racial gaps in unemployment, hits smack in the face of individual preferences: blacks have a taste for crime (or, identically, have a preference for risk). Perhaps it is out of a sense of ethnic chivalry that authors hesitate to make this claim, especially when it relates to crime or unemployment. Yet the resort to individual preferences is the only logical last resort when all else fails if one is to believe in rational models of man.

Why then do authors fail to pounce upon the frail rationality assumption? The opportunity is certainly there. Take, for example, Blau's insightful revelation about criticisms of the Becker discrimination model. After reciting the standard implication that, in the long run, Becker-type discrimination cannot survive, Blau poignantly observes that rejection of the Becker model of discrimination "is a double-edged sword." We can dispute whether observed sex differences in market outcomes arise because of "tastes for discrimination," just as do adherents to sexism or segregation theories. But the failure in the long run of the Becker model is no surprise to those who are skeptical about the responsibility of market discrimination for these sex differences in the first place. For this last group, somewhat less chivalrous than the "liberal neoclassicalists," coining the term Kathryn Allen used elsewhere in this book, the sex differences in market outcomes arise because of diverging commitments to the labor market vis-a-vis home production (i.e., housework) and because of different motivations, aspirations, and so on. In a word — preferences.

Malveaux essentially by-passes the challenge of rationality and preferences. Why do blacks invest in so little education? Why, within a search theory perspective, is it that blacks have high turnover rates? Malveaux steadfastly avoids giving credibility to the claim that blacks invest less in education than comparable whites do because of differing preferences. She similarly and conspicuously overlooks the possibility of black quit rates and turnover rates as being determined by some sort of perverse set of tastes. For all of her peripheral objections to the human capital and search models, Malveaux succumbs to the charms of the neoclassical rationality assumption.

Dickens, a pioneer in the development of rational models of irrationality (see his stimulating coauthored paper on cognitive dissonance, Akerlof and Dickens, 1982) is less quick to fall to the charms of conventional postulates of consumer rationality. He recognizes two deviants: (1) failure to calculate accurately probabilities of uncertain events, and (2) failure to believe those probabilities even if they are calculated accurately. What is especially pungent are his speculations about pathological behavior. Dickens boldly suggests the possibility that self-destructive behavior might be at the root of workplace accidents. There is probably much more pathological behavior than economists have been willing to admit — why else are there so many more psychologists and psychiatrists than there are economists? There is no reason to believe that pathological or, at minimum, nonutility maximizing behavior is confined to consumers, in any event. It is particularly disturbing, then, that Dickens refuses to apply his important insights on irrationality to the theory of the firm. Further, his explicit efforts to model consumer and producer decisions regarding safety ignore completely the deviation from normal rationality even when his discussion of imperfect information seems to dictate it.

In order to stimulate new debate and discussion on the topics reviewed by Blau, Dickens, and Malveaux, I will state some alternative hypotheses, based on a nontraditional notion of rationality, about how labor market participants behave. As a background for this exercise, a brief review of the economic rationality issue is warranted.

The standard notion of economic rationality to which I refer — self-interested, individualistic maximizing behavior — was enshrined by Adam Smith. In arguing that self-interest motivates cooperation, Smith relates

> . . . man has almost constant occasion for the help of his brethren, and it is in vain for him to expect it from their benevolence only. He will be more likely to prevail if he can interest their self-love in his favour, and show them that it is for their own advantage to do for him what he requires of them. (1937, p. 15)

Moreover, Smith argues that this self-interest, far from being damaging, instead promotes the public good

> Every individual is continually exerting himself to find out the most advantageous employment for whatever capital he can command. It is his own advantage, indeed, and not that of society, which he has in view. But the study of his own advantge naturally, or rather necessarily, leads him to prefer that employment which is most advantageous to the society. (1937, p. 421)

This view of the natural state of man has as its modern counterpart "the criterion of purposive activity", or the idea that man acts with a possession of logic ensuring efficiency of his actions given whatever limitations and constraints he faces.

Philosopher Maurice Godelier (1972, p. 252) incorrectly lumps together von Mises, Robbins, and Samuelson with Polanyi and Dalton in his list of adherents to this view of economic rationality. Wrong or not in associating an Austrian and a couple of neoclassicalists with economic anthropologists, Godelier clearly contrasts this polar view of rationality with a Marxist one

> [Maximization is a form of] economic rationality [that] is the product of a special historical evolution and is characteristic of developed capitalist societies in which the control and accumulation of capital constitute the strategic point of social competition. . . . the capitalist form of economic rationality differs fundamentally from the forms of rationality of primitive societies in that in it the structure of the field open to social competition is such that the struggle for control of the factors of production play the decisive role. . . . (1972, p. 293)

This characterization is an elaboration and expansion upon Oskar Lange's indictment of economic rationality as being the historical product of capitalist enterprise.

One speculates that even a Marxist would fail to reject the neoclassical notion of rationality when the subject matter is a well-structured capitalistic labor market. It is no surprise, then, that many radical labor market paradigms such as those concerning segmented or internal labor markets have difficulty rejecting the rationality assumption. These theories either blame differential opportunities for diverging labor market outcome or they point to the preference-altering structures within the labor market as causes of differing responses of otherwise equally rational labor market participants.

Other scholars, particularly organizational theorists, who are less concerned with defending and upholding the tradition of economics than with describing how people actually behave, have questioned the appropriateness of the economic rationality assumption.

The locus classicus of the organizational theorist's challenge to the standard rationality assumption is Herbert Simon's *Administrative Behavior* (1947, 3d ed., 1976). This document laid the groundwork for the development of an important alternative to theories of utility and profit maximization. Do firms really maximize profits, or do they pick a level of sales that provides a satisfactory share of the market? Simon (1979) in his Economics Nobel Lecture argues that rational models of the firm and labor market fail miserably in predicting real-world outcomes. Irrational behavior (or at least nonrational behavior, or "bounded rationality," that deviates from utility-profit maximizing behavior) does explain what we see, according to Simon.

Rather than trying to fit neatly the axioms of rationality into a more complex model of organizational behavior — e.g., by invoking uncertainty, asymmetric information, imperfect competition, and so on — the approach of Simon has been to construct a theory that begins with a description of how decisions are actually made in organizations. The theory is designed to link together executive decisions with responses of the lowest-ranked workers. Cyert and Marsh (1963) who build upon this theory provide a succinct analysis

> The theory tends to subdivide, then, into two main parts, each concerned with a certain class of decisions of significance to organizations. The first subdivision views the organization as a clearinghouse through which transfer payments are arranged among participants (e.g., workers, investors, customers). The theory describes the "decision to belong," and specifies the conditions of organizational survival in terms of methods of motivating organizational participants.
>
> The second subdivision aims at the development of theory explaining how decisions are made in organizations, with special emphasis upon the processes of executive influence and the impact of organizational positions on individual goals and perceptions. (p. 18)

The key to the "bounded rationality" perspective is that producers and consumers do not necessarily maximize. Because of often conflicting goals and expectations of individuals in organizations, decisions reflect more often than not an element of consensus or suboptimal satisfying rather than a global rationality in the sense of an efficient competitive equilibrium. I will call such decisions and the behavior that underlies them irrational (although other types of behavior could also be considered irrational, e.g., Dickens' "self-destructive pathological behavior").

The most obvious candidate for theory revision via challenge to the economic rationality assumption is Dickens' model of safety provision in the workplace. In a vast majority of work environments posing safety hazards, teams of laborers are involved. On the automotive assembly line, in the mechanics' workshop, on the construction site, in the fire station, and under the glaring sun over the cucumber patches, workers often work in groups. Workplace safety is a function, in part, of how well these groups perform.

An illustrative example is that of fire departments. Injury on the job — being struck by falling debris, slipping off a ladder, getting trapped in a smoke-filled room — is related ultimately to cooperation and shared trust among members of the team. If one is to avoid an accident, others must be looking out for you.

It is entirely possible that accidents with a known probability distribution across all team members befall some members with greater frequency than others. How does one explain this? In a broader context how does one explain the frequently recited allegation that some individuals are accident prone? Answers to these questions require a model of organizational behavior and the rationality assumption has been shown to be too strong in many instances for characterizing the team production that must be understood in order to understand these questions.

Exploring alternative behavioral models when analyzing occupational safety hazards may generate some hertofore interesting — indeed unraised — hypotheses. Do racial tensions among workers on construction projects increase the probability of accidents? Does mechanization and use of robots in automobile plants lead to such perverse worker responses as short-circuiting man-replacing machines and other actions that pose serious safety hazards? In other words, can meanness, alienation, sabotage, and just plain destructive behavior be fundamentally related to industrial safety? Perhaps research using notions of "bounded rationality" will be helpful in answering these questions concerning workplace safety.

Another critical issue in labor market research that "bounded rationality" may be useful in understanding is occupational segregation. In her useful reminder about the pitfalls of using "residual discrimination" statistical tests, Blau points out that there are many factors such as preferences or unmeasured characteristics frequently overlooked by researchers that could plausibly explain diverging labor market outcomes between men and women. What Blau fails to point out concerning this empirical research is that occupational segregation is never modeled in residual discrimination tests. She realizes that occupational segregation is a central factor that ought to be accounted for when she concludes

> On the basis of the existing evidence, it appears that sex segregation is an important mechanism for producing sex differences in earnings. (p. 40)

A guess as to why empirical tests of the discrimination hypothesis have failed to include explicitly a model of sex segregation is found in Blau's own words

> . . . occupational differences between men and women do not seem to be consistent with optimizing behavior on the part of women. (p. 41)

The guess is that the discrimination model is a model of rational choice, and Blau recognizes that something other than self-interested, individualistic, materialistic decisions are behind the puzzles of women's economic position.

Interestingly, Blau also gives a full-blown treatment to the role that preferences might play in theoretically determining sex differences in employment. She recognizes that child-bearing and child-rearing decisions can alter labor force participation patterns and even generate productivity differences that eliminate discrimination as an explanation for women's low wages. Of course, Blau is assuming standard rationality. Yet even Gary Becker (1963) has recognized that what appears to be rational may indeed be irrational behavior constrained by limited opportunities and resources. Perhaps because of sheer inability to forestall child bearing in favor of continued work experience some women choose to stay home and disinvest in their human capital.

This line of reasoning is in contrast with Blau's. She agrees that sex differences in economic returns to experience and marital status may reflect tastes or preferences. She feels that discrimination by employers could contribute to these differences as well. The question is which factor plays a more important role? Blau, weakly, opts for the employer discrimination explanation. That is understandable. The human capital model within which the discussion occurs only admits one sort of rationality: a stark economic rationality regarding marriage or child bearing. Apparently, for Blau, this assumption is difficult (impossible?) to accept.

It seems that a top priority in labor market research on occupational segregation should be to discover what it is about behavior in organizations that results in significant concentrations of females in certain occupations. Rather than look at individual tastes and employer discrimination — factors predicated upon economic rationality — researchers should probe into the behavior of the larger group in organizations. One hypothesis that might be tested is that segregation is maintained by inequality of power within an organizational structure. For example, there are power inequalities between secretaries and executives and between nurses and surgeons. Do female executives and surgeons act in the same manner as their male counterparts in maintaining the power inequality? Alternative notions of rationality will help answer this question.

Malveaux, ironically, comes closest in rejecting the standard rationality assumptions. She muses

> Our concepts of rational decision making, of occupational choice, of the linkage between employment and the quantity and quality of education seems reflective of the labor market experiences that we as economists have ourselves . . . A more realistic theory of the labor market might note that most workers choose jobs by occupational accident, not by deliberate occupational choice.

There are, as we have suggested before, alternative concepts of rationality. Deeper probing of the models that Malveaux finds unable to explain racial differences in unemployment rates might have unveiled these alternative concepts earlier.

Take, for example, the discussion of job search. Unemployment differentials can be decomposed within a search model into aspects of hiring and quitting — involuntary and voluntary turnover — and searching, or duration of unemployment. Quite clearly both the costs of search, affected in part by opportunities and initial wealth, and preferences or tastes affect turnover and duration of unemployment. Malveaux identifies the difficulty that the search model has in explaining the persistence of racial differentials through time. This finding is surprising because the search theory has all of the ingredients to "explain" black unemployment.

Do young blacks have high unemployment rates? Yes, search theory tells us. Why? Because black youth have high turnover rates due to high quit rates arising from (1) low opportunity costs of search, (2) alternative income-generating options (e.g., crime, welfare), or (3) misjudgment of the distribution of wage offers. It is possible that Malveaux has overemphasized the failure of this model to explain a continued racial gap in unemployment. The model seems to say very clearly that blacks have higher unemployment rates than whites, in part due to differing opportunities, preferences, tastes, and/or perceptions. And these facts together ought to explain virtually anything.

What is ironic is that other models of search are at the heart of alternative theories of organization. These models do not assume economic rationality or optimization. The search process described by them, while quite realistic, is also quite complex.

In the simple search model, when the offer wage exceeds the workers' reservation wage the job is accepted. Of course, the formation of these offers and reservation wage functions follows from a decision rule employed by employers and workers. It just so happens that by convention the decision rule assumed by most labor economists is one obtained from the maximization of a relevant criterion function. But intuitively we know that alternative decision rules will result in different search strategies by firms and workers. And since optimizing behavior need not prevail, it is possible that the simple rule of accepting jobs whenever the offer exceeds the reservation wage will be violated. Is this sort of irrational search behavior observed in reality? Recent research suggests that it is.

Kenneth Phillips and I (1979) reported on a study of job search among CETA workers. We concluded that wage offers were generally higher in the suburbs than offers in the city and were virtually identical for blacks and whites. But controlling for race, distance from job to residence, and a host of other factors, potential workers in the sample were less likely to show up for scheduled interviews with these very same high-paying suburban employers. It is possible to patch-up the old rationality model to make sense out of this: imperfect information, perverse preferences for inner-city life, grossly misaligned perceptions, and the like. Or one can resort to more complex notions of rationality and decision making.

Patching up the old rationality-based model has become habit forming these days. The rush to modify old models is an act of saving face. Edward Lazear (1982) puts it bluntly

> There are a large number of actual institutions and personnel practices that are embarrassments to labor economists because their simple competition models do not easily explain these phenomena. (p. 15)

There are many other wrinkles that need to be ironed out before labor market models become realistic. Why are some workers, like presidents of corporations, paid more than they are worth? Why is it that other workers, like young employees, are paid less than they are worth? Lazear and others have labored long hours to mend, cajole, and doctor the neoclassical labor market model to derive consistent answers. (The answer to the first question, incidentally, is that promotion is a prize associated with winning a labor market contest and, although a wage-marginal productivity gap results, the compensation scheme is shown to be economically rational since wage spreads affect effort levels. The answer to the second question follows similar lines of reasoning. Younger employees work hard to assure that they are retained and thus will be paid higher wages in the future.)

The chapters by Blau, Dickens, and Malveaux suggest that the patch-up efforts to date are less than successful. The chapters do leave open a sliver of hope that better modeling of rational decision making under uncertainty, imperfect information, segmented markets, and the like may provide better explanations for observed labor market phenomena. That optimism is probably misplaced.

Good public policy on safety in the workplace, sex differentials in wage, and racial differentials in unemployment should begin with a challenge to the assumptions underlying our old models. The direction of labor market research should be toward construction of a new model based on empirically verifiable assumptions about work-force behavior. Organizational theorists have provided a wealth of case studies from which it should be possible to infer a limited domain of reasonable assumptions about man's central motivating behavior in the workplace. It would be no surprise if such efforts lead to the rejection of the standard rationality assumption. These organization behavior exercises should not be performed uncritically, however.

Whether agents in labor market transactions do or do not behave rationally will still be a matter of heated debate. Do participants know all of the variables and equations, or lower and upper bounds of the models built to describe their behavior? Do they really have preference functions, the maximization of which define the goals of the decisions our models purport to study? The late Ragnar Frisch in his 1970 Nobel Lecture argues that they — decision makers in both developing and industrially developed countries — most certainly do. But what of the case studies that show decision makers actually have targets that they try to realize? The standard retort is, "But they act as if they were maximizers." What of the interviews that reveal the expansive gap between what executives think they do and what they actually do? Frisch responds

> It is well known that people will not always behave in an actual situation exactly in the way they *said* in an interview question they *would* behave in such and such a situation. But still, I think, it remains that valuable information may be obtained through interview questions, provided the questions are widely formulated in a *conversational manner*, and not simply carried out by some youngster in the opinion poll trade. (1981, p. 7) (emphasis in original)

In other words, do not believe the results of poorly conducted interviews.

In the final instance, then, recognition of the frailty of the rationality assumption in models of labor market behavior is not enough. The alternative models, of course, will need to be subjected to as much rigor or critique as there is rigor in defense of the standard model. Future research on labor markets that accepts this challenge will help reverse the trend identified by Dickens of the proliferation of policy without theory.

Note

1. My colleague, Frederick Thayer, an expert on administrative and organizational theory, disputes this point, however. He claims, "I do not see where 'standard' organization theory is at odds with economics. All decision-making models are of microeconomic rational choice." Either this is evidence of widespread acceptance of 'nonstandard' organization theory among organization behavioralists or a major misunderstanding of microeconomic rational choice among adherents to the 'standard' theory. I am grateful, in any event, to Professor Thayer for providing me with a classic quote on Taylorism "All men are naturally lazy" that sums up still another dispute between economists and organizational theorists.

References

Akerlof, George A., and Dickens, William T. "The Economic Consequences of Cognitive Dissonance." *American Economic Review* (June 1982), 307–319.

Becker, G.S., "Crime and Punishment: An Economic Approach," *Journal of Political Economy* Vol. 76 (1968), 189–217.

Becker, G.S. "Irrational Behavior and Economic Theory," *Journal of Political Economy* (February 1962), 1–13.

Cyert, Richard M., and Marsh, James G., *A Behavioral Theory of the Firm*. New Jersey: Prentice-Hall, 1963.

Frisch, Ragnar. "From Utopian Theory to Practical Applications: The Case of Econometrics." *American Economic Review* (December 1981), 1-16.

Godelier, Maurice. *Rationality and Irrationality in Economics*. London: NLB, 1972.

Lazear, Edward P. "Analytic Approaches to the Understanding of Institutions in the Labor Market." *NBER Reporter* (Fall 1982).

Myers, Samuel L. "Black-White Differentials in Crime Rates." *Review of Black Political Economy* (Winter 1980), 133-52.

Myers, Samuel L., and Phillips, Kenneth E. "Housing Segregation and Black Employment: Another Look at the Ghetto Dispersal Strategy." *American Economic Review* (May 1979), 298-302.

Simon, Herbert A. *Administrative Behavior: A Study of Decision-Making Processes in Administrative Organizations*. New York: Free Press, 1976 3rd edition.

Simon, Herbert A. "Rational Decisionmaking in Business Organizations." *American Economic Review* (September 1979).

Smith, Adam. *The Wealth of Nations*. New York: Random House, 1937.

OCCUPATIONAL SAFETY AND HEALTH REGULATION AND ECONOMIC THEORY: COMMENT

Stephen A. Woodbury

The need to understand occupational hazards is clear enough. In 1980, 4,400 workers lost their lives on the job, over 5.6 million occupational injuries and illnesses were reported, and over 41.8 million work days were lost as a result of employment hazards (Bureau of Labor Statistics, 1982). The optimistic expectations that accompanied passage of the Occupational Safety and Health Act of 1970 (OSH Act) — "a substantial reduction in work-related death, illness, and injury," in the words of Congressman Carl Perkins — have not been realized. We have witnessed neither a gross reduction in work-related injuries in the last decade, nor has any study attempting to control for other influences on employment injuries found any significant independent effect of the efforts of the Occupational Safety and Health Administration (OSHA).

Therefore, William Dickens' paper on occupational safety and health (OSH) regulation is a timely and welcome contribution. Although avoiding for the most part the empirical work that has been done on OSH, Dickens nicely reviews the theoretical literature on OSH and provides some insights of his own. By and large, his review is a faithful and helpful guide; it needs no comment. Nor is there any pressing need to critique his new theoretical results, although it may be helpful to review some of those results in a general way and to flag a few of the curiosities surrounding them.

Dickens draws special attention to three results offered in the third section because of their alleged relevance to policy and because they seem in some sense surprising. The first result is that the imposition of a safety standard on a monopsonist can improve the well-being of workers, even if the monopsonist initially is providing an optimal amount of job safety. The relevance of this result for policy aside, it has an immediate intuitive appeal that makes it not so surprising. Consider first the result shown by Walter Wessels (1980): In a competitive labor market in which the employer is free to adjust nonwage benefits — including job safety — in response to the imposition of a minimum wage, the disemployment effect of the minimum wage will be mitigated because the employer will at least partly offset the wage increase by reducing nonwage benefits. Consider next the textbook monopsony model: Imposition of a minimum wage increases both employment and the wage. Putting these two results together gives Dickens's result, which makes eminent sense: Under monopsony, so long as wage and nonwage benefits are imperfect substitutes, a mandated floor under one component of compensation (the wage) should increase employment and thus improve workers' welfare, and so, too, should a mandated floor under another component of compensation (such as job safety).

The second result to which Dickens gives special attention is his demonstration that, under certain circumstances, improving the information workers have about the job hazards they face may make them worse off. This is indeed a counterintuitive result, but Dickens' demonstration of it is both elegant and convincing. Yet he is careful to note the stringency of the assumptions needed to obtain the result, concluding that, "Since it is unlikely that misperception could persist for long with many people [realizing the ill effects of a job hazard], information is unlikely to make people worse off unless the hazard is new and there is a long delay between exposure to the substance and the onset of the symptoms of the disease."

Third, Dickens shows, again under certain assumptions, that imposing uniform safety standards on firms will be more welfare-improving than levying taxes on injuries or exposure to toxic substances. This is decidedly at odds with the policy prescriptions of many economists (Smith, 1976, and Nichol and Zeckhauser, 1977, in particular) who advocate an injury tax to create incentives for firms to improve workplace safety and to do so in the least costly and most effective way possible. The circumstances under which uniform standards are preferable are, in Dickens's view, rather unusual: Workers have prior beliefs about the hazards associated with working in a given firm but have no prior knowledge of which jobs in the firm are safe and which are unsafe — that is, they have no knowledge of the relation between job characteristics and job safety. Firms will possess monopsony power when information is imperfect in this way, and thus policies that reduce monopsony power will improve welfare. Imposition of uniform safety standards will reduce the monopsony power of firms, but an injury tax will not, because it would allow firms to adjust their safety levels according to the cost of doing so, and hence give rise to different safety levels in different firms. Hence, standards are the preferred policy. The result is intriguing and rather neat, but again, Dickens seems to feel that the assumptions generating it are rather unrealistic. He seems to view it more as a theoretically interesting result than as an insight with implications for policy.

Throughout his treatment, Dickens emphasizes the dependence of results on assumptions. This dependence, of course, goes without saying, but Dickens is unusually candid about the extreme sensitivity of his and others' theoretical results to assumptions about information, the character of the labor market, and the behavior of employers and workers. Naturally, he finds this dependence — which results in much ambiguity about the predicted effects of various policies — rather annoying, remarking in response to the question of whether giving workers more information will make them better off, "Once again, the answer is a frustrating 'it depends'."

Dickens' solution to this frustrating dependence of the predicted effect of policy on the assumptions embodied in models is "to test the important assumptions," as he states in his introduction. Formulation of good policy, we are told, depends on knowledge of how labor markets will react when the assumptions of perfect competition fail to hold. Hence, he concludes that the most important goal of empirical research should be to identify the importance of the different possible types of market failure. Implicitly, then, empirical economists will tell us which assumptions are valid, and then the theorists will tell us, by referring to an appropriate model, which policy will achieve the most desirable outcome.

This approach to policy research and its implications for applied work are, I believe, methodologically untenable and wholly out of sympathy with the current direction of empirical research on labor markets. Testing assumptions simply is not on the economic research agenda for at least two reasons. First, no one appears to know what it means to test an assumption, as Blaug (1980, chapter 4) has noted. In an assumption invalid if it is deemed unrealistic? And what would make an assumption unrealistic? Lack of descriptive accuracy, abstractness, or neglect of every relevant variable? Failure to specify properly the motives of economic agents? And second, what if we could test an assumption — for example, the assumption of workers' a priori complete knowledge of job risk — and were to find that we could partly, but not completely, reject its validity? Or what if the valid or correct assumptions about information and market structure found by empiricists proved to be cumbersome or intractable? Where would these circumstances leave the theorist? In view of these problems, it is not surprising that discussions of the validity of assumptions have generated far more heat than light — witness the marginalist controversy of the 1940s or the controversy over human capital theory that followed its advent.[1]

The purpose — at least intended and claimed — of empirical work is to test hypotheses, to test the implications of models, and to measure so-called structural relationships, not to test the assumptions of models. Theoretical models are rejected or confirmed (or tend to be confirmed) depending on whether the economic outcomes they imply are observed, not depending on the validity of their assumptions. One need only glance at the voluminous literature on labor supply, labor demand, and compensating wage differentials to see that the concern of labor economists in the last twenty years has been to test the implications of models and to measure structural coefficients like elasticities, not to test assumptions. I would argue strenuously that reversion to testing assumptions would be methodological retrogression.[2]

In fact, research over the last decade has taught us much about the predictive validity of the competitive labor market model and about the effects of alternative OSH policies. The accumulated evidence falls naturally into two categories: (1) evidence on the magnitude of compensating wage differentials for job hazards, and (2) evidence on the effects of various policies on reported occupational injuries. Each is discussed in turn.

A large literature, reviewed by Smith (1979) and Brown (1980), has attempted to measure the responsiveness of wages to changes in the risk of death and to a variety of other job characteristics. The research strategy here has been to estimate, using any of a number of the rather rich data files on individual workers and households, a reduced-form wage function of the form

$$w_i = a_0 + a_1 r_i + \sum_{j=1}^{J} b_i x_{ij} + \sum_{k=1}^{K} c_i z_{ik} + e_i \qquad \text{(C.1)}$$

where w_i is the wage (often the natural logarithm of the wage) of worker i; r_i is the risk of on-the-job death faced by worker i; x_{i1} through x_{iJ} are independent variables corresponding to the characteristics of worker i (age, schooling, race, sex, and on so); z_{i1} through z_{iK} are characteristics of worker i's job other than risk (industry, occupation, unionization, whether work is repetitive or requires strength, for example); e_i is a normally distributed random error; and a_0, a_1, the b_i's, and c_i's are linear coefficients.

Various studies, using different data and a variety of specifications of equation C.1, have found differing values of the wage premium received by workers facing risk, but all have found a significant positive relation between risk and the wage. To cite two representative examples, Thaler and Rosen

(1976) found that the weekly wage premium for a one one-thousandth increase in the yearly probability of on-the-job death was between 2.7 and 3.9 percent; and looking at wage premia for nonfatal accidents, Olson (1981) found that a one percentage point increase in the probability of experiencing an on-the-job accident results in a weekly wage premium of 0.92 percent and, further, that a one-day increase in the average number of work days lost per injury results in a weekly wage premium of 0.4 percent.

These estimated wage premia are substantial, but recent work by Mellow and Sider (1982 and forthcoming) indicates that they may well have a downward bias and understate the risk premia that actually exist. The reason is that existing surveys of individuals often include little data on the characteristics of the job held by the worker including, of course, risk. Hence, data on a worker's industry and occupation must be appended to that worker's record based on responses to questions about his or her occupation and industry. In the notation of equation C.1, individual characteristics (the x_{ij}'s) are from a micro survey but job characteristics and the risk faced by a worker (the z_{ik}'s and r_i) are industry or occupation averages from another source that are merged into the micro data file. The problem is this: If an individual's response to a survey question about industry or occupational affiliation is inaccurate, incorrect values will be attached to that worker's record and empirical work based on the resulting data file will suffer from response error. The latter is a special case of measurement error.

Mellow and Sider measure the bias induced by response error by examining differences between a worker's description of his or her job and the description provided by the employer. They use two different data sets, the Current Population Survey (CPS) and the Employment Opportunity Pilot Project Survey (EOPP), and find — using the standard approach of equation C.1 — that an increase of one workday lost per worker-year results in a wage premium of 4.0 percent (using the CPS data) to 11.7 percent (using EOPP). But after correcting for response error, they find the premium to be 6.1 percent (using the CPS data) to 14.6 percent (using EOPP). Thus, as they note (p. 7), "Errors in the matching process . . . appear to lead to substantial downward bias in estimates of the wage-risk trade-off" — on the order of 25 to 50 percent to be specific.

The weight of the evidence indicates that the labor market does indeed generate substantial compensating differentials for risk. But are these differentials in some sense large enough? There are two senses in which observed differentials might not be big enough. First, we might make a judgment on ethical grounds that a three of four percent wage differential (or any wage differential) is inadequate to compensate for a one one-thousandth increase in the probability of death on the job. This is an ethical matter about which economists as economists have little to say. But second, we might want to know whether the observed differentials are as large as would be generated by a competitive labor market or if they are depressed by power on the employer's side of the market. This is a task that surely is within the scope of economics, but it will require more information than we now possess about workers' preferences for risk and other job attributes, on the one hand, and about the costs incurred by employers in reducing work hazards, on the other. Work on these issues is of relatively recent vintage and has some distance yet to go.[3]

If risk premia should be inadequate to fully compensate workers for the work hazards they face, then clearly some policy may be in order. There are basically two alternatives: first, direct regulation, of which the OSH Act is an example; and second, the creation of financial incentives for employers (and perhaps also workers) to improve occupational safety and health.[4]

The presence since 1970 of direct regulation, in the form of OSHA, has led to special interest in gathering information on its effects. A serious data problem — the method of collecting injury data was changed with the implementation of the OSH Act — has hampered these efforts, yet several researchers have found ingenious ways around the inevitable difficulties.

Smith (1979) and McCaffrey (1983) have both examined the lost work day injury rate in firms inspected by OSHA. They compare the injury rate (in a given year) of firms inspected early in the year (March or April) with the injury rate of firms inspected late in the year (November or December), reasoning that inspection early in a year might have an appreciable effect on the year's injury rate whereas inspection late in the year would not. Smith found that 1973 inspections had a statistically appreciable effect on accident rates in small firms (those with fewer than 100 workers) but none on injury rates in medium and large firms. Further, he found that 1974 inspections had no significant effect on injury rates at all. McCaffrey's follow-up to Smith's study found no significant relation between inspections and injury rates in any of the years examined (1976, 1977, and 1978). His conclusion (1983, p. 145) is that "no convincing evidence exists that OSHA inspections reduced injury rates in inspected firms from 1974 to 1978."

Similarly, three other studies, using different approaches, have found a small to nonexistent relation between the efforts of OSHA and injury rates. Another study by Smith (1976, appendix C) concluded that industries targeted by OSHA in 1972 and 1973 experienced the same injury rates as they would have had they been subject to no special scrutiny. Viscusi (1979), using a pooled cross-section of industries from 1972 through 1975, found that neither OSHA inspections nor proposed penalties bore any discernible relation to planned or actual investment by employers in safety and health. Further, Viscusi found no impact of OSHA inspections or penalties on actual injury rates. Bartel and Thomas (1982) used data covering 22 states from 1974 through 1978 to estimate the determinants of OSHA inspections, compliance with OSHA standards, and lost work days on an industry-by-industry basis. Their findings show a statistically nonzero but very small effect of inspections on the rate of lost work days — a 100 percent increase in inspections would result in a 4 percent reduction in lost work days per worker.

Why does all the research on the impact of OSHA lead to the conclusion that the effects of OSHA standards have been small to nonexistent? The authors of the studies cite several factors (see especially Smith, 1976, pp. 59–67): low probability of inspection, minimal financial penalties for violation of standards, difficulty in uncovering plant safety violations and enforcing remedies, and a tenuous link between the standards set by regulators and actual workplace safety. Both Smith (1976, p. 67) and Viscusi (1979, p. 131) admit that they would have been surprised to find that OSHA had more than a negligible effect on injury rates or efforts by employers to improve workplace safety.

Turning to the evidence on the effects of incentive mechanisms — injury taxes levied on employers and experience-rated workers' compensation premia — we find fewer studies but findings that are nonetheless substantial. Chelius (1977), who is perhaps the champion of a reformed workers' compensation (WC) system as the most effective workplace safety policy, emphasizes that incentives to reduce injuries must bear on both workers and employers. He contends that the actions of both affect the number of injuries that occur. He marshalls empirical evidence to show that WC systems, which place the liability for workplace accidents partly on the employer and partly on the worker, are related to lower death rates than are systems that place strict liability on employers. He also shows (1977, Appendix C) that improved WC benefits are significantly related to higher industrial-injury rates, which seems to support his belief that workers do change their behavior depending on incentive — if it is less costly to suffer an accident, workers will do less to prevent accidents. Chelius thus argues in favor of a system of shared liability such as WC (appropriately reformed) as an effective workplace safety program.

But WC also must offer incentives to employers to invest in accident prevention. Russell (1974) has shown that, as currently set up, WC premia paid by employers are not responsive to changes in the accident rates experienced by companies, especially small companies. She suggests changes in the so-called experience-rating formula so that employers will pay smaller premia if their safety records improve, providing an incentive to reduce on-the-job hazards.

To what degree would employers actually respond to improved incentives to reduce injuries and disease — to an injury tax or WC premia more tightly tied to the number of accidents in a given workplace? Sider (1981) finds that, in four of the six industries he studies, imposition of a tax of $4000 per injury would result in a six to ten percent decrease in the number of injuries. Smith (1976, p. 80) finds that a $4000 per injury tax would lower the manufacturing injury rate by between 18 and 25 percent. These responses to financial incentives are not dramatic, but they are far greater than the minimal to nonexistent responses to direct regulation that researchers have found.

This brief review of statistical evidence on compensating differentials and the impact of various policies is not intended to show that our empirical knowledge in these areas is complete, unflawed, or even that such research has reached the point of diminishing returns — far from it. Most notably lacking is evidence on equalizing differences for occupational disease (as opposed to injury) and on the relative effects of various incentive mechanisms on occupational health (as opposed to safety). But the evidence accumulated over the last decade does seem to show, first, that labor markets do generate measurable compensating wage differentials for occupational injury and work-related death; and second, that occupational injury rates are more responsive to the financial incentives generated by policies such as an injury tax or workers' compensation than to direct regulation. In short, the experience with OSHA seems to teach the same lesson that undergraduates learn in most courses in comparative economics — that coordinating economic activity by plan and command, except in unusual circumstances, is more difficult than coordinating it by price incentives.[5]

There remains plenty of room for further research. Above all, we need more empirical work on workers' preferences for safety and health, on employers' costs of providing improved safety and health, and on the effects of the various safety and health policies. That means we need better data, wider use and innovation of appropriate techniques of estimation, and theory that has empirical content that can be used to frame and guide applied research.

Notes

1. On the marginalist controversy, see Lester (1946) and Machlup (1946); on human capital, see Chamberlain (1969).

2. This is not to say that efforts to measure the degree of monopsony in labor markets, to analyze how workers form their perceptions of job risk, or to ascertain the degree of worker ra-

tionality are wasteful or out of place. On the contrary, such research is of inherent interest and an invaluable aid to choosing among alternative explanations of phenomena we observe. But this is different from the role Dickens envisions for such research — that is, as a way of deciding which models are most realistic.

3. Rosen's (1974) model spells out the importance of workers' preferences and employers' costs in generating a market-equilibrium trade-off between wages and job risk. For evidence on workers' preferences for nonwage benefits, see Atrostic (1982) and Woodbury (1983). For evidence on employers' costs, see Sider (1981).

4. Provision of more and better information is another policy option often mentioned, but there appears to be no empirical evidence on it, at least in this context.

5. That economists may seem to be gratifying their professional penchant for incentives over direct regulation does not necessarily impugn their empirical findings.

References

Atrostic, B.K. "The Demand for Leisure and Nonpecuniary Benefits," *American Economic Review* (June 1982), 428–440.

Bartel, Ann P., and Thomas, Lacy Glenn. "OSHA Enforcement, Industrial Compliance, and Workplace Safety." Working Paper 953, National Bureau of Economic Research, Cambridge, Mass., August 1982.

Blaug, Mark. *The Methodology of Economics.* Cambridge: Cambridge University Press, 1980.

Brown, Charles. "Equalizing Differences in the Labor Market." *Quarterly Journal of Economics* (February 1980), 113–134.

Chamberlain, Neil W. "Some Further Thoughts on Human Capital." In G.G. Somers and W.D. Wood (eds.) *Cost-Benefit Analysis of Manpower Policies.* Kingston, Ontario: Queen's University, 1969, 230–248.

Chelius, James R. *Workplace Safety and Health: The Role of Workers' Compensation.* Washington, D.C.: American Enterprise Institute, 1977.

Lester, Richard. "Shortcomings of Marginal Analysis for Wage-Employment Problems." *American Economic Review* (March 1946), 63–82.

Machlup, Fritz. "Marginal Analysis and Empirical Research." *American Economic Review* (September 1946), 519–554.

McCaffrey, David P. "An Assessment of OSHA's Recent Effects on Injury Rates." *Journal of Human Resources* (Winter 1983), 131–146.

Mellow, Wesley, and Sider, Hal. "Accuracy of Response in Labor Market Surveys: Evidence and Implications." Working Paper 133, Office of Research and Evaluation, Bureau of Labor Statistics, Washington, D.C., December 1982. (Forthcoming in *Journal of Labor Economics.*)

Nichols, Albert L., and Zeckhauser, Richard. "Government Comes to the Workplace: An Assessment of OSHA." *The Public Interest.* (Fall 1977), 39–69.

Olson, Craig A. "An Analysis of Wage Differentials Received by Workers on Dangerous Jobs." *Journal of Human Resources* (Spring 1981), 167–185.

Rosen, Sherwin. "Hedonic Prices and Implicit Markets: Product Differentiation in Pure Competition." *Journal of Political Economy* (January/February 1974), 34–55.

Russell, Louise B. "Safety Incentives in Workmen's Compensation Insurance." *Journal of Human Resources* (Summer 1974), 361–375.

Sider, Hal. "Work-Related Accidents and the Production Process." Working Paper 117, Office of Research and Evaluation, Bureau of Labor Statistics, Washington, D.C., April 1981.

Smith, Robert S. *The Occupational Safety and Health Act: Its Goals and Achievements.* Washington, D.C.: American Enterprise Institute, 1976.

______. "The Impact of OSHA Inspections on Manufacturing Injury Rates." *Journal of Human Resources* (Spring 1979), 145–170.

______. "Compensating Wage Differentials and Public Policy: A Review." *Industrial and Labor Relations Review* (July 1979), 339–352.

Thaler, Richard, and Rosen, Sherwin. "The Value of Saving a Life: Evidence from the Labor Market." In Nestor E. Terleckyj (ed.) *Household Production and Consumption.* New York: National Bureau of Economic Research, 1976, 265–298.

Viscusi, W. Kip. "The Impact of Occupational Safety and Health Regulation." *Bell Journal of Economics* (Spring 1979), 117–140.

Wessels, Walter J. "The Effect of Minimum Wages in the Presence of Fringe Benefits: An Expanded Model." *Economic Inquiry* (April 1980), 293–313.

Woodbury, Stephen A. "Substitution Between Wage and Nonwage Benefits." *American Economic Review* (March 1983), 166–182.

U.S. Department of Labor, Bureau of Labor Statistics. *Occupational Injuries and Illnesses in the U.S. by Industry, 1980.* BLS Bulletin 2130, Washington, D.C., U.S.G.P.O., April 1982.

A COMMENT ON THE MARKET IN LABOR POWER

Paul Zarembka

Of the five chapters by Allen, Blau, Datcher, Dickens, and Malveaux (the chapters seen by this reviewer) only the Allen chapter correctly indicates that economic theories are based on the class interests the theorists defend. Allen, however, seems most interested in a managerial class which is supposed to be distinct from the capitalist. While she introduces Marx cursorily in a few pages at the end of her chapter and even concludes that "the scientific analysis of unemployment . . . can be found in the pages of *Capital*," nowhere does she confront whether Marxism is consistent with a managerial theory. Her chapter, in fact, does not go deeply enough into the issues to be able to discuss the question of consistency, and it is very unlikely that the managerial mentality and art of persuasion that she introduces at the beginning will help. In any case, her own approach would have been more effective if she had shown how "the three distinct interpretations of the labor market [she discusses in the second section] . . . are rooted in the broader ideological framework of the class from which they arise: the managerial class" (p. 1).

The Blau, Datcher, and Malveaux chapters all take Becker's works as their starting point and never really break from that perspective, although both Blau's and Malveaux's chapters are intelligent enough to conclude on limitations of traditional theories, and Malveaux shows sensitivity to Marxist ideas. Datcher's chapter is little more than an empirical literature survey and even her title is unclear. Dickens' chapter is too deep in neoclassical economics to make it worthy of attention.

So, let us return to first principles and suggest another approach to the type of questions that concern the authors. First of all, if one reads anthropological literature (on native Americans, for example) and historical literature (on antiquity, for example) it becomes immediately apparent that there are very many societies which have absolutely no labor market or a very limited one. Therefore, a labor market is not innate in being human. It must be socially produced. Consequently, when one wants to address questions of the level of employment, of racial and gender characteristics, and so forth, one must first know in whose interests this market was created.

Second, the word labor market which dominates all neoclassical labor economics is already a bourgeois conceptualization. For the market is not in fact in labor — the activity of work — but rather in the capacity to do work, a capacity possessed by a laborer. The activity itself is decided by someone else — the employer, the capitalist. In other words, it is a market only in *labor power* (reserving the word *labor* for the actual activity of work). This is important because the sellers of labor power, who are then told what to do, are quite different social agents from those who buy labor power and then decide how actually to utilize this capacity for work. Without the distinction, the specific class nature of the transaction disappears.

It may be useful to pause and ask how the bourgeoisie so often gets away with getting economists to substitute "labor market" for "market in labor power." First, capitalism is a system of generalized commodity production — not only is everything produced for sale (not direct use) but also laboring activity is commoditized since labor power is sold by workers and bought by capitalists. Given that all of us grew up with this daily experience of deep commoditization, we initially think that society is eternally so commoditized. Therefore, collapsing labor power onto labor conceptually does not seem to lose anything in understanding — except that this whole system was created in a particular class interest. The second reason is that economists are hired directly by the bourgeoisie or else by the state and universities. The bourgeoisie would simply fire an economist who consistently made the distinction between labor and labor power. And so would the state, which is dominated by the bourgeoisie. University economists, however, can be rather accurately described as petit bourgeois since typically they do not directly hire labor power but do have a rather stable access to their profession (their means of production). Yet their professional advancement generally is not aided by exposing the system all live under. In sum, conceptual frameworks for intellectual understandings are circumscribed by the interests of the dominant class. Whether an individual economist is conscious of his/her being dominated by a class interest is of no particular moment in the fact of the dominance.

Be that as it may, the market in labor power is in fact a market resulting from all means of production being controlled and owned by the capitalist class facing a working class which controls and owns no means of production. While capitalists could work their own means of production and let others starve, they in fact exploit the weakness of the workers by having them do all the work but only returning a fraction of their working day via wages Wolff, 1977, p. 103 calculates only 25 percent for the United States in 1967! Indeed, the workers are weak not only because they do not control and own the required means of production but also, and consequently, because they are not even guaranteed any work at all. In fact, it is the function of this *reserve army of laborers* to hold in check the ambitions of labor — and the fear of unemployment is a very disciplining force indeed.

So, how would we assess developments of the reserve army in the capitalist world today, more particularly in the United States? It certainly should be a dominant question for those interested in workers.

One comment should be made initially. The officially recognized unemployment rate is only a symptomatic reflection of Marx's concept of the reserve army of labor. Besides pauperism, Marx divides the reserve army into three components; the floating, the latent, and the stagnant. The floating refers to those willing and able to sell their labor power to capital and would certainly include all those officially listed as unemployed. But also included would be those looking for employment outside state channels as well as those who would accept employment but have given up an active search. The latent reserve army refers to those being squeezed out of precapitalist agriculture and who are looking for minimally favorable employment conditions under capital. While this category is still very important in the Third World, housewives in the United States responding to financial pressure on the family could be assimilated into this category. The stagnant reserve army refers to those with extremely irregular employment who work the longest hours and for the lowest pay when work is found. Also very important in the Third World, in the United States some portion of the minority population often can be included here (for example, Chicano migrant agricultural laborers). In sum, the officially recognized unemployment rate is only a symptom of the general level of the reserve army.

To analyze the determinants of the level of the reserve army in the United States, it is useful to recall some basic propositions of Marx's analysis of capital. First, *value* is produced only by proletariat labor subject to the domination by capital in either those industries producing means of production (Department I) or means of subsistence for the working class (Department II). A measure of the newly created value each year is the total labor hours of work in these two branches. *Surplus value* is then the difference between this newly created value and that portion of the value that is embodied in the labor time required to produce the goods that the working class is able to purchase with the wages it receives for selling its labor power. The labor time required includes both direct labor time and time required to replace means of production used up.

Surplus value is used most fundamentally for *accumulation of capital*, i.e., to purchase more labor power to be attached to more means of production produced by previous labor. Yet there is a deep contradiction in the accumulation of capital that is particularly important for understanding the twentieth century. The principal historical means of having more laborers available for domination by capital is the penetration of precapitalist forms of production through the development of productive forces. And this development of productive forces — what Marx calls production of relative surplus value — also reduces the labor time that is required to produce the goods consumed by workers already subject to the domination of capital. So, as the world comes more fully under the hegemony of capital (i.e., more proletarianized), the enormous mass of surplus value has increasing difficulty in finding new accumulation possibilities. Capitalists as individuals see this as restricted markets for their products.

The Great Depression of the 1930s was the clearest expression of this contradiction of capitalist accumulation, also called the crisis of overproduction of commodities — the inability to sell what had been produced. But we are living this contradiction every day that the capitalist mode of production persists, and most Third World countries live its continuing reality. However, the American bourgeoisie also learned from Nazi Germany how to move that contradiction to another plane — develop mass amounts of *unproductive labor* in the military, which absorbs surplus value that otherwise could not find outlets and also aids in maintaining the bourgeoisie against working-class pretensions at home or abroad. Those political forces in the United States that try to convince the bourgeois state that state money spent on the military creates less jobs than the same amount spent on social services — and so suggest a change in priorities — completely miss the significance of the fact that the lowest levels of the U.S. unemployment rate after the Great Depression were during World War II, the Korean War, and the Vietnam War.

To give some idea of the importance of unproductive labor in the United States, we can examine the calculation of Wolff (1977). Within unproductive labor, he includes wholesale and retail trade (as Marx specifically asserted), finance and insurance, real estate rentals, business services, nonhousehold (business) amusements, nonenterprise government employees, domestic help, and a couple of property income categories. While it seems that the important category of labor time in production of military hardware is inappropriately included as productive, nevertheless 32 percent of labor time was unproductive in 1947 and rose to 45 percent in 1967 (the last year of his calculation, p. 109). Stated differently, without substantial unproductive labor in the United States, unemployment would be enormous.

The Republican administration now is expanding further military expenditures as well as reversing those concessions/bribes made to American labor since the Roosevelt administration — concessions/bribes made in return for neutralization of struggle against, or even support of, its imperial designs. This administration is undertaking the military policy in the name of the international "communist" menace and the Soviet military build-up. In reversing the concessions/bribes to its working class, it restricts consumption of the masses, raises the rate of surplus value, and exacerbates overproduction. The American working class is given higher unemployment and a much more developed military. On the one hand, the American bourgeoisie thus seems to be setting American labor up for a repeat of the Depression begun under the Hoover administration, then World War II — smash the working class with the Republican Party; make concessions/bribes with the Democrats later in the decade or in the 1990s in return for support for World War III. On the other hand, the success of the re-industrialization of Western Europe and Japan after World War II led to a slowly rising competition for American capital and concessions/bribes to American labor may be less possible for the remainder of the century. If internal class struggle then sharpens, given the type of government the U.S. state has supported in Vietnam, Indonesia, Iran, Chile, El Salvador, Israel, and South Africa (to take a few extremes), there are no grounds to believe that the U.S. state would not do here, if necessary, what it found necessary elsewhere and even here earlier (for example, Haymarket, 1886; Ludlow, 1913–14; Little Steel, 1937; Kent State and Jackson State, 1970).

We seem to have moved away from the market in labor power. But not really. For these systemic questions vitally condition the total situation, including issues of racism and sexism. As we know, heightened militarism, racism, and sexism all went together in the rise and development of Nazi Germany as one response to the consequences of a massive reserve army. As the reserve army continues to expand in the United States, one political line here will be similar. If so, a crucial political struggle is blocking a rise of fascism — represented by, but definitely not limited to, the American Nazi Party, the Ku Klux Klan, and/or a military takeover of the U.S. government, as was unsuccessfully attempted in 1934 (see Zilg, 1974, pp. 292–298) during our Great Depression.

References

Wolff, E.N. "Unproductive Labor and the Rate of Surplus Value in the United States, 1947-1967." In P. Zarembka (ed.) *Research in Political Economy*, Vol. 1. Greenwich, Conn.: JAI Press, 1977, 87–115.

Zilg, G.C. *Dupont: Behind the Nylon Curtain*. Englewood Cliffs, N.J.: Prentice-Hall, 1974.

Author Index

Subject Index

Contributing Authors

Kathryn Allen is a candidate for a law degree at the University of Texas at Austin who has done extensive research in the area of law and economics.

Francine Blau is Professor of Economics and Labor and Industrial Relations at the University of Illinois at Urbana-Champaign.

William Darity, Jr., is Associate Professor of Economics at the University of North Carolina at Chapel Hill.

Linda Datcher is a Post-Doctoral Fellow at the Kennedy School of Government at Harvard.

William Dickens is Assistant Professor of Economics at the University of California at Berkeley.

Samuel Friedman was formerly a sociologist with the Vera Institute of Justice.

Saul Hoffman is Associate Professor of Economics at the University of Delaware at Newark.

Julianne Malveaux is Assistant Professor of Economics at San Francisco State University.

Samuel Myers, Jr., is Associate Professor of Economics at the Graduate School of International and Public Affairs at the University of Pittsburgh.

Rhonda Williams is Assistant Professor of Economics at the University of Texas at Austin.

Stephen Woodbury is Assistant Professor of Economics at Michigan State University.

Paul Zarembka is Professor of Economics at the State University of New York at Buffalo.

GPSR Compliance

The European Union's (EU) General Product Safety Regulation (GPSR) is a set of rules that requires consumer products to be safe and our obligations to ensure this.

If you have any concerns about our products, you can contact us on ProductSafety@springernature.com

In case Publisher is established outside the EU, the EU authorized representative is:

Springer Nature Customer Service Center GmbH
Europaplatz 3
69115 Heidelberg, Germany

Batch number: 10830937

Printed by Printforce, the Netherlands